STRATEGY
IN ACTION

Contents

Preface and Acknowledgments

In the research and writing about strategy and also in business practice, it is the formulation of strategy that receives most of the attention. Execution gets short shrift. To date, we have been so preoccupied with devising the plan that scant attention is given to carrying it out. But now managers in company after company are reporting serious difficulty in making their best-laid plans come true.

This book focuses on ways to close this gap between expectations and actual results. What can managers do to increase the odds that their investment in strategic planning will pay off?

The evidence is clear that a new strategy needs structured support. Organizations do not change easily. So as the central message of this book we lay out a series of adjustments, or moves, that will buttress the choice of a fresh direction.

> To implement a new strategy: thrusts must be programmed, organization needs to be refocused, committed executives have to occupy key posts, and incentive packages may have to be redesigned and control systems realigned to match the revised goals. Many failures of strategy can be traced to absence of such matching of structure and strategy.

This is the heart of the book—as we first conceived it.

We soon discovered, however, that strategy formulation could not be given the terse treatment that we originally intended. Difficulties in execution often have roots in the vagueness of the plans. The way in which strategy is developed and especially the form of its expression are critical forerunners of success in implementation. This led to expansion of the introduction into what is now Part I. Our aim in this Part is not to review the growing literature on wise selection of strategy; instead, we concentrate on getting strategy formulation into an *action-oriented mode*.

> Action-related strategy has several characteristics. Broad goals are restated in terms of "strategic thrusts"—key moves that should be started immediately. Financial targets are not merely attractive ratios; instead, they are carefully predicted outcomes of positioning each business-unit in a particular vantage point in its competitive setting. Corporate strategy is more than juggling portfolios; it also requires active and selective resource inputs to operating units.

A drawback of discussing elements, or steps, separately as we do in Part II is seeming to propose fragmented effort. Quite the contrary. Integration of moves supporting a new strategy is crucial. This aspect of "strategy in action" is developed in Part III.

> Especially in a large organization all these supports for strategy must be fitted into a unified structure—even though we know that new conditions will require revisions of this structure. The moves of management should be coordinated and phased so that each reinforces the other. Moreover, as normal changes in strategy occur, the whole interacting structure must be reshaped to suit new needs.

Much of what we propose involves the proper use of well-recognized management concepts. The critical task is to bring many diverse influences into a selected sharp focus. In addition, a number of less familiar concepts are woven into the total approach. These include:

Resource conversion model.
Prepared opportunism.
Corporate input strategy.
Key actor analysis.
Internal entrepreneurs.
Broad-stroke programming.
Focused climate.
Stock option equivalents.
Steering control.
Synergistic fit.

The meaning of these terms and their contribution to an integrated approach will become clear when the appropriate section is read.

Because we want the message of this book to reach busy executives, as well as students of strategic management, considerable effort is made to avoid academic jargon. Interlarding of frequent references is avoided for the same reason. Nevertheless, the ideas presented are compatible with—and often flow out of—the latest scholarly research. Much of this research is exciting, but flagging all the linkages to that literature calls for a different sort of book. The annotated references for each chapter—which again have an action-oriented bias —are intended to help readers dig fruitfully into a selected issue.

Many managers and colleagues have helped shape the ideas presented here. The richest source (of both effective and poor practice) has been consulting relationships. We wish to acknowledge this debt and express the hope that our more systematic treatment of strategic management will recompense in a small way those who have kindly provided grist for our mill. The Strategy Research Center at the Graduate School of Business, Columbia University, supplied technical support. Camilla Koch converted messy copy into clean manuscript. Phyllis Mason located and annotated most of the selected references. South-Western Publishing Co. is permitting us to use some material which appeared earlier in one of their books. For all this cooperation we are very grateful.

B.Y.
W.H.N.

STRATEGY
IN ACTION

PART I

THE TRAJECTORY
Sharpening the Strategic Focus

The Realm of Strategy

THE WORD *strategy* means many things to different people—ranging from on-side kicks for football fans, to naval blockades for military commanders, to any alternative for operations researchers, to recognition of China for heads of state. Thus in this opening chapter we need to identify the distinctive role of business strategy in the management of a company.

Turning the concept of strategy into an effective managerial tool requires considerable skill—as we shall show in later chapters. But before embarking on the main message of the book, we want a common understanding of what the shouting is all about.

PLACE OF STRATEGY IN SHAPING AND GUIDING A COMPANY

What Strategy Is Not

Discussions about strategy with many executives have revealed several sources of confusion. If we immediately set these aside, the nature of strategy becomes clearer.

1. Strategy is *not* a response to short-term fluctuations in operations or the environment, nor is it the response to the frequent short-term reports on, for example, sales, labor turnover, weekly output, or competitors' prices that every manager receives. Instead, strategy deals with the predetermined direction toward which these quick responses are pointed. It is concerned with the longer-term course that the ship is steering, not with the waves.

2. Strategy is *not* a set of numbers merely projected out three to five years; it is not an extrapolation exercise based on this year's balance sheet and profit-and-loss statement. Rather, the emphasis in strategy is on the quality and texture of the business. New services, the focus of research, market position, foreign sources of materials, government sharing of high risks—these are the kinds of issues that are molded into a verbal statement of where and how the company hopes to move. General Electric and several other companies, for instance, insist that the qualitative strategic plan be a separate document from the subsequently prepared financial projections.

3. Strategy is *not* a rationalization of what we did last year or of what appears in next year's budget. With a bit of imagination and artful wording, a statement that looks like a strategy can be written around almost any set of activities of a going concern. An actual strategy, in contrast, is a longer-term plan that sets the direction and tone of the shorter-range plans. Unless the strategy provides underlying guidance, its preparation is mere window dressing.

4. Strategy is *not* a functional plan, not even a long-run one—such as a five-year marketing plan or a seven-year production plan. Rather, strategy involves the integration of all these functional plans into a balanced overall scheme. In some circumstances one function may drive the others—product development, say, may determine marketing efforts or vice versa. Nevertheless, it is company strategy that sets the priorities and weighs or minimizes the risks. An overall viewpoint is essential.

5. Strategy is *not* a statement of pious intentions or optimistic wishes. Merely envisioning a future world and selecting an attractive position in that world is not a strategic plan. Instead, a strategy must be feasible in terms of resources that will be mobilized, and it must identify ways by which at least some form of superiority over competitors is to be achieved.

6. Strategy is *not* a cluster of ideas in the minds of a few select leaders of the company—ideas labeled *strategy* if and when they are voiced because they come from key individuals. Rather, the concepts

are disseminated and understood by all managers to at least the middle
levels of the organization and perhaps below. Unless there is such
widespread understanding, coupled with acceptance and preferably
commitment, not much progress toward strategic goals will occur.

This list of "is not's" sets some helpful boundaries on the meaning of
company strategy. By weeding out what may mistakenly be called
strategy, we can focus on the potential power of the main concept. Of
course, the converse of the "is not's" generates a set of positive characteristics—namely, that strategy focuses on basic longer-term direction, is primarily qualitative, provides guidance for preparation of
short-term plans, integrates functional plans into an overall scheme for
the company, is realistic and action oriented, and is understood
throughout the top and middle levels of the organization.

REALISTIC MISSION ANCHORED TO ACTION PROGRAMS

The nature of company strategy can also be suggested by sketching in
broad strokes the analytical process by which a particular strategy is
formulated. Methods and problems in designing a strategy are explored in Chapter 6; here we are making a quick pass to show the
qualities of the end product.

An essential feature of all strategic planning is a forecast of the
world ahead—or, at best, a forecast of those parts of the environment
that will have significant impact on the company's successes and
failures. Of course, there will be a variety of uncertainties, and our
strategic planning will have to deal with them. Nevertheless, forecast
we must if we are to grasp full advantage of the changes that lie ahead.

This scenario of the future should cover social, political, and technological changes as well as economic shifts (see Figure 1–1). Ideally,
we would like to spot each change that will create significant opportunities or threats to our industry and then relate that external change
back to the particular parts of our operations that will be affected.
Analysis of these anticipated developments should enable us to decide
what strengths or capabilities, such as access to low-cost materials or
strong market position, will be crucial for future success. Conversely,
the forecasts should warn us of weaknesses that would spell disaster.

A second kind of forecast and analysis focuses on our company's
strengths and weaknesses relative to present and anticipated competition. Future actions by these competitors sharply impacts on the
strategy that makes most sense for us.

Then, we need to be creative and skillful in identifying future op-

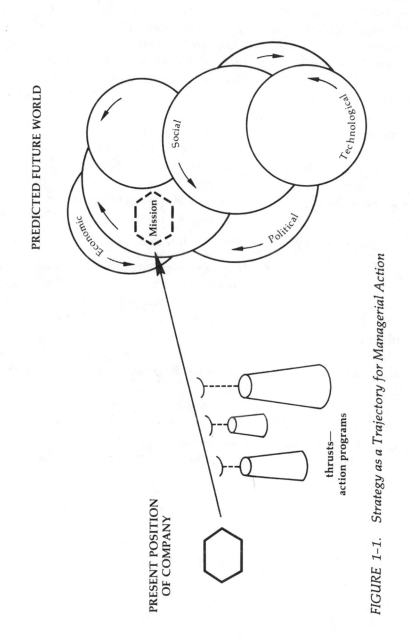

PREDICTED FUTURE WORLD

Social

Economic

Mission

Political

Technological

PRESENT POSITION
OF COMPANY

thrusts—
action programs

FIGURE 1-1.   Strategy as a Trajectory for Managerial Action

portunities where our relative strengths give us a comparative advantage. On the down side, we try to spot declining or unprofitable segments that require a fresh approach or withdrawal.

From such a set of forecasts and analyses—which, in fact, are much more complex, as will be seen in later chapters—a picture emerges of where and what we would like our company to be in that future world. What are the particular products or services we believe we can provide to what markets in a distinctive manner with the resources we can mobilize? This becomes our strategic mission. As events unfold we may adjust the target, but at any point in time the strategy tells us the best direction to move.

A desired position in a predicted future world—that is, a company "mission"—can be treated as the bulls-eye or target of the strategy. But the main role of strategy is to evolve a *trajectory* or flight path toward that bulls-eye. Typically, a company must initiate at appropriate times a whole series of programs or action plans if it is to attain its desired domain. As Figure 1–1 suggests, to move from our present position to the desired position may require launching new products, building a reservoir of technically trained people, negotiating a merger, or perhaps liquidating part of our present operations. When and how to move aggressively on these programs is an important aspect of the strategy. The tie to current activities comes largely, though not entirely, through these *thrusts.*

This essential tie between mission and thrusts can be compared to the realities of a chess game. A series of smart moves without some broader strategy will not finally win the game against a capable competitor, and a grand design without a series of moves to achieve it remains but a twinkle in the loser's eye.

THE USE OF STRATEGY

Crown Cork & Seal Company presents a classic case illustrating the process just described. When J. F. Connelly became president, the company was on the verge of bankruptcy, with only a small part of its product line—bottle caps and related closures—earning a modest profit. The outlook for its major business, tin cans, was dismal. The product was mature, with total demand growing slowly; glass, paper, and plastics were making inroads in this market and threatening to make even more; competitors had excess capacity, and price competition was severe. But there were a few brighter spots in the total picture, and Connelly decided to concentrate on one of these. Cans that could hold contents under pressure were more difficult to make and consequently were not subject to cutthroat competition. Moreover, the growth prospects for these were better than average, with aerosols and beer the major users. As for beer containers, Connelly predicted that metal cans would take market share from glass bottles. Thus serving this special *niche* became Crown Cork's target.

Several major programs were necessary to develop a comparative advantage in the niche. All thought of a full line was abandoned, and the regular can business was liquidated (this provided some capital to pacify the bankers). On the other hand, Connelly tooled-up to give excellent service to his selected customers; this involved locating plants close to customers, installing some new equipment, and organizing very fast response to customer needs. Also, overhead was trimmed far below the industry average.

The results at Crown Cork have been dramatic. Volume did grow much faster than the total can industry—not only in beer but later in soft drinks as well. Crown Cork's service has enabled the company to obtain an increasing share of this volume. Meanwhile, the low overhead gives the company the best profit margin in the industry. Granted, this market concentration and low overhead has made the company somewhat vulnerable. But for over two decades in the company's major line of business there has been a clear, realistic mission anchored in action programs.

For a recent example of well-conceived strategic action, Citibank's decision to serve worldwide corporations as a special group of clients is impressive. For years Citibank has had a network of branches in foreign countries. Traditionally, each country had a strong manager who ran the local operations with a high degree of decentralization. But several environmental changes have raised questions about the amount of local autonomy that is desirable. Multinational corporations have grown rapidly and account for an increasing share of world trade. In addition, modern communication devices have made rapid, frequent contact with all cities of the world commonplace. These developments, in turn, have led multinational corporations to centralized management of cash balances, foreign exchange transactions, funds transfer, short-term borrowing, and the like. Citibank predicts that the multinationals will seek increasing efficiencies through coordination of their fiscal operations.

These developments create an opportunity for banks that can provide integrated services worldwide tailored to the specific needs of individual multinational corporations. And Citibank, with its well-developed branch network, has a comparative strength. Seizing the opportunity, Citibank decided to serve this niche with distinction.

But picking the mission is not enough. Citibank has to assure that its widespread facilities do, in fact, serve the coordinated needs of each major customer. For this purpose Citibank created a new World Corporation Group charged with relationships with about 450 multinational clients. Work with these clients was transferred from the foreign branches (and the New York international division), and a single officer was placed in charge of serving each client. However, to avoid costly duplication, the global account officers—like account executives in an advertising agency—call on the local branches to perform any work that is needed.

A delicate matrix form of organization has emerged. There are continuing problems of the allocation of scarce resources—notably, money for loans in developing countries. Nevertheless, the strategy is clear. The initiative for planning and control of services to these clients is centralized. This means some interference with service to local overseas clients, but Citibank believes that in its relative position the gains from improved service to multinational corporations will outweigh losses on the local front.

In this segment of its operations, then, Citibank has identified a mission and established programs (primarily organization and personnel in this instance) necessary to pursue that mission. To date the results have been good. Like any strategy, however, the wisdom of continuing that direction depends on the accuracy and monitoring of the forecasts—or *premises*—about future environmental conditions.

RISING NEED FOR STRATEGIC DIRECTION

The concept of company strategy has been set forth in the preceding pages—first by noting what strategy is not, next by briefly sketching the strategy formulation process, and then by giving two quick examples. The need for this kind of strategic management is increasing. Managing a company, always a challenging task, is becoming more difficult, and careful strategic analysis is vital to cut through the maze. Among the forces that are making strategy crucial are these:

1. Managers are being confronted by a *wider range of external pressures* that must be taken into account in their major decisions. These pressures to which management is now expected to be responsive include environmental protection, employment opportunities for

minorities and all sorts of disadvantaged, shielding the consumer, and conforming to increasing government regulations.

2. *Shorter payout periods* are necessary for most investments. The more frequent shifts in technology, consumer preferences, resource availability, foreign exchange rates, and so forth trim the time available to recoup investments. Consequently, better forecasting and faster responses to external changes have to be built into the planning process.

3. *Improved communications* aid competitors, suppliers, customers, and ourselves alike. Jet travel, photo-phones, television via satellite, electronic computers, worldwide news services all increase the range of factors to be considered and the speed of responses to events everywhere. And they add to the information explosion. One result is that strategic shifts must be more discerning and more frequent.

4. *Growing intensity of competition* quickly removes any slack in the system. World trade means competition from anywhere; advancing technology encourages cross-industry competition. Consequently, strategic planning must consider who our *future* competitors will be, not only who is here today.

5. *Larger enterprises* require more levels of management and usually embrace more diverse kinds of businesses. This size itself leads to antitrust complications, potential synergies, hedging risks, more formal internal systems, and less first-hand experience in the industries managed. And strategy should incorporate these factors.

6. *Changing values* of members of the organization complicate strategy formulation. Attitudes toward leisure, self-fulfillment, mobility, insecurity (future shock), ethical behavior, "participation," and loyalty to one's employer affect the alternative strategies proposed and the commitment to new ventures. Moreover, growing sophistication of techniques within each function (finance, marketing, production, and the like) increases the danger that highly specialized technicians will pursue narrow goals, that is, suboptimize. Strategy helps to integrate these specialists.

7. *Professionalization of management* arising from an increasing separation of owners and managers impacts on managerial styles. Tomorrow's managers will be even more sophisticated about available planning and control techniques, subjected to more formal controls, open to conflict-of-interest questions, and perhaps more averse to risk taking. One important function of strategy is to counteract a tendency of professional managers to become too conservative and bureaucratic.

Each of the trends just listed will probably continue, and, in so doing they will make forward planning increasingly complicated. They compound the problems of adjusting to new opportunities and new threats. That complexity, however, heightens the need for company strategy, because strategy becomes the beacon light that guides most other planning. It cuts through the fog. It provides a direction and a sense of purpose in practical operational terms.

SOCIAL RESPONSIBILITY AND STRATEGY

If strategy sets the direction and lays out major thrusts for companies, as we have argued, then we cannot evade the question of social responsibility. History tells us that no socially devised institution as powerful and pervasive as the private enterprise system can survive unless it serves society well. Therefore, we must ask ourselves whether the strategy formulation process we are exploring leads to socially responsible behavior.

Social responsibility is neither a mere academic issue nor a fashionable buzzword. Business enterprises, especially the very large ones, are being challenged along with other parts of the "establishment." If executives hope to retain such management prerogatives as they still have, they must be clear in their own minds and make clear to others that they are acting in a socially responsible manner.

Our conviction is that sound strategic management contributes to socially responsible behavior—not perfectly, but overwhelmingly. The reasoning that leads us to this conviction is outlined in the next few pages, and we hope you agree. A secondary purpose of spelling out this analysis here is to emphasize a range of external relationships that must be weighed in formulating strategy. Not least is the integrating and balancing role pictured for the central manager as an essential feature in shaping strategy. Thus even if you are calloused about social responsibility, the analysis should deepen your understanding of the nature of strategy.

Resource Conversion—The Prime Responsibility

One constructive way to merge social obligation with a managerial view of strategy is the *resource-converter* model. Here we step back and examine briefly the role business-units* play in society.

---

* As explained in the next chapter, by *business-unit* we mean a single-line company or a division of a multiproduct corporation that operates as a distinct business.

Broadly speaking, each business-unit mobilizes resource inputs of diverse sorts and converts these resources into direct and indirect outputs that have a greater net value to society than would alternative uses of those resources. As a self-made plant manager said, "We've got to send more out the door than we take in." But the total process is much more complex than this generalization implies.

The relationship of a business-unit with each resource contributor always involves a two-way exchange. Figure 1–2 shows these flows for five typical outside groups—material suppliers, labor, the community, suppliers of capital, and customers. For a specific company there will be a wider variety of subgroups, but the underlying concept is the same. Each group of contributors—sometimes called *stakeholders*—provides a needed resource and receives in exchange part of the output flow of the enterprise.

Much more than money is involved. Typically, an array of payoffs provides the basis for continuing cooperation. Employees, for instance, are concerned about meaningful work, stability of employment, reasonable supervision, future opportunities, and a whole range of fringe benefits in addition to their paychecks. Suppliers of materials want a continuing market, sure and prompt payment, convenient de-

FIGURE 1–2.   *Enterprise = Resource Converter*

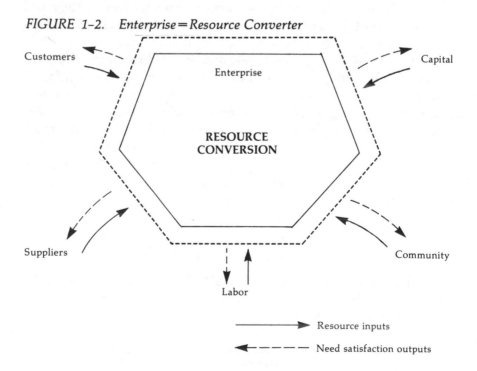

livery times, quality standards suited to their facilities, minimum returns, and the like. Investors are concerned about uncertainty of repayment, security, negotiability of their claims, veto of major changes, and perhaps some share in the management. For each resource contributor, mutual agreement about the conditions under which the exchange will continue is subject to evolution and periodic renegotiation.

Note that most of the widely discussed social-responsibility issues deal with some modification of previous conditions of resource exchange. Examples are equal opportunity for minority labor groups, public disclosure for investors, environmental protection for communities, and quality guarantees and informative labeling for consumers.

The true essence of social responsibility, in our view, is not simply making concessions in company contributions to one or more resource groups. Rather, it is ensuring the *maintenance of resource flows on mutually acceptable terms.* A business-unit and its managers are performing vital social functions as catalysts and integrators of resource conversions.

From society's point of view, profits are not "the name of the game." Instead, the aim is continuing resource conversion—which provides a flow of jobs, markets for materials, taxes and other support for the community, goods and services for consumers, and effective use of capital. Indeed, profits are essential to attract the necessary capital, but also essential are satisfactory markets, good jobs, acceptable products, and other outputs. The real "name of the game" is keeping the conversion process flowing. This is a very difficult but tremendously important task in modern society, particularly in a free society seeking to operate by consent rather than by edict. That assignment is by far the foremost responsibility of managers.

Winning continuing cooperation of each resource contributor has its price. In addition to monetary payments for products/services contributed, various guarantees, timing of actions, veto rights, alternative actions foresworn, and similar limitations may be granted. Now, if the concessions made to one resource group place too heavy a burden on the company, it may become impossible to grant the *quid pro quo* desired by other contributors—or *stakeholders.* The simple example of this problem appears in cash flows; a drastic jump in energy costs or wage rates (or drop in selling prices) may absorb so much cash that other demands for payment cannot be met. Employment guarantees or restrictions on how capital is used, to cite two more common examples, may be demanded by the labor or capital contributors, but these demands may place the company in an untenable position in meeting the wishes of other outside groups.

Basically, the managers of a business-unit serve as mediators between the various claimants. But since the resource contributors rarely meet face-to-face, it is the central managers who must consider the impact of demands of one group on the ability of the business to comply with other demands. This is a complex but vital social service.

FINDING AN ADVANTAGE IN RESOURCE CONVERSION

The ability of a company to reconcile diverse desires of its resource contributors is largely shaped by its strategy. In finding a distinctive mission—an untapped source of materials, a new service for customers, a better way to finance leased equipment, or early adaptation of new technology are examples—the company increases its social output. This additional margin helps the company to meet competition for resources on all fronts. Contrariwise, if the strategy poorly adapts the company's skills to its total environment, the capability of the company to satisfy all its contributors' exchange claims is weakened. Such an enterprise may be unable to fulfill its prime social function, namely, continuing resource conversion, and go out of existence, to the detriment of all.

It is folly to attempt to excel in all things. Instead, as noted earlier in this chapter, each business-unit should select a particular mission and a basis for differential advantage. For instance, IBM has always stressed customer service, customer orientation in product design, and liberal treatment of its employees. Humble Oil (now part of Exxon) rose to prominence because it gave high priority to acquiring a large crude oil (energy) base. Merck and Boeing stressed building a better mousetrap—ethical pharmaceutical goods and aircraft, respectively.

Each business-unit singles out perhaps one but more likely a few areas having synergistic ties in which it hopes to excel. In these areas it tries to develop an unusually favorable relation with the selected resource groups as compared to that of competitors. Typically, it pioneers in a new form of service or unique benefit that is attractive to the key contributor group, and couples this with a compatible internal technology. (For example, Crown Cork coupled special service to beer producers with a new technology for manufacturing two-piece cans.) The internal conversion technology and organization reinforce in a symbiotic way the external relationship being stressed. And, the business-unit's primary social contribution will probably arise in these areas. If the business-unit is wise (or lucky), it selects relationships for emphasis that will become especially important strengths in the future competition within its industry.

For the many external relationships not selected as a source of differential advantage, a business-unit *satisfices*; that is, it seeks with each of these resource suppliers a continuing relation that is at least adequate. Often the business-unit is too small to attempt any more than following general industry practice; its location, history, personal preferences of key executives, or existing resource base may not provide a good springboard, or management may deliberately decide that effort applied in other directions will be more rewarding. These secondary relationships cannot be neglected; they must be adequately maintained—like Herzberg's hygiene factors. Moreover, the secondary relationships should be designed so that they support or are at least compatible with the primary thrusts of the selected strategy.

In other words, using the resource-converter model we can say that a business-unit is acting in a socially responsible manner when it is able to sustain a continuing inflow of resources and outflow of services. It is not the prime responsibility of a business-unit to improve social values (although some do); rather, the primary task is finding ways to adjust to shifting pressures so that vital, satisfaction-generating exchanges will continue. Earning an adequate return on capital is one necessary condition and thus—perhaps paradoxically—a reasonably valid measure of social performance, but there are many others.

Strategy of each business-unit points the way that unit has selected out of a myriad of possibilities to demonstrate its justification to continuing existence. Idealistic but unworkable strategies are as antisocial as cynical strategies that defy social norms.

Summarizing, the preceding line of thought shifts the role of central managers away from the single-minded profit maximizers pictured in economic theory; it also undercuts the illusion of all-powerful dictators whose special interests block social reforms. Instead, from a social viewpoint:

1. Central managers assemble and integrate resources of many sorts for purposes of conversion into desired outputs; they are essential as catalysts.
2. In so doing they must mediate incompatible demands to keep the conversion process moving.
3. Because the claimants for, say, less pollution, more jobs, lower

prices, or absolute safety do not confront each other directly and are seldom concerned about the trade-offs involved in the pursuit of their provincial goals, managers bear the brunt of negotiating on all fronts.

4. Managers' most constructive task is conceiving and executing strategies that adjust resource conversions to new threats and opportunities while at the same time using a conversion technology that creates an optimum mixture of socially desired outputs.

Performing these interrelated tasks well is a great social contribution, and adept strategy formulation and implementation is a vital part of the process.

FROM CONCEPT TO PRACTICE

Strategy is a potentially powerful tool of management. As we have noted, it can give a company direction in the buzzing confusion of a topsy-turvy world. It encourages integrated and concentrated effort on a clear mission. It helps managers serve social needs. It puts lofty objectives into an operational form. All this and more is the realm of strategy.

A wide gap exists, however, between this general concept of company strategy and purposeful, committed behavior on the front lines of action. In fact, moving from concept to practice has turned out to be elusive for most companies. Thus the aim of the following chapters is to explore ways to close this gap.

The scope and form of a company strategy strongly influence its impact on other kinds of planning. Also, the process of developing the strategy to be followed affects its acceptance. More specifically:

1. A clear distinction needs to be recognized between business-unit and corporate strategy, because they concern quite different issues. (Chapters 2, 3, and 4 deal with this question of multilevel planning.)

2. Although strategy deals with the posture and thrusts of "our" enterprise, a significant part of the content focuses on relationships with other enterprises. (Chapter 5 explores these external alignments.)

3. Strategy is not God-given, as the Ten Commandments to Moses. Rather, strategy emerges from much give-and-take,

primarily among the executives who will either disregard it or put it into effect. (Chapter 6 examines the birth and nourishment of a new strategy.)

In addition to these important issues in strategy formulation, the force of any strategy is closely tied to the consistency and reinforcement of other managerial practices within the company. Too often a bridge is lacking between the selected strategy and short-run action. Among the critical links are:

4. Strategy ⟷ programming (action plans) in each department as well as for special projects.
5. Strategy ⟷ resource allocation—especially when it is focused on short-run results.
6. Strategy ⟷ policies and accepted values that have a sustained and pervasive influence on the way business is conducted—and often are slow to change.
7. Strategy ⟷ organization structure that either obstructs or facilitates moving in new directions.
8. Strategy ⟷ selection and motivation of key executives who can make or break the venture.

Building these linkages between the strategic concept and managing the daily business is discussed in Part II—Chapters 7 through 11. Then, because even the best-designed schemes may falter or fail to keep in tune with unexpected events, periodic evaluation is needed. Important here are:

9. Controls that measure progress and monitor external developments and feedback of these data for progressive revisions of strategy. (Chapter 12 tackles this task.)
10. Through all this "make-happen" effort, balance and reinforcement are critical, yet flexibility must be maintained. (That is the subject of Chapters 13 and 14.)

Clearly, strategy is no separate device that can be merely grafted onto an existing organization. If it is to be effective, it must be made an integral part of the total management process and system.

Strategic Direction of a Business-Unit

T oo often in the past, company strategy has been little more than resounding words. The statements have failed to provide executives with positive guidance for concrete action. Frequently, the strategy was stated in such general terms that it seemed irrelevant to the decisions and other actions being taken by line managers.

One way to make strategy meaningful is recognition of *different levels* of general management. The strategic issues facing the manager of a business-unit differ from those facing the CEO of a diversified company. Each level needs its own strategy. These strategies will be related but nonetheless distinct, because they address a different set of problems.

A second way to help tie strategy to the personal priorities and efforts of executives running business-units is to be sure to cover all *four key parts* of a well-thought-out strategy. One bright idea is not a strategy. That idea(s) needs to be fleshed out into an integrated scheme.

Dealing with the fear that future uncertainties are too great to permit strategic planning is a third means. For most executives, provision for *coping with uncertainty* transforms strategy from worthless speculation into prudent preparation.

Exploring these three ways of making strategy operational is the purpose of this chapter.

FOCUS ON BUSINESS-UNITS

Diversified companies need two levels of strategic planning. On the first level each distinct product line faces questions about how it can best serve its customers. Then at the corporate level quite a different set of questions arises about how to combine the various operating units into an optimum overall pattern. Of course, single-line companies do not have the second tier (although the very search for a second line may well require this duality), but for the large number of corporations that do operate distinct businesses, separate strategic planning is crucial.

Size is not the determining factor. Passenger airlines and electric utilities, for instance, typically are single-line enterprises even though their assets may be very large. Some much smaller companies, on the other hand, have several businesses, each of which needs its own strategy. A book publishing company, for example, that sells college texts, elementary and high school texts, and trade books has three separate businesses. Each has its own authors, its own customers, its own competitors, and its own requirements for success. What the publisher does in one branch of the industry need not dictate what it must do in the others.

Compelling reasons exist for focusing most strategic planning effort at the business-unit level. These self-motivated operating units are the centers for fitting together a whole array of transactions—with employees, bankers, suppliers, customers, governments. This organization level calls for the greatest sensitivity in allocating resources, assuming risks, and making trade-offs—all with an eye to future service, balance, and survival.

Although there may be advantages to combining several business-units, as we shall see in the next chapter, the underlying strength of any such combination comes from the units themselves. Adding a superstructure is no substitute for performing needed services, and that is done—well or poorly—at the business-unit level.

For purposes of strategic management, it is clearly desirable to think *first* of each distinct business as though it were a separate firm. Each of these businesses must find some basis of distinction over its competitors. In the long run, each business must attract its own resources. Problems of integration and balance, of stability and aggressiveness, must be reconciled internally and also fitted to the specific environment of each particular business. Whatever the stock ownership and affiliations, a strategy must be devised that will make the business-unit workable.

By *business-unit* we mean either a single-line, self-contained company *or* a division within a larger company that operates as a distinct business. For strategic management, business-units within a corporation can be differentiated from one another when each (a) has its own single-line or homogeneous cluster of products or services, (b) serves a separate and reasonably homgeneous market, and (c) employs its own reasonably homogeneous technology.* Even when only two of these characteristics are present, that portion of the company should be treated as a strategic-business-unit, to use General Electric terminology, with its separate strategic plan.

A management consulting firm, to cite a service rather than manufacturing example, had for years helped some of its clients locate new executives when no suitable person was available for promotion from within. However, this service was always treated as a stepchild and received intermittent attention. Finally, executive recruiting was separated from counseling. The executives in charge of the new unit sought a much wider market than the firm's consulting clients; they also devised much more systematic searching and screening methods. Now forced to develop their own strategy, they ran a very successful business. The consulting firm presently has two business-units, each with its own services, market, and technology; each pursues a strategy designed to serve particular needs better than competitors

The application of strategic analysis at the business-unit level has an internal as well as an external benefit. The whole process is much closer to actual operations, and "front-line" participants are involved. Market and competitive facts are more intimately known; threats and opportunities include those that seem relevant to operating executives; adjustments can be made promptly; the "not-invented-here" hurdle is minimized. In other words, several of the difficulties of getting strategy formulated *and* put into practice are reduced. An outside prod may be needed—as will be discussed in Chapter 6—but the bridge between strategy and operations is not as long as when planning is focused at the corporate level. Finally, managers' motivation in making a strategy happen is almost certain to be much higher when they have had a direct hand in its evolution.

* The organizational issues of business-unit boundaries are discussed in Chapter 9.

FOUR VITAL PARTS IN
A BUSINESS-UNIT STRATEGY

Some reverie and hoping are usually mixed in with the early forecasts when new strategy is first considered. Often a vision of what the company might become emerges, at least in a few venturesome minds. Perhaps after some checking the vision turns to a mission with sustained aspiration and commitment. Many successful people tell of forming such goals early in their career.

But strategy is made of sterner stuff. The underlying assumptions have to be examined, alternatives considered, risks appraised, ramifications and side effects weighed. A strategy is a course of action to which valuable resources (including one's own energies) will be committed. It is the basis for doing some things rather than others today. The company's future will be altered because of it; survival may be at risk. Consequently, strategy should be earthy and realistic.

Very briefly, *the strategy of a business-unit stakes out its mission and indicates the main distinctive means to be used in fulfilling that mission.* As a guide to all key people in the business-unit the strategy should be stated in terms that have operational significance.

Too often senior managers fail to move their strategy thinking from the broad-aspiration stage. The head of a small, successful electronics firm, for instance, said in a statement to employees:

> Our strategy is to become a leader in our industry—peripheral equipment for computers. Starting with a present base in printout devices, we intend to grow at least 20% per year. To do that we will add new lines, through acquisition if necessary. Growth is the key to better job opportunities for our employees and increased profits for stockholders.

The president of a Midwest fast-food chain was even more general. He stated:

> Our strategy is to be a growth company. We plan to grow about 25% each year, expanding on a regional basis. Because growth involves start-up expenses we will not try to increase our ROI above a constant 15%, but the prospect of future earnings should make our stock prices move up faster.

Neither of the above statements provides adequate guidance. One simply identifies an industry in which the company will operate and the growth goals, but little else. The other cites goals but fails even to mention the industry, market, or product. In fact, neither concern is close to its targets, and the electronic-device company is being acquired rather than absorbing other firms.

A well-developed business-unit strategy should include four basic elements:

1. *Domain sought.* What products or intangible services will the business-unit sell to what group of customers?

2. *Differential advantage in serving that domain.* On what basis—such as access to raw materials, better personnel, new technology, or low costs and prices—will the business-unit seek an advantage over competitors in providing its products or services?

3. *Strategic thrusts necessary and their approximate timing.* To move from where the business-unit now is to where it wants to be—as laid out in (1) and (2)—what moves will be made early and what can be deferred?

4. *Target results expected.* What financial and other criteria will the business-unit use to measure its success, and what levels of achievement are expected? *

By covering all four of these elements, lopsided emphasis on just one aspect is avoided. On the other hand, the strategy still can be highly selective on the specific conclusion it contains.

Domain Sought

The starting point in clarifying the strategy of almost any business-unit is to define the domain it seeks, its product (or service)/market scope. Selecting an industry is the first narrowing step—say, the health-care industry or the coal industry. (In fact, most business-units have their resources and strengths so deeply committed to an industry that they have only limited choice in this matter.) The chief issue, however, is picking a *propitious niche* in that industry. The niche may be a segment of the total products (or services) offered by the industry, or it may be a selected group of customers defined in terms of size, income, location, or some other characteristics. Obviously, each business tries to select a niche in which the growth and profit prospects are attractive and in which it has strengths relative to competitors.

Crown Cork & Seal Company, to continue an example cited in

---

* By listing targets as the fourth element, rather than the first, we place emphasis on the operational content of strategy. The more abstract goals—such as growth—usually serve better as criteria of acceptability than as guides for action. In practice, possible strategies are debated back and forth so often that no clear priority exists between target results and mission.

Chapter 1, was so bound up in the container industry that it could not move out and survive the transition. So it sought one or more niches that were more attractive than the average and that matched Crown Cork's capabilities. Pressurized cans used by breweries and aerosol product manufacturers met these criteria. That particular market became the primary domain sought by the company.

The Franklin National Bank switched the domain it sought during its exciting history. Starting as just a small country bank on Long Island (New York), it grew under the guidance of a single CEO to become the thirteenth largest bank in the United States. Its first domain was commercial banking, serving consumers and local business in the limited area of Long Island. Having become the leading bank in this domain, Franklin National expanded its goals (as soon as the state law permitted). It then moved into Manhattan and sought to become a truly national and international bank, with an array of services matching Citibank, Chase Manhattan, and the other giants. This enlarged domain drastically altered the character of the bank—with results explained in the following sections.

A redefinition of one's industry or niche within that industry sometimes suggests an attractive domain. The classical examples of redefinition—breaking down conventional boundaries—are total transportation instead of railroading and packaging instead of glass containers. Such a shift in perspective enabled O. M. Scott & Sons to expand from grass seed into an array of fertilizers and herbicides, all related to lawn care. Of course, the recasting of the concept of an industry is only a start; the need to select an attractive niche within that new scope remains.

Clear identification of a desired domain enables a business to concentrate on the particular activities necessary to serve that domain well. Especially important is anticipating changes in demand, supply, and regulation in the domain and preparing in advance to meet these new requirements. A secondary benefit of a well-defined domain is as a guide on what not to do. Activities that are irrelevant to serving the domain can be pushed aside.

The desired domain does not remain static. The nature of markets and competition in those markets frequently change. Products mature. A business may achieve a dominant position in one niche and have to look elsewhere for growth. But until a change is decided on, the selected domain provides positive direction to other business-unit planning.

The strategic advantage of picking a niche very carefully does not necessarily mean that a company should confine its activities to a single niche. Synergistic benefits may be obtainable from serving closely related niches. An expansion matrix, shown in Figure 2–1, suggests possibilities. Clearly, expansion arising from fuller use of productive capability would lead in quite different directions than providing the same services to a wider range of customers. With respect to synergy, as a firm moves farther away from its present customers and/or its present productive capability, the prospects for synergistic benefits diminish. At the extreme (lower-right corner of Figure 2–1), if new customers are to be served with a completely different knowledge and facilities, synergy tends to disappear; the firm is then involved in conglomerate expansion. And, moving in a diagonal direction increases the risk, since both factors become less familiar.

Of course, not all opportunities for synergy are suggested by the diagram. For instance, vertical integration may provide economies in marketing, purchasing, and production scheduling.

If a business-unit elects to serve two or more niches, it is highly desirable to analyze and plan for each separately. In this way the benefits that come from concentrated attention will not be lost. When and if the volume of work in a single niche can support its own organization, and if economies of scale permit separate marketing and production activities, an additional business-unit may be wise. This question is examined in Chapter 9.

Early writers on business strategy gave almost exclusive attention to this task of finding attractive niches suited to company strengths—and to building a large market share in such niches. In fact, the Strategic Planning Institute's analysis of factors leading to profitability

FIGURE 2–1. *Expansion Matrix*. Reprinted by permission of South-Western Publishing Co. from W. H. Newman and J. P. Logan, *Strategy, Policy and Central Management*, 8th ed. (Cincinnati: South-Western, 1981).

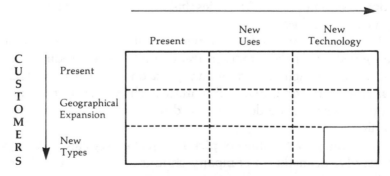

shows domain to be crucial to success. Experience with strategic management, however, shows clearly that being well situated in an attractive market is not enough; business-unit strategy should include three additional elements, which are now described.

DIFFERENTIAL ADVANTAGE IN SERVING SELECTED DOMAIN

The second essential pillar in a business-unit strategy is identifying one or more bases in which superiority over competitors will be sought. If our particular unit is to continue to attract customers and resources, we must perform at least some parts of the total industry task with distinction. New product design, quick deliveries, low production costs, better personnel policies, fewer fights with environmentalists—these examples only suggest the many possibilities.

Returning to the two companies used as illustrations in the preceding section, Crown Cork seeks a differential advantage in the pressurized can niche by (a) giving fast, personalized service to each of its customers at a level its full-line competitors cannot afford and (b) keeping its overhead expenses far below those of competitors. Franklin National Bank differentiated itself during its Long Island growth phase by (a) promptly opening branches in expanding residential areas and (b) offering unusual services first (its firsts included parking for customers, drive-in windows, evening hours, and prompt FHA home mortgage loans). However, when the bank moved to Manhattan, it found itself in a "me-too" situation, running hard to catch up with the services offered by established competitors. Consequently, the primary differential advantage it found itself forced to adopt was the granting of higher-risk loans. And this latter practice led directly to the Franklin National's collapse.

A differential advantage in one niche may be a handicap in another. For instance, Island Creek Coal Company appealed to steel companies and other metallurgical customers on the basis of its low-sulfur, high-volatile coking coal (coming from underground mines) which was carefully washed, sized, and graded to meet technical requirements. The metallurgical market, however, is mature. The big surge in demand for coal is coming from electric utilities, and here low-cost energy rather than technical quality control is the main basis for differential advantage. Island Creek's undergound mines and more elaborate surface treatment add to costs, and thus they are a detriment in the high-growth segment of the industry.

Some companies seek a differential advantage in their external alignments, as suggested in our brief discussion of social responsibility in Chapter 1. Sohio oil company, for example, badly needed to overcome a relative disadvantage in obtaining crude oil, so it adopted a strategy of participation in Alaskan oil exploration. The major discoveries there potentially give Sohio a significant differential advantage. However, the huge investment that has been necessary to remain a major partner in the production and transportation of this oil has placed the company in a strained financial position.

Unless a business-unit can devise a strategy that couples an obtainable differential advantage with an attractive domain, the domain is likely to be captured by a competitor.

STRATEGIC THRUSTS

Normally, a gap exists between the present position of a business-unit and the domain and differential advantages it seeks. Obstacles to closing that gap will vary in magnitude and over time, and the business-unit will have limited personnel, capital, existing external relationships, and other resources to use in dealing with these obstacles. Consequently, a third basic strategic consideration is deciding what major thrusts to make and how fast to press for changes. Besides identifying what these major thrusts should be, this element of strategy also involves steering a course between too-much-too-soon and too-little-too-late.

A few years ago, Crown Cork faced a threat to its strong position in high-pressure cans. The aluminum companies began producing a two-piece aluminum can. This new can has a differential advantage over the conventional three-piece steel can such as Crown Cork, American, Continental, and National can companies were making: it is lighter in weight; it has less possibility of leaky seams; the remote chance that lead on the seams produces lead poisoning is avoided; and printing on the can looks slightly better. Crown Cork did not want to switch to the aluminum can, because it would then find itself buying raw metal (roughly half the cost) from companies that would also be its competitors for the end product. A possible alternative was a two-piece steel can.

Thus a new thrust, vital to maintaining Crown Cork's position in the can business, was forged: the development of a low-cost technology to manufacture a two-piece steel can. This involved high-speed drawing of a thin steel sheet into the sides and bottom of the can, a task previously believed impratical. A complicating factor was that Crown Cork's low overhead policy meant that it normally spent very little on manufacturing process R&D. So a joint engineering venture with steel companies—which obviously also had a substantial stake in the outcome—was launched. Five years later a technology that involves both steel making and can making emerged. The two-piece steel can is now a viable competitor with the two-piece aluminum can.

A second issue then arose. How fast should Crown Cork convert to manufacturing two-piece steel cans? A large investment in machinery was involved: the technology might change; excess three-piece capacity would create price pressure in the total market; and the environmental agitation against nonreturnable containers could swing demand back to glass bottles. In spite of these drawbacks, Crown Cork decided to beat its competitors in building two-piece steel can lines. As a result of this second thrust, the company already has over half of the installed capacity for making the new steel cans.

Clearly, these two moves have been crucial points of Crown Cork's strategy. They illustrate what we have called thrusts and some other people term initiatives, or key programs. A strategic thrust is a vital, positive undertaking that moves a company toward its differential advantage in its desired domain.

Failure to include thrusts in a strategic plan may leave the selected objectives floating; it is probably the major "missing link" in moving strategy from ideas to action. This was a contributing weakness in Franklin National Bank's move into Manhattan. In addition to taking risky loans, Franklin National failed to tool up to do the broader business it said it wanted. There was no thrust focused on developing and/or acquiring a pool of talented personnel necessary for the new tasks, and there was only slow recognition of the need to modify the informal centralized organization, which suited Long Island, to a complex, sophisticated organization for a major bank of world stature. By contrast, note that when Citibank adopted its strategy to go after more business from world corporations it recognized the organization and personnel hurdles and established thrusts to overcome them.

The sequence and timing of thrusts can be tricky. Some actions obviously must precede others, for example land acquisition before plant construction. But often a strategic choice can be made. In the British Petroleum move into the United States market, the company deferred heavy commitment in marketing until a source of United States crude oil was in sight. To have started marketing alone and relied completely on local purchases of finished products would have exposed the company to very high risks. In this situation we can also note that building or acquiring refining capacity came even later; clearly, refining capacity was not regarded as a critical factor—it could be manipulated later without paying high penalties.

A different sequence is being followed by a manufacturer of fiberglass boats. A low selling price is a key feature of the marketing strategy, and to achieve costs permitting this low price, a large modern plant is necessary. The company's current sales are not large enough to keep such a plant busy. Nevertheless, the management decided to build the plant and to be in a strong competitive position. While market demand is being built up, the company has taken on several subcontracts at break-even prices and is even selling some boat hulls to another boat builder to help cover overhead costs of the plant. Here is an instance of moving first into large-scale production facilities, hoping that demand will catch up.

Even after a sequence has been selected, the manager has to decide how fast to move. It is quite possible to be too early. A leading East Coast department store, for example, correctly predicted a major shift of population to the suburbs, and it became a leader in establishing suburban branches. However, at the time it selected branch locations, few of the large, modern shopping centers with their vast parking spaces were in existence. Consequently, the store established branches in locations that are now being passed by. The irony of the situation is that the management of this store was more farsighted than several of its competitors, yet because it moved too soon, it is now at a relative disadvantage in suburban operations.

Although difficult to do wisely, the timing of thrusts does provide a desirable flexibility in the execution of strategy. Delaying or even shifting the sequence of major moves permits postponement of especially heavy commitments. This introduces a degree of flexibility without a total change in strategy with each change in the wind.

In dealing with thrusts, even more than with differential advantages, a business-unit strategy should be highly selective. The highlighting of critical moves, in contrast to all sorts of minor maneuvers, is a significant part of the guidance that strategy provides.

Target Results Expected

The three elements of business-unit strategy just described deal primarily with what to do when—and by implication what not to do. They are guides to more detailed planning and action which are to follow. This emphasis leaves out one important dimension of strategy.

If these things are done (and the environment is largely as predicted), what results are expected?

A small manufacturer of testing instruments for metallurgical industries, for instance, adopted a strategy of major commitment to research in the use of lasers. Translated into targets of anticipated results, this research commitment meant aiming for (a) a breakthrough on testing equipment in two to five years, (b) a reputation as a technical leader in this field within three years, and (c) a break-even on company profit and loss during the next three to five years. Note how much clearer the strategy is when we state both the means (laser research) and the ends (the three targets).

There are several reasons why strategy should include some statement of anticipated results. The people who must endorse the strategy, especially those who contribute resources, can reasonably hold back until they get some feel for what the situation is likely to be as a consequence of all this activity. Also, the individuals designing the strategy will have their personal objectives and values, and they, too, will be concerned about how results are expected to match these criteria. By no means least important, target results set the stage for shorter-run targets and controls, which are essential ingredients of effective implementation.

Taking the viewpoint of the senior manager who is responsible for the selection of strategy, how does he or she decide, "Okay, that's it"? Fundamentally, the process involves: (a) selecting the criteria for judging the strategy, (b) translating and stating the expected results of the strategy in terms of these criteria, and (c) deciding whether the expected results (the targets) meet acceptable minimum levels of achievement and are better than expected results of alternative strategies.

Criteria to be Considered. Several criteria are often used to evaluate a strategy, such as:

1. Return on investment (usually this is profit related to financial investment, but it might be the return on any critically scarce resources).
2. Risk of losing investment of scarce resources.
3. Company growth (in absolute terms or as a percentage of the market).
4. Contribution to social welfare (in one or more dimensions).
5. Stability and security of employment and earnings (of all employees and/or of executives).

6. Prestige of the company and of company representatives.
7. Future control (or influence) over company decisions.

Different individuals naturally stress one or two of the above criteria—finance people, the return on investment; research people, the company prestige; marketing people, the company growth; and so forth—and occasionally they may wish to add other criteria such as cash flow or international balance of payments. Fortunately, doing well on one criterion does not necessarily detract from all the others, so a specific strategy has not one but a whole set of results, and the only practical way to judge a strategy is to consider several criteria simultaneously. To expedite the evaluation process, three or four of these various criteria should be singled out as dominant in the specific situation.

Expressing Strategy in Terms of Criteria.   Meaningful strategies must be conceived in operational terms—products to sell, markets to reach, materials to acquire, research to perform, and the like. However, such actions take on value only as they contribute to desired results, and the pertinent results are defined by the criteria just discussed.

So to relate strategy to the selected criteria, a conversion or translation is needed. For instance, the actions contemplated in a strategy have to be expressed in anticipated costs and revenues, which give us an estimated profit. Similarly, the proposed actions have to be restated in manpower terms to estimate their effect on stability of employment (if that is one of the key criteria), and likewise for other criteria.

These restatements of anticipated results become the targets at which the strategy is aimed. But because the success of any strategy is never certain, these targets will be surrounded by many if's and maybe's. Often they should be expressed as a range, not a single point, with subjective probabilities attached. Nevertheless, tentative though the estimates may be, this is the currency in which a strategy will be evaluated.

Are Targets Acceptable?   Now, with criteria selected and the anticipated results of strategy expressed in terms of these criteria, the manager is in a position to say "Let's go" or "That's not good enough." Rarely is there a choice among several strategies, each of which is quite attractive. Instead, the pressing question is whether any proposed plan is acceptable at all. The reason for this scarcity of attractive choices is that all of us have high aspirations, at least for one or two criteria. Thirty percent profits, no real risk, worldwide prestige, half of industry sales—any and all of these may be part of one's dreams. The blunt facts are that few of these dreams will be realized by any strategy we can conceive. So we have to decide what *level of achievement* will be acceptable for each of our criteria.

This picking of acceptable levels is complicated by differences in values held by key executives. For instance, strategy A may promise a thirty percent return on capital but with a fifteen percent chance of complete loss and a sure transfer of ownership; whereas strategy B promises only a fifteen percent return on capital but with small risk of total loss and little danger of change in control of the company. Many quantitative techniques exist for computing optimal combinations. Reality, however, indicates that personal perceptions and values strongly affect the decision. The chairman of the board—say, a wealthy person and a large stockholder—may prefer strategy A; the president—who came up from the ranks, is fifty-two years old, and owns little stock—may prefer strategy B. Or, if the chairman likes the prestige of his position and the president thinks the chairman is too conservative, the preferences may be reversed.

It is difficult to generalize about whose values will predominate. Generally, the most active and aggressive senior executives will establish the pattern, provided their objectives meet at least the minimum acceptable requirement of each interest group whose withdrawal of support could paralyze the company. In the language of Chapter 1, the output of the strategy must enable the company to fulfill at least minimum needs of resource contributors.

Thus, though there is no simple resolution of how high targets should be, we obviously should not evade the translation of operational plans into key targets (or vice versa). A strategy expressed in terms of targets alone is little more than wishful thinking. On the other hand, an operational strategy that is not translated into targets is primarily an article of faith. A well-developed strategy has both an operational plan and targets.

All four parts of a business-unit strategy—the domain sought, differential advantages, major thrusts, and target results—are interrelated. Figure 2–2 stresses this interdependence. Each of the four parts contributes an essential dimension; together they set a clear course.

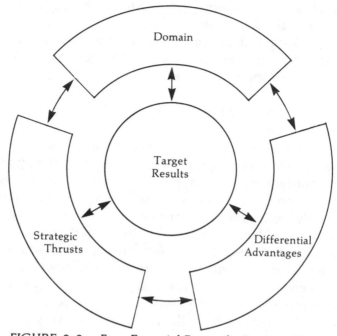

FIGURE 2-2.   Four Essential Parts of a Business-Unit Strategy

COPING WITH UNCERTAINTY

Two ways of making the strategy concept more workable have been recommended—(a) concentrating first on a separate, tailor-made strategy for each business-unit, and (b) designing business-unit strategies that include four key parts: domain, differential advantage, thrusts, and target results. Coping with uncertainty is a third way.

Line executives who are working hard to meet monthly goals and overcome short-run hurdles often resist strategic management because, "Nobody knows what will happen three years from now. Why waste time on imagined problems?" So, unless strategic planning includes practical means for dealing with future uncertainty, a lot of managers will be reluctant to give it attention.

Strategy is always surrounded by uncertainty. The future has been uncertain since long before Joseph advised the Egyptian pharaoh on the first national food stabilization plan. The environment five to twenty or more years in the future is sure to differ from the present; competitors' actions and reactions are unknown; even the business-unit itself is changing. In the face of such shifting sand, how can a manager be expected to lay out a strategic plan?

Four kinds of help come to the aid of the strategic manager: good environmental forecasts, limits on exposure to adverse risks, progressive revisions of strategy, and *prepared opportunism*.

Good Environmental Forecasts

Executives handling day-to-day affairs of a business-unit are rightfully skeptical about forecasts of the problems they will face, say, five years in the future. "Who knows whether our major competitor will hold his price of imports from Korea? Consumers are fickle—last year sports cars were hot; this year Mrs. Cabot wants a pickup truck! Even a three-months' budget gets out of date."

Indeed, the specifics do change, but experience indicates that most of the broad trends affecting business-unit strategy can be predicted within a useful range. There is sufficient momentum in society to make sudden turnabouts rare, and new discoveries take quite a while to have widespread effects—as the history of satellite communication or equal rights for women bear witness.

One helpful approach is to think in terms of the four types of underlying forces listed in the previous chapter—economic, social, technological, and political. First ask what particular elements in each of these categories are already changing in a way that has important impacts on our business, and second, where in our operations is the impact being felt? The aim of this exercise is to identify a limited number of elements that, at least at present, are significant. Then with this list as an agenda, we can forecast how those elements are likely to behave in the future.

To illustrate with a mature product—passenger automobile tires— several basic forecasts can be made for the 1980s with considerable confidence. Technologically, belted tires, which have already been around for a decade, will achieve a more dominant position. Lighter cars will reduce tire wear. Politically, safety will continue to be stressed. Socially, both potential car owners and cars per capita will continue to increase, but at a slower pace. Economically, the replacement tire market will flatten out, because of longer life of belted tires, lighter cars, and some driving restraint (because of high gasoline prices). Also, the original equipment market will continue to be dominated by a few large, low-cost producers; except for Michelin, no new producers will have the clout to enter the original equipment business.

Each part of this forecast is based on a development already taking place and is likely to continue for several years. Each can be backed up by substantial quantitative and qualitative support. The reader may wish to qualify or add to these terse statements, but the point is that this kind of forecast is available to the strategy-formulation process.

Even in relatively new domains, some of the important parameters can usually be forecast. Consider heart pacemakers, which are implanted in patients' chests for the balance of their lives to assure regularity in heartbeat. Socially, the demand will increase as the total population gets older and as more surgeons learn to perform the operation. Technologically, atomic-powered pacemakers will become much more popular than battery units because of their smaller size and longer span of life before replacement is necessary. Politically, government aid in meeting large medical expenses—such as a pacemaker involves—is very likely. Economically, costs should fall substantially, because the three leading producers are just at the beginning of the experience curve; moreover, because barriers to entry are high—as with many medical products—profit margins should be attractive.

This sort of forecast has reasonable reliability because of inertia—the energy required to stop a prevailing force and the energy needed to launch an alternative. Of course, time spans must be considered. If a business-unit strategy will take five years to execute and five years to "harvest," then an environmental force likely to persist for at least a decade is long enough. However, if the inertia may run out in five years and the business-unit needs fifteen years for a full cycle of development and harvest, future uncertainty jumps sharply.

Several words of caution must be added. (a) A mathematical model is not being suggested. Our experience indicates that identification of several key elements and qualitatively relating such elements to factors in a strategy is as far as this approach should be pursued. (b) Some but not all the issues to be weighed will emerge in this approach—as a business-unit and its competitors undertake different activities, additional environmental elements must be included on the agenda. (c) Within the general drifts that are identified, cyclical and other short-term ups and downs will also occur. Timing of moves remains a delicate problem, even when the general direction is clear.*

---

*Many managers lament their "lack of data" for good environmental forecasting. For most strategy choices, however, substantial quantities of data do exist. When looking back at "surprises," several large companies discovered that they had possessed warning data, but this information was in some other department, or it was not recognized as relevant. The forecasting task of general drifts over the relevant time-span is more

Our basic argument in this section is that a substantial portion of environmental uncertainty can be resolved, with sufficient reliability for strategy formulation, by the systematic selection and study of key elements within the economic, social, technological, and political sectors. Useful predictions can and should be made. Frequently, although not always, the practical difficulties with strategic management arise more with the use of forecasts than with their accuracy.

LIMITS ON EXPOSURE TO ADVERSE RISKS

A second general way to deal with uncertainty is limiting potential losses. If we are unsure what will happen, we then try to maintain a position in which we can bear the adverse results if unpredictable events turn out badly for us. Insurance, hedging, postponing commitment to action, even foregoing an opportunity are all possibilities.

Complete risk avoidance, of course, is neither possible nor desirable. Instead, we look for a strategy that (a) has almost no chance of complete catastrophe and (b) has a down-side risk, if present, that is substantially smaller than the potential up-side gain. The exposure sought is suggested in Figure 2–3.

Theoretically, at the moment of decision (year 0) we would estimate the array of possible results, the probability of each, and the value we attach to each. Figure 2–2 merely shows outside limits; an expected value would fall in between. In practice, the computation of numerical values is virtually impossible, because the combinations of numerous uncertainties and of intervening actions soon boggle the computer as well as one's mind. Nevertheless, the underlying concept of keeping the potential consequences of uncertain events in a favorable balance and within a lower limit is often applicable to strategic alternatives.

Contingency plans are a device for limiting losses. They provide a fallback alternative if the main goal is unattainable. For example, an energy company interested in coal gasification estimated that it could sell the output of its new coal mines to public utilities if the gasification process did not prove to be as efficient as hoped. Although the sale of coal would not provide a very attractive return on investment, it

---

digging out information, recognizing its significance, and interpreting its impact. Moreover, consultants who are acquainted with available data can be tapped. We do not underrate the difficulty of forecasting, but we do observe that, frequently, lack of data is more an alibi than an insurmountable hurdle.

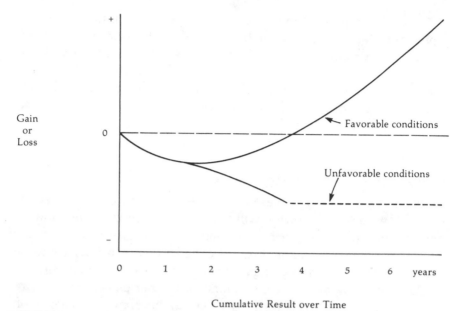

Cumulative Result over Time

FIGURE 2-3.   Limiting Down-Side Exposure to Loss

would prevent out-of-pocket losses. Incidentally, military planners frequently prepare contingency plans.

Note that all these "What if . . .?" approaches to uncertainty increase the number of predictions we must make. The number of factors to consider and the need for intuitive judgments have actually increased! So, the benefit is not in sidestepping the hazards of forecasting. Rather, we have introduced a way of thinking about the risks that accompany uncertainty. Once the range of possible outcomes is grasped, a lower limit of exposure can be set.

Progressive Revisions of Strategy

The primary way to deal with uncertainty, by far, is progressive revisions. With new knowledge—and to that extent the uncertainty is reduced—a plan made last year is updated this year.

In these revisions we do two things. First, we reconsider the predictions on which the current strategy was based. If recent events call for a change in the forecasts, then the strategy is modified accordingly. In other words, revising the game plan is a built-in feature of the plan itself. We are willing to proceed with a strategy based partly on shaky assumptions because we know those assumptions will be reexamined as soon as better supporting data are available.

A second feature of strategy revision is to fill in gaps. In any strategy, in pursuit of flexibility—as mentioned earlier—we deliberately postpone decisions, and especially commitments, for aspects of the plan that can be settled later without significantly affecting actions that have longer lead times. For example, a marketing plan (but not the market) or a plan for capital financing for an exciting new product need not be settled until R&D work has progressed from the lab to the pilot-plant stage. But now, with product feasibility almost assured, what could previously be treated as tentative options must become a current thrust.

A strategy, then, is continuously evolving from bold, though realistic, aspirations through an explicit general plan and early steps of implementation, into an array of concrete moves necessary to make the dream come true. In the process, the original dream is clarified and modified—partly because the original forecasts were inaccurate and incomplete and partly because the world changed and the original plan needed to be modified. Uncertainty abounds; revisions are repeatedly made.

Revision also involves measuring progress along major thrusts to see if they are still possible or whether new, different ones must be added. The monitoring and control necessary for this kind of adjustment are discussed in Chapter 12. But there is sufficient persistency of general direction so that the business-unit engaged in strategic management is much closer in tune with opportunities than its competitor that merely reacts on a short-term basis and thus drifts with the changing tides.

PREPARED OPPORTUNISM

Environmental forecasting, balancing recognized risks, progressive revision—these approaches deal with uncertainty of increasing degree. But what can be done when the future appears so cloudy that we can't form a target mission sufficient for even the progressive revision approach?

Prepared opportunism is the best answer. It is a loose strategy that extends beyond the planning horizon for specific strategies. It involves conscious preparation, even though the desired domain and basis for differential advantage of the business-unit are still unsettled.

Planning at the Suburban Medical Center illustrates prepared opportunism. Here, central managers have predicted that governmental and economic pressures for regionalized health services (in contrast to each hospital offering a full line of services) will grow, but who will do what and how such assignments will be decided is very unclear. The Suburban Medical Center board is ambitious and wants a significant role but is uncertain how it should proceed. In this instance, an opportunity arose to merge with a local rehabilitation clinic, and Suburban Medical Center seized the opportunity, partly because such an affiliation might provide a competitive edge in sparring for regional status.

Prepared opportunism involves the creation of an ability to adjust—to take advantage of new situations—to pounce on new opportunities. Such ability can be generated in three ways:

1. Developing reserve resources (capital, skilled manpower, production and/or distribution facilities, R&D capability, and so on). Reserves can be achieved through:
   (a) excess over present needs;
   (b) access to added resources;
   (c) flexibility to withdraw from present uses.
2. Monitoring—keeping in touch with changes in potential arenas.
3. Cultivating a capacity for rapid reaction; this relates to psychological, social, and organizational structures.

The resource base suggested in (1) above should be tied to scenario forecasting. On the basis of, say, three scenarios, a business-unit selects one or more tentative offensive or defensive strategies, and then it identifies the resources it would need. Such a line of thought guides the character and size of the resource base to be developed. Without at least an informal projection of this sort, building available resources rests on just blind faith in their future values.

Typical examples of resource bases for prepared opportunism include unused borrowing capacity, mining rights or other access to raw materials, and a metal-can company's small venture in plastics to get a feel for that technology.

With respect to capacity for rapid reaction, item 3 above, Michael Kami* has argued that the chief value of long-range planning is the preparation of managers to deal with unforeseen opportunities (not the execution of the plan they originally devised). This preparation involves (a) a mental and emotional willingness to think about and do things differently than at present, (b) an awareness of where adjustments must be made and who should be consulted about such adjust-

* Former Director of Long-Range Planning for IBM and Director of Corporate Planning for Xerox.

ments, and (c) some practice in devising a new scheme and hence a bit more speed and finesse in doing so. The military analogy is "war games," but a particular business-unit may try other ways to develop the desired flexibility.

The obvious drawbacks to prepared opportunism are (a) the cost of getting prepared—the unused resources, monitoring, and building adjustment capability and (b) the difficulty of maintaining such capability in fighting trim without actually using it. Here again, military preparedness is a close analogy—except in degree; we are willing to bear the burden of military preparedness as insurance and also as a source of political clout, but few businesses can afford comparable outlays for contingencies.

In the business field, prepared opportunism ranges from the simplest form—in which strategic action beyond a one-year budget is confined to perhaps building a strong equity, developing marketing muscle, or investing in a large engineering staff—to its elaborate form—where it gets very similar to strategic planning with built-in provision for revisions. The distinction lies in the clarity of the business-unit's mission. In prepared opportunism, the mission remains undecided, whereas with a strategy plus frequent revisions the mission is expressed, even though it probably will be modified over time. A designated mission subject to periodic revision leads to higher morale and also to a tendency for more investment and other commitments. Prepared opportunism has more uncertainty, more flexibility, and a lack of a rallying cause.

Concluding comment: These means of coping with uncertainty— good environmental forecasts, limits on exposure to adverse risks, progressive revisions of strategy, and prepared opportunism—can help any business-unit; they confront a prickly problem and deal with it constructively. But neither they nor the strategy formulation they help shape create the uncertainty. Most of the unknowns and unknowables are inherent in our complex, dynamic society. Every enterprise makes decisions that shape its future, even though its executives may be unwilling to admit the long-term implications because of the surrounding uncertainty. Strategic management accepts uncertainty as inevitable, and then tries to turn this ambiguity into an advantage through strategic planning.

Strategic planning for a business-unit has been the focus of this chapter. It is the business-unit that has the intimate interaction with the environment, that grasps opportunities, that develops differential advantages which lead to success, that selects and integrates resources creatively. And because the business-unit is such a center for dynamic action, we believe strategic planning should focus first and foremost on it. Diversified companies do face an additional set of strategic issues, to which we turn in the next chapter, but these are secondary, in the sense that they are concerned with aiding, harmonizing, and guiding the basic units in which the primary action takes place.

Portfolio Strategy for a Diversified Corporation

BUSINESS–UNIT VERSUS CORPORATE STRATEGY

Strategy for a single business-unit has been our focus in Chapter 2. These single-product-line, self-contained "companies" are the dynamic building blocks of our economic society. Each requires individualized attention. Our prime attention on the creation of strong business-units is more than a convenient analytical approach; it reflects the cardinal importance of these units.

Nevertheless, successful business-units often outgrow their original mission. Their market may have matured; they may have strengths that can be applied to related businesses; a broader base may be needed to match competition or spread risk; assurance of supplies may become critical; perhaps an irresistible deal may present itself. For such reasons as these, many corporations find themselves engaged in several different businesses.

Sooner or later the benefits of combining the collection of business-units within a corporation must be assessed Potentially, the federation of units will be stronger than the sum of each business operating independently. But this does not happen automatically. We need a *cor-*

porate strategy that focuses on the selection and the interrelation of units that will, in fact, yield the benefits of union.

Corporate strategy, in contrast to business-unit strategy, applies to a different level of organization, and it differs in content. Broadly speaking, corporate strategy has two parts. The first part deals with selecting and developing a collection of business-units. This is usually called *portfolio strategy*. Portfolio issues are widely discussed; in fact, many people assume that portfolio choice is the only strategic problem at the corporate level. However, most diversified corporations deal with a second set of strategic issues centering around the question, "What should the corporation do to add extra strength to its business-units?" We call this *corporate input strategy*.

A basic approach to formulating both parts of corporate strategy is indicated in Figure 3-1. A careful appraisal of the business-units presently owned is the first step. For each unit the results to date, the standing relative to competitors, threats and opportunities in its environment, and projected future results based on existing plans should

FIGURE 3-1.   *Approach to Corporate Strategy.* From W. H. Newman and J. P. Logan, *Strategy, Policy, and Central Management,* 8th ed. (Cincinnati: South-Western, 1981), p. 353. Used by permission of publisher.

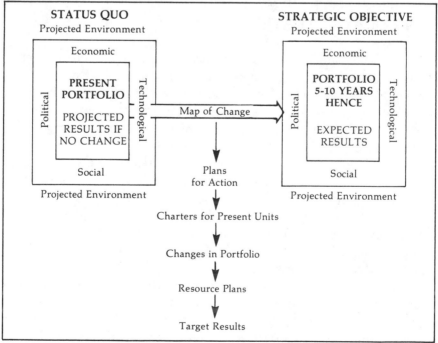

be studied. Moreover, the projections for all business-units should be combined into a consolidated picture of what the corporation will be and do if the status quo is maintained.

If this combined picture is not entirely satisfactory, then the second broad step is to decide what doable changes, executed within the projected environment, would put the corporation in the best balanced position. This becomes the strategic objective. It stipulates the desired portfolio of business-units five to ten years hence, their relative competitive positions, the individual unit results, and the combined results for the corporation as a whole. Also, it stipulates the distinctive inputs the corporation will make to the business-units.

To move from the status quo to the strategic objective will require some supporting changes along the way. The main features of these planned changes, which become part of the corporate strategy, deal with charters for present units (domains, expectations, constraints), changes in the portfolio, resource plans (including sources and allocations of capital), and target results at intervals along the course.

The main elements in a corporate strategy, then, include:

1. The desired portfolio of business-units five to ten years hence.
2. The distinctive inputs by the corporation that will help give its business-units a differential advantage.
3. Major moves (thrusts) to get from present situation to the holdings pictured in (1):
   (a) charters for business-units to be retained;
   (b) additions or deletions of business-units, including desired acquisitions;
   (c) consolidated resource mobilization and allocation plans.
4. Target results.

The chief issues and hurdles in developing the corporate portfolio strategy are discussed in this chapter, leaving review of corporate input strategy to Chapter 4.

PORTFOLIO DESIGN

A popular approach to corporate portfolio analysis is the four-cell matrix stressed by the Boston Consulting Group (BCG)—see Figure 3–2. The earlier BCG version focused only on cash flow and simply looked at industry growth versus company market position. The implications of this chart are that *dogs* should be sold or liquidated, while

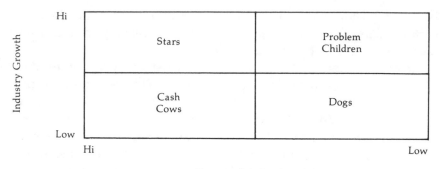

Company Market Position

FIGURE 3-2.   Simple BCG Portfolio Matrix. From W. H. Newman and J. P. Logan, *Strategy, Policy, and Central Management*, 8th ed. (Cincinnati: South-Western, 1981). Used by permission of publisher.

cash cows should provide the capital to foster growth of *stars* and improved market position of *problem children.*

In practice, this framework has proved to be a gross oversimplification. More factors should be considered in placing a business-unit on the matrix, and more than cash flow is involved in building a desirable portfolio.

A good portfolio has several dimensions. Four are always significant: (a) growth and profitability of the business-units considered separately, (b) synergy among the units, (c) risk and profit balance, and (d) cash-flow balance.

First Ingredient: Attractive Business-Units

The business-units within any diversified corporation will naturally vary in attractiveness. Industry growth rates change; competitors expand capacity; risks assumed turn out well or poorly; and so forth. Thus an initial step in reviewing portfolio strategy is to compare the relative attractiveness of present units—especially in terms of their future prospects for growth and profitability. Corporation resources will be limited, with respect to central management time, perhaps also capital. Consequently, guidance is needed on where to place the "bets."

A useful way to highlight such a comparison of business-units is on an evaluation matrix. One such matrix, adapted from layouts used by General Electric and Royal Dutch Shell, is shown in Figure 3-3. Here each business-unit is evaluated on the basis of its industry attractiveness and its competitive position in that industry.

Placing a business-unit on such a matrix involves many subjective

COMPETITIVE POSITION OF BUSINESS-UNIT

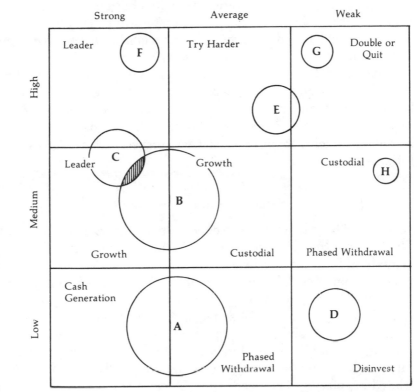

Note: Area within circles indicates relative size of business-units

FIGURE 3–3.   Evaluation Matrix. Area within circles indicates relative size of business-units. From W. H. Newman and J. P. Logan, Strategy, Policy, and Central Management, 8th ed. (Cincinnati: South-Western, 1981). Used by permission of publisher.

judgments. Both the subfactors to be included and the outlook for each factor have to be decided. Among the subfactors that determine an industry's attractiveness are: market growth rate, stability of demand, availability of resources, product and process volatility, number of customers and suppliers and the ease of entry, governmental support/regulation, gross and net margins, and inflation vulnerability. A similar set of subfactors bears on the competitive position of a business-unit. These include: relative market share, product/service quality and reputation, favorable access to resources, R&D strength, relative productivity and costs, and community and government relations.

The matrix is designed to provoke strategic thinking. For instance, in the example shown on Figure 3-3, business-unit D clearly should be divested, and A—the corporation's original business—has such poor prospects that it should be used to generate cash as it is phased out. In contrast, units E and G may warrant significant resource inputs, because they are in attractive industries.

This sizing up of the business-units separately, of course, builds on the thorough strategy planning done within the respective units. Each business-unit should have its own plans that, if successful, may change its present location on the evaluation matrix. At the corporate level harsher judgments about their relative prospects are needed as a basis for allocating scarce resources.

SECOND INGREDIENT: SYNERGY AMONG BUSINESSES

A good portfolio is more than a collection of attractive business-units. The fact that the units are associated under a single central management should add extra value. Often a unit when viewed separately has only medium appeal, but when combined with other holdings it may add unusual strength. Synergy and balance are both involved.

Four potential sources of synergy deserve attention:

1. First is the ability of corporate executives to manage (serve as "outside director") various kinds of businesses with acumen. Historical data show that the more-successful diversified companies stick to related businesses. Thus Federated Department Stores in its diversification stays with retailing, because its central managers understand that type of activity. In contrast, Teledyne in its initial growth phase concentrated on new high-technology businesses. The rationale is that the experience gained and the competence needed in guiding one part of the portfolio will be especially valuable to other business-units in related fields.*

2. Synergy may be possible from the broader use of a particular strength of one of the business-units. The Campbell Soup Company provides a well-known example. Over the years this company has built up a strong national selling organization for its soups. When it acquired Pepperidge Farm, an East Coast producer of specialty breads, cookies, and the like, it used its marketing strength to give Pepperidge Farm products national distribution. In another case the R&D capabil-

---

* This argument also has negative connotations. As we shall see, considerations of balance may suggest that unrelated businesses be assembled, but if this is done, part of the cost will be added complexity in management. (We return to this issue in Chapter 9.)

ity of a production-systems company helped a machine tool business develop electronic controls for its equipment. Similarly, the national repair service organization of a printing-press company is a great boost to the sale of Swiss-made auxiliary equipment.

3. Vertical integration is another potential source of synergy. For instance, an assured supply of paper periodically becomes critical for magazine publishers. Time, Inc. has its own paper subsidiaries which provide supply protection. At the same time, Time's paper mills are assured of a large, steady customer with a minimum of selling effort.

4. When business-units are relatively small, the parent may be able to provide a centralized resource more efficiently than the units could obtain that resource independently. The prime example, of course, is raising capital in major financial markets on terms that separate units could not command alone, but there are many other possibilities. Small commercial banks, when they are combined into one group, find substantial economies in electronic processing of checks, deposits, billings, and so on. (The local unit is also able to make larger loans because the total capital that sets size limits is larger.) The central room-reservation service provided by hotel and motel chains is a significant advantage to local units in maintaining occupancy.

Care must be exercised in seeking synergies. Some possibilities run into antitrust barriers. Also, obtaining a synergistic benefit clearly implies that two or more business-units will operate within certain constraints, and over time that requirement may become a serious drag. Many vertical-integration schemes, for instance, tend to limit flexibility—as rubber companies tied to obsolete national rubber plantations discovered.

Nevertheless, the prospect of synergistic benefits may influence decisions of which business-units to retain—or add—in a total portfolio. The potential impact of ability to manage, use of special strengths, vertical integration, and central resource pools should be at least considered.

Portfolio selection may create the potential for synergy. The actual achievement of synergistic benefits, however, calls for special managerial action. Typically, the necessary synchronization of operations occurs only when central executives "make it happen." We return to this need for follow-up action in the next chapter.

THIRD INGREDIENT: RISK AND PROFIT BALANCE

A third consideration in portfolio strategy is the degree of risk and the resulting fluctuation in profits that is acceptable. The mix of businesses selected clearly affects the overall uncertainty about the stability and size of sales and profits.

Prevailing norms provide some guidance, but what best serves the diverse interest of various stakeholders is ill-defined.

Generally, survival takes precedence over less risky liquidation. This is reflected in two portfolio guides. First, companies in mature businesses are expected to shift investment to new lines of business to provide continuity, even though the new businesses are more risky than the present ones. For example, Handy & Harman's traditional activity of processing silver and gold is "mature," because major new uses of these venerable metals is unlikely, and rising metal prices dampen much increase in the physical volume of present uses. So Handy & Harman has adopted a long-run objective of deriving half its future profits outside the precious metal area. It is steadily adding business-units in other high-value-added industrial processes. This is an explicit strategy of reducing the risk associated with remaining in its primary field.

Another indication of the importance attached to survival is the concept that a corporation should not bet its existence on a single, risky venture. No publicly owned firm relies entirely on the success of drilling a particular off-shore oil well; it gets other investors to share the risk on that well, and then it diversifies to part ownership in other wells, probably in other geographical areas.

Hedging against cyclical risks is often proposed. If you are in the construction business, the idea is also to enter a business that goes up when construction goes down. In practice, cyclical hedges are very difficult to find. A corporation supplying auto manufacturers, for example, may enter the replacement-parts market, because this has a much more steady demand, but the replacement-parts industry is at most stable, not contracyclical, so the combined result is only a dampening of the auto production fluctuations. To return to the Handy & Harman example, that corporation does have a large refinery for secondary recovery of precious metals, so that when metal prices rise, the refinery is busy, even though the processing mill is slack.

In a shorter-term view, some revenue stabilization can be achieved by balancing seasonal products. The old nostalgic coal-and-ice business can now be seen in Head's production of skis and tennis rackets, ski clothing and shorts.

In each of the above examples one specific risk is offset (to some extent) by another with counterbalancing characteristics. The aim is greater stability of revenue and profits—even though the average result may be lower than the "expected" returns from one of the ventures alone. Carried to the extreme, this averaging of risks leads to a conglomerate in which a catchall collection of business is assembled with no special effort to match one against another. (Full diversification gives a corporation an average growth about the same as the GNP—a growth rate unacceptable to many managers and investors.) However, even the high-flying conglomerates rarely admit to such indiscriminate averaging. Instead, some other rationale dominates portfolio selection—such as synergy—and risk balancing is a constraint to bring total exposure down to a level acceptable to major stakeholders.

Fourth Ingredient: Cash-Flow Balance

Growing businesses typically absorb cash—for working capital as well as plant and equipment—even when they are highly profitable. In fact, companies do fail because their cash resources cannot support a very successful takeoff of their product. Mature and declining businesses, in contrast, often generate cash as assets are gradually being liquidated. Such net investment flows vary widely by kind of business—being very sharp in mining, for example, and reversed in magazine publishing, where consumers pay in advance for subscriptions.

One additional dimension, then, in building a portfolio is balancing cash flows. Internal generation of needed cash is the aim. Of course, this is not the only potential source of cash; new equity and loans can be secured for profitable ventures, and declining ventures rarely need to justify new infusions. Nevertheless, our tax system makes internal generation of cash a significant advantage. Cash paid to stockholders as dividends is subject to personal income tax; even if the stockholders are willing to reinvest it in the corporation, they have much less—maybe only 50%—to so invest. However, if the company itself makes the reinvestment directly, the personal income tax bite is avoided. (Underwriting expenses are also avoided.) Moreover, if a new business-unit is showing a loss that can be offset against a profit of some other unit, then to that extent (and temporarily we hope), the corporate income tax can also be avoided until the loss carry-over is used up.

Because internally generated cash is a comparatively inexpensive and convenient way to finance growing business-units, one or more *cash cows*—as cash generating units are often called—are attractive segments in a portfolio, even when their long-run prospects are poor. This ability to shift cash flows from cash cows to stars and wildcats can provide an enterprise with immortality—Ponce de Leon's fountain of youth!

Summarizing: The design of a desired portfolio considers several different factors, including: attractiveness of the business-units separately, synergy, balanced risk and profits, and cash flow. The weight attached to each factor depends on the strengths the corporation already possesses, environmental opportunities, and personal values of its key executives.

MAJOR MOVES TO ATTAIN DESIRED PORTFOLIO

CHARTERS FOR PRESENT BUSINESS-UNITS

The portfolio strategy for a diversified corporation blends several different considerations, as we have just seen. The long-run strength and direction of the consolidated group is the dominant criterion. The various business-units are assigned roles in terms of what is good for the family as a whole.

In this composite plan some business-units are destined to grow rapidly; others have to modify their emphasis, overcome particular weaknesses, or demonstrate improved capability before they will be strongly supported; a few may be encouraged to take high risks because the potential gains are great; several have the role of cash cows; one or two may be retained largely for the protection or strength they give one of the stars; and so on.

With this overall concept in mind, it is possible to negotiate a *charter* for each existing business-unit. This charter will be an agreement between corporate executives and the senior management of the business-unit regarding:

1. The *domain*—the product/service/market scope—in which the business-unit will operate.
2. The *expected results*, including sales growth, competitive position, productivity, profitability after interest and taxes, cash generation, R&D output, community leadership, and perhaps other objectives. Some of these will be numerical and sharp; others may be intangible and soft.
3. *Constraints* regarding expected interaction with other business-units of the company, external behavior norms, required man-

agement systems, and the like. These, too, may be quantitative or qualitative.

4. *Resources* that will be made available from the corporation and those the unit is free to acquire itself.

Such charters are the bridges—the connecting links—between corporate strategy and the strategies of the various business-units. They define the mission of each unit insofar as that mission is shaped by corporation-wide considerations. As with all strategy, the content is selective, focusing on vital issues while deliberately excluding procedural and personal relationships. For each business-unit its charter sets the scope and broad objectives of its activities, and for the corporate office, each charter provides the major guidelines for approving or disapproving various proposals for specific actions.

We should note that business-unit charters are not holy words passed down from omniscient corporate officials. Rather, they emerge from recurring give-and-take discussions between executives at the corporate and business-unit levels. Business-unit executives must be active participants, because they know most about possibilities and problems of the business and because they must psychologically accept the challenge that the charter provides. At the same time, a location within a family of business-units inherently creates needs that must be fitted into the more specific strategies of the respective units.

This meshing together of the formulation and the execution of the various strategies is so important that it receives repeated attention throughout the rest of this book. It is one of the most effective educational devices available to managers: corporate executives really learn about business-units, and unit executives can appreciate corporate constraints, expectations, and needs.

Changes in the Portfolio

In addition to providing a basis for charters for existing business-units, corporate portfolio analysis flags the need for additions and deletions in the portfolio. Which of the present units are irrelevant and a drag? What gaps need to be filled with split-offs or acquisitions? If acquisitions are called for, in what directions to look?

Opportunities for new synergy or improved balance may stand out during the careful portfolio analysis outlined above. Or proposals from internal entrepreneurs or outsiders may call attention to ways the overall portfolio could be strengthened. Once recognized, such potential additions become *opportunity gaps* for strategic planning.

The next question is whether to try to fill the opportunity gaps by internal growth or acquisitions. Sometimes there is little choice. For example, when Pan Am recognized that its international bookings were being jeopardized by the lack of coordinated domestic flights, merger with an existing domestic airline was the only realistic alternative. To start its own domestic flights was neither economically nor legally feasible—a tie-up with a company like National Airlines was the direction in which to move.

In other circumstances, gap filling by acquisition is impractical. Procter & Gamble learned that antitrust barriers prevented it from getting a running start in the bleach business through an acquisition of Clorox. Clearly, for legal reasons the bigger the parent company, the more it will have to rely on internal growth in new businesses that are closely related to its existing businesses. Moreover, in a brand-new industry acquisition candidates may not exist. When Western Union moved into satellite communications, for example, the necessary satellites were not yet in orbit.

Between these extremes, however, a choice often exists. In many states commercial banks can increase their geographic coverage either by opening new branches or by acquiring existing banks in the desired location—to cite one example. Acquisitions provide faster entry and perhaps some resources (such as people, market position, trademarks, or patents) that would be difficult to assemble. On the other hand, acquisitions often bring with them unwanted assets or traditions; they may foreclose taking other attractive steps; they may be more difficult to meld into the family; they may be expensive.

During the late 1960s and early 1970s, many corporate planners fell in love with acquisitions. Corporate strategy and acquisition plans were treated almost as synonymous. Now a more balanced view prevails. A total portfolio strategy is developed, as outlined in this chapter, and acquisition criteria and opportunities grow out of this broader picture. Acquisitions often are a significant facet of corporate strategy, but they are only a part.

Divestments are the other side of the coin, hence also a part of strategy. The matrix analysis suggested in Figure 3–3 identifies business-units that both now and in the future make little contribution to corporate goals. Further study of synergy and of risk and cash-flow balance refine this diagnosis. In any turbulent environment some business-units will become either a continuing drain on resources or at least a drag on energies that could be better directed elsewhere.

In practice, divestments are usually made too slowly. Even outstanding companies are reluctant to get rid of—in BCG language—their "dogs." RCA held on to its venture in computers until losses were in the hundreds of millions; General Foods dabbled first in gourmet delicacies, then in the fast-food business, well beyond the point of no return; Johnson & Johnson kept TEK brushes long after that unit failed to serve the evolving corporate strategy. Such tardiness is explained partly by waiting for a propitious opportunity to sell or liquidate the unit. The primary cause, however, is personal. There is no inside champion for disposal, as typically is present for an acquisition; some people will lose their jobs, and senior executives are reluctant to admit that they cannot make a success of anything they direct.

Without clear strategic direction, these normal pressures for inaction are likely to dominate. To avoid the high cost of inaction, both corporate strategy and effective execution are needed.

RESOURCE PLANS AND TARGET RESULTS

A well-conceived corporate strategy provides several kinds of guides. It leads to coordinated charters for existing business-units and also to plans for additions to and deletions from the present lineup—as we have just seen. In addition, two other forms of guidance should be developed.

The projected courses for various business-units will generally call for resources from the central corporate pool—notably capital and perhaps executives or central services. To help assure that these resources will be available when needed, a summary program of the expected flows to and from the business-units should be prepared. Such a program will alert corporate officials of any prospective need for obtaining new resources. A revision in capital structure may be involved, and if so, groundwork for the issuance of new securities should be laid. Contingency plans reflecting shifts in capital markets may be advisable. And, corporate input strategy (see next chapter) can be factored in.

Also, the resource plans will show in approximate numbers how much will be allocated annually to each business-unit for what purposes—at least as future developments are now conceived. These allocations will probably be revised as wants unfold. Nevertheless, the strategy provides guideposts, and any major deviation in resources needed will call for a review of the continuing wisdom of the strategy. Meanwhile, the various business-units can proceed with their planning on the working assumption that the projected resource allocations will be made available to them over the next several years.

A final set of guides tied in with the strategy are the *target results*. Every strategy is designed to reach certain goals by given dates. These are the expected consequences of the stipulated actions. Some of these target results will be financial: perhaps sales, profits, return on investment, or earnings per share. Other targets may be more qualitative: market position in selected industries, community endorsement, product leadership, resource base, and the like. Such targets are good for keeping on course, motivation, and control—as we shall see in Part II.

FROM CONCEPT TO PRACTICE

Corporate strategy as described in the preceding pages is a powerful tool. It pulls together the actions of the various business-units into a balanced, synergistic program; it channels scarce resource; it endorses missions for operating managers; and it sets targets for overall results. But it is a difficult tool to use.

THE LURE OF EXCEPTIONS

Cynics say that most corporate portfolio strategy is merely a high-sounding rationalization of acquisitions already made. Somehow—the argument runs—among risk balance, cash flows, and synergy you can justify any combination. It is true that many promoters who are guided by little or no consistent strategy do dress up their actions with the language of strategic management. However, the possibility of such chicanery does not reduce the strength of strategic management for those who sincerely use it as a way of harnessing their own behavior. We don't forego medical treatment just because a few quacks exist.

The real difficulties in practice are more subtle. A common problem is the temptation of a "good deal." For example, a proposed acquisition may offer attractive short-run financial benefits. One company may have a large tax-loss carryover, and if a profitable unit can be merged into that company, the taxes that the profitable unit would otherwise have to pay can be avoided.

Acquisition of companies for far less than their replacement cost is also tempting—even though replacement would be a serious mistake.

Mergers may be suggested solely because of differences in price-earning ratios. Suppose the stock of the Apple Company is selling at twenty times its earnings per share and the stock of the less glamorous Orange Company at ten times its earnings. Then if Apple acquires Orange and its price-earnings ratio stays at twenty, the capitalized (market) value of Orange's earnings has doubled.

The acquisition of privately held businesses may be focused primarily on inheritance and estate taxes. Or, a proposal may pivot around the predilections of a few key individuals. Indeed, the resourcefulness of matchmakers is an impressive display of human ingenuity.

"Good deals" are fine—*provided* they also are compatible with corporate strategy. The danger is that managerial energies and other resources will be sidetracked onto ventures that are alluring at the moment but do not contribute to a strong, balanced portfolio. In contrast, if a corporation has thought through its strategy, then it already has a screening mechanism to quickly decide which proposed deals warrant further attention. Too often the strategy is fuzzy, and the "good deal" is embraced as an exception.

The reverse also occurs. Actions that should be taken are postponed—as exceptions. Here the common examples are sick business-units in which drastic action is unpleasant. A *Fortune* 500 corporation turned down an opportunity to sell (at a loss) one of its oldest business-units that was clearly in a declining industry; because of its long affiliation, an exception to the recognized strategy was made. Losses increased, and three years later the division was liquidated, because no buyer could be found. In another corporation an ailing division with dim prospects was nursed along for seven years, as a "special case." The serious cost in this instance was the required time and attention of senior management which could have been much more productive if it had been spent on growing businesses.

Because exceptions to beautifully designed plans are sometimes warranted, the tough judgment is which special benefits are great enough to justify intentionally going off course. Our observation is that exceptions too often win the day.

BAFFLING UNCERTAINTIES

In designing corporate strategy, many uncertainties must be resolved. Somehow—through some combination of facts, expert opinion, and intuition—forecasts of business conditions, industry outlooks, and business-unit success must be made. Of course, revisions and contingency plans may be included. But without agreed-upon forecasts, a full-blown strategy cannot be formulated.

Many forecasts can be made with reasonable confidence—at least within the time span and tolerance limits necessary for strategic planning. Other factors such as international political developments or finding a cure for cancer are baffling. When several key factors are interdependent, scenario forecasting is often the best we can do. For example, the attractiveness of a company planning to produce manganese from modules lying deep on the ocean floor depends on technological advances, world price of manganese, and international agreements on a law of the sea—to name only three related uncertainties. Forecasting in such areas is hazardous, and when a parent corporation is largely dependent on a naturally biased business-unit for assessment data, the evaluation becomes even tougher.

Two dimensions that are increasingly frustrating for international investment are rates of inflation and foreign exchange rates. Inflation is pushing long-range planning away from profits based on conventional accounting to annual cash flows. In the international area the cash-flow estimates have varying value because of shifts in exchange rates—assuming that transfer of the money will be permitted. Government regulations also are a major source of uncertainty, at least on lead times. The cumulative uncertainty in such computations may well exceed the tolerance of practical planning.

In such circumstances some parts of a corporate strategic plan may have to retreat to prepared opportunism, discussed in the preceding chapter. The future is seen too dimly to lay out market positions and other expected results. Yet a conviction remains that truly attractive opportunities will develop, and those firms ready to serve such opportunities will benefit from an early start. Thus the corporate strategy seeks to position one or more business-units where they can move promptly as the prospects become clearer. Such a strategic position may involve frontier technology, local marketing and distribution systems staffed with indigenous personnel, transportation facilities, skill and favorable reputation in managing joint enterprises, ties to world markets, or access to raw materials.

Under prepared opportunism a particular business-unit may be encouraged—its charter may provide—to develop along certain lines that the unit acting alone would shun. Within the parent corporation's total portfolio may be several such business-units, each building strength on a particular front. Then as events unfold, those strengths that prove to be valuable can be forged into a more specific plan. Rarely will all the specially directed units find a significant role in the final program, and to this extent effort and investment will have to be discarded. The hope, of course, is that the strengths actually used will be sufficiently valuable to offset losses on the others. Moreover, while "taking out insurance" the enterprise can "learn" what is involved in developing specific strengths—a learning experience that may prove valuable in the future.

Such a strategy lacks the completeness, neatness, and efficiency of a fully developed plan. It does have the virtue, however, of feasibility in the face of baffling uncertainties.

WORKABILITY TEST

No strategy is well conceived until its workability is weighed. If the chances of it being carried out are remote or the cost of doing so is very high, then the strategy itself should be at least reassessed.

A wide range of strategy-implementation problems are examined in Part II of this book; these problems relate to both business-unit strategy and corporate strategy. Two additional implementation issues are directly created by the corporate portfolio choices we have been exploring in this chapter. Because they can be serious enough to lead to a modification of portfolio strategy, they should be noted here.

Sometimes corporate strategy makes demands of a business-unit that are inconsistent with the strategy the unit would follow if it were independent. For example, the business-unit may wish to expand, whereas the corporate strategy wants it to be a cash cow. It is natural for unit executives to feel that they should be permitted to use the cash they generate to strengthen their own position, instead of denying themselves for the benefit of a small, upstart activity.

In other cases business-units are asked to incur risks (or avoid risks) because doing so helps corporate balance. Synergy may require that a business-unit refrain from developing its own raw materials, or prepared opportunism may call for a form of expansion that is very expensive from the unit viewpoint. Such corporate demands seem especially onerous to managers of a business-unit when they arise unexpectedly because of some other activities of the corporation and the cause is unrelated to their own situation.

Now, in a decentralized corporation the commitment of local executives to their strategy is very important for successful results. If to the business-unit executives the corporate guides "don't make sense," foot-dragging or misleading information or other maneuvering is likely to occur. The conviction unit executives have that a corporate-imposed strategy "will never work" can very easily become a self-fulfilling prophecy. The basic point is that there is a practical limit to which the business-units can be "pushed around," and this limit is a constraint on what corporate strategy is workable.

Portfolio strategy may create a second kind of workability strain. Each business-unit strategy calls for a managerial system (planning, organizing, leadership, and controlling) that is suited to that strategy. A large cash-cow unit needs a different management system than a unit experimenting with coal gasification. The desirable management system for a commercial bank differs from that for an aircraft manufacturer. The more diverse the units within a portfolio, the more heterogeneous will be their management systems.

Few corporation managements have the capability of understanding, melding, and skillfully directing widely diverse management systems. Such diversity raises temperamental and management style issues as well as difficulties of intellectual grasp. "We just don't know how to run that kind of business" is a frank and perceptive comment often heard.

Here again is a practical constraint on corporate portfolios. Cash flows and risk balance may appear desirable, but not beyond the point where effectively administering the diversity of units is no longer feasible.

CONCLUSION

Merely the outline of this chapter and the next one clearly shows that we believe that corporate strategy is often viewed too narrowly. More than opportunism and cash flow should be considered in selecting a portfolio of business-units, and the total corporate strategy should embrace more than portfolio selection. Especially when we consider how corporate strategy can be translated into guides for action, the scope of vital issues broadens.

The present chapter has focused on developing a strategic portfolio of business-units to be in the corporate family. Four criteria are important in this portfolio design: (a) attractive business-units, each considered separately in terms of its industry and its competitive position, (b) synergy that will arise from having a particular mix of business-units within a single corporate group, (c) the combined balance of risk and of short- and long-term profitability, and (d) the prospects of internal generation of cash by some business-units that will help finance projected expansion of other business-units.

Several types of additional strategic plans should be derived from the portfolio design. (a) For each business-unit to be retained a charter can be negotiated, covering domain, expected results, constraints, and resource support from the corporate pool. (b) Desirable acquisitions, spin-offs, and divestments of business-units should be indicated. (c) From the charters and the corporate input strategy to be considered in the next chapter, the total financial, critical personnel, and other corporate resource pools required can be estimated; then plans can be laid for mobilizing and allocating these resources. (d) Consolidated results targets can be set for intermediate and longer-range periods. Such supporting plans, coupled with the portfolio design, constitute the corporate-strategy package.

Carrying out such a corporate strategy calls for unusual persistence. In addition to the array of unexpected events affecting the several business-units, alluring opportunities to make acquisitions that deviate from the portfolio design may arise. Also, the business-units cannot be treated like pawns on a chessboard; the morale and responsiveness of managers within the business-units may significantly affect what can be done with those units. Consequently, compromises and adjustments in corporate strategy are likely. Nevertheless, some integrated and consistent direction is far better than mere opportunism or passive drift.

Corporate Input Strategy

CORPORATE STRATEGY INVOLVES more than the choice of a good port-folio. Developing an attractive array of business-units is vital—as the whole discussion in the preceding chapter attests—but it is an incomplete view of good corporate strategy. Most corporations do more than make investments and then passively await results. Rather, they seek synergies among the business-units and with the corporation—the progressive corporation does "bring something to the party."

So, a second vital dimension of corporate strategy is: What should be done by the corporation to strengthen its various businesses? Low-cost capital, a supply of outstanding managers, assured access to markets are possibilities. As a result of such inputs from the corporation, most—if not all—of the business-units should gain greater differential advantage than they could muster if they operated independently.

Our focus here is on major inputs. Every corporation provides minor services for its operating units—stockholder relations, filing consolidated reports with governmental agencies, a logo to place on the letterhead are typical examples. But the minor, usually necessary, activities do not significantly affect the fate of the business-units. Even such work as central purchasing or institutional advertising typically is helpful but far from determining the growth or demise of specific business-units. Corporate strategy concentrates on actions that are fundamental to success. It adds yeast, not just seasoning.

The central issues of corporate input strategy are:

1. Selecting a few kinds of contributions the corporation will make to its business-units—contributions of such quality and value that the business-units gain a significant advantage over their competitors.
2. Finding ways to develop a differential advantage in the production or delivery of such services.
3. Integrating these strengths into portfolio selection and corporate mission, and into the design of charters for business-units.

Note that this view supports the concept, already stressed, that business-units are the primary operating segments of a diversified corporation. To the extent it is practical, operating activities should be placed within these business-units. We would transfer operating activities to another division or to the corporate level only when the benefits of doing so are very high. In this sense, *corporate inputs* run counter to the basic pattern of decentralization. They are exceptions. Nevertheless, experience shows that when wisely selected and carefully administered, corporate inputs can be a powerful asset.

CORPORATE RESOURCE ARSENAL

Diversified corporations can strengthen their business-units primarily in two ways—(a) by providing one or more valuable resources on attractive terms, and/or (b) by central management of synergies among the business-units. The following examples—answers to the question posed in Figure 4–1—illustrate the possibilities of strategic inputs.

Low-Cost Capital

By far the most widely recognized aid that a parent corporation gives its operating units is growth capital. As is very clear in the cable television–interactive television arena, for example, a new business-unit often incurs losses for several years before it can build a profitable niche. And even an established venture needs working capital and fixed capital to grow.

A cash-rich parent is very convenient in such situations. Growth

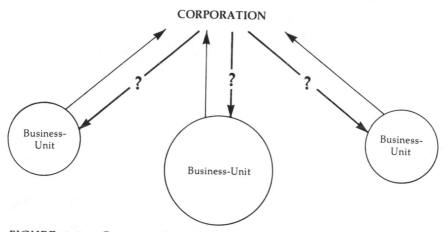

FIGURE 4-1.   *Corporate Input Strategy*

can proceed as rapidly as technology, markets, and environmental conditions warrant. Often a jump on competitors is possible.

The parent corporation need not have cash in the bank (or flowing from owned cash cows), if it can raise new funds at a favorable cost. If its capital structure permits more borrowing and it enjoys a favorable credit rating, interest will be a taxable expense, and thus the net cost of capital will be relatively low for a new venture. Or, if the parent corporation enjoys a high price/earnings (P/E) ratio on its stock, equity capital may "cost" less than the business-unit would have to pay. In this manner financial strategy of the corporation builds a resource that strengthens the business-units.

Of course, not all diversified corporations are in such an enviable condition. They may already be saddled with debt and have a low P/E ratio. Indeed, a large and well-known business-unit with an exciting new product or with extensive collateral may be able to raise capital on better terms than its parent. So, the crux is whether the diversified corporation can and will give its operating units a differential advantage with respect to the supply of capital.

Outstanding Executives

Other corporate inputs may be as invigorating. For instance, a few corporations go to great lengths to develop a pool of unusually well-qualified managers. The high-sounding expression, "Our greatest strength is our people" may be accurate. Selection, training, and know-how are designed to give managers in such corporations a competitive edge.

To cite two examples, both General Electric and IBM spend a lot of effort and money on executive development. The clear aim is to have outstanding managers who can be moved into various business-units—with the expectation that these managers will be able to run their units better than their competitors.

When a corporation develops enough "depth" of able general managers, it (a) can move immediately instead of searching for an outsider, (b) need not devote time and effort "socializing" a new executive to the corporate culture, (c) doesn't tip off plans to outsiders by searching for a particular kind of manager in the open market, and (d) reinforces the message that this corporation provides great opportunities for its own people.

This is an ambitious strategy. It deals with a soft asset, compared with capital. The people are mobile, and competitors may seduce them. There is doubt about how transferable to other kinds of business some of the skills and know-how will be. Nevertheless, the potential rewards are high. If a corporation does, in fact, succeed in staffing its business-units with executives who can outdistance their competitors, a whole array of other strengths may be promoted.*

Corporate R&D

Useful, creative ideas, scientifically tested, are scarce and expensive. For most laboratories to be effective, a "critical mass" (minimum size) is necessary. One way to seek a flow of such ideas and specialized laboratory service, without loading high costs onto each business-unit, is through a centralized R&D division.

For years Bell Laboratories served the various operating companies of the AT&T system in this manner. The worldwide pharmaceutical firms also typically centralize their research work (although separate problems may be studied at separate locations). Other examples are well known. The aim is to create a powerful research group at the corporate level that makes contributions to the operating divisions—contributions that the divisions acting alone would be unable to achieve or even unlikely to investigate.

Centralized R&D has its drawbacks. Lack of responsiveness to operating needs, pursuit of inconsequential questions, reluctance to piggyback on research of competitors, and similar issues are often raised. The more diversified the operating divisions, the more difficult

---

*The problems of finding executives well suited to execute a selected strategy are explored in Chapter 10.

these problems become. Nevertheless, the overall success of such corporations as DuPont with centralized research does indicate that this can be a workable corporate input strategy.

CENTRALIZED MARKETING

The basic concept of a business-unit places control of major functions—engineering, production, marketing, and the like—within the unit. To a large extent the unit is self-contained and autonomous; it runs its own show. Coordination between the functions and adjustments to the environment of each particular business are decentralized.

Occasionally, however, a corporation seeks strength by defying the usual pattern. One possible exception is to withdraw parts of marketing from the business-units and to perform these particular activities in a corporate marketing division. In fact, this was the original strategy of General Foods Corporation. Each of the several companies that were merged into General Foods—Post Cereals, Jell-O, Maxwell House Coffee, and so on—continued to buy, manufacture, package, price, and ship products as they had previously done. The key contribution of the new corporation was nationwide selling and nationwide promotion for all the products. By combining selling and promotion into a single division, the corporation provided the several operating companies much more complete coverage and skillful promotion than any company could muster when acting separately.

The large Japanese trading companies operate in a roughly similar way for the manufacturing companies they represent, although here the manufacturers maintain a more independent existence.

The Coca-Cola Company, to cite another variation, leaves most marketing functions with its local distributors but it centralizes control over promotion of the trade name. That name is a great corporate resource. Distributors gain a powerful competitive benefit when they are authorized to use this resource.

Such centralized marketing activity creates numerous problems of coordination, adequate attention to each product, and accountability. As the product lines grow in size and diversity, the differential benefit of the pooled service diminishes. But again we observe the corporation searching for some special input it can provide to its business-units so effectively that they enjoy a comparative advantage over competitors.

Note that in each of these examples—low-cost capital, outstanding managers, R&D capability, central marketing—the corporate strategy is to focus on just a few resources. These resources are not complete businesses; instead, they have value only as they are distinctive inputs to the business-units. In effect, the corporation develops an arsenal of exceptional resources. By drawing from that arsenal to supplement their own resources, the business-units gain strengths they cannot muster alone.

Theoretically, corporate input strengths may be so great that they dominate diversification moves. The possibility of benefiting from a particular corporate input may be the prime factor in selecting new businesses to add to the corporate portfolio.

Many diversified corporations, in fact, provide few strategic inputs to their business-units. This is especially true of "conglomerates"— assemblies of already established firms that have little relation to each other and are merely clustered in a passive holding company. The pressure to generate short-term profits and cash flow is often so great that the parent corporation is not even a good source of capital. Moreover, the development of a truly outstanding corporate resource is difficult, time-consuming, and frequently expensive. Long-term commitment to a corporate input strategy is necessary. For these reasons, corporate management must select with care any input resources in which it undertakes to excel.

CORPORATE MANAGEMENT OF SYNERGIES

In addition to providing strategically valuable corporate inputs, diversified corporations may seek differential advantage from synergy among their business-units.

Building synergy is a strategy goal of many diversified corporations. Copper firms combine mining with smelting and extend on into wire drawing. Airlines own resort hotels (often to their regret), and newspapers form ties with local radio stations. The aim—as suggested in Figure 4–2—is to dovetail operations of two or more business-units in the corporation's portfolio in a way that generates extra benefits.

Of course, in selecting businesses for the portfolio, potential synergies are among the factors considered. However, the actual achievement of synergy usually requires strong guidance. The interaction between business-units has to be shaped so that the desired reinforcement does occur. Corporate strategy sets this direction.

A quick review of several possible sources of synergy among business-units will illustrate the role corporate strategy can play.

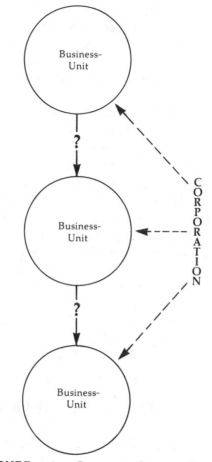

FIGURE 4-2.   Corporate Synergy Potential

VERTICAL INTEGRATION

A corporation that publishes several monthly trade magazines bought out the firm that did most of its printing. The chief aim of the acquisition was to assure fast, adaptable printing service for the magazines—at normal industry prices. Under the guidance of the parent corporation CEO, this service objective is working well. The manager of the printing business, however, is not entirely happy. He is expected to obtain outside business to keep his shop busy when not printing magazines, yet he is not permitted to make major investments in equipment for that purpose unless it can also be used for the magazines. Clearly, in this simple case the corporate strategy to stress vertical integration takes priority over independent operation of the printing business. Although the printing unit is constrained, the total effect on all the business-units combined is a net gain.

AMAX's entry into aluminum production was more complicated. At that time, the more profitable processing stage in the aluminum industry was mining and primary reduction. But entry into mining was blocked by well-established firms, and to build a new mine and plant without at least some assured outlet would have been very risky. So AMAX first acquired fabricating companies—with the clear intention of using these as a base from which to integrate backward "upstream." Attention next focused on electrolytic refining, but this required crude aluminum (alumina) and preferably ore (bauxite). Various joint ventures were discussed, options obtained, and mills planned. Each venture was to be a business-unit, but throughout the ten-year period when all this planning occurred, AMAX was seeking roughly balanced vertical integration. The interrelations between the various operating units were a crucial feature of AMAX's strategy.

During the long planning period environmental obstructions arose; supply caught up with demand; unexpected joint ventures opened up; AMAX became short of capital. So finally AMAX spun off all its aluminum holdings to form a new company with Mitsui of Japan (who wanted a foothold in aluminum in the United States).

The AMAX saga certainly cannot be explained in terms of a simple portfolio matrix. Each business-unit, in addition to its own viability, was viewed as a link in a vertically integrated system, and AMAX corporate strategy was the dominant force driving that system.

Full Utilization of Raw Materials

Related to vertical integration is complete use of raw materials. To paraphrase an old meat-packing quip, synergy comes from utilizing every part of the pig but the squeal. A more recent example is found in the forest-product industry. Peeler logs for plywood come only from the trunk of trees, so a lumber mill is added to use the smaller pieces. Then pulp and papermaking is tied to lumber operations to utilize even smaller pieces, and some of the sawdust finds its way into particle board.

Each of the products—plywood, lumber, pulp and paper, and particle board—may be managed as a separate business-unit. However, the parent corporation is also concerned that the operations be dovetailed in a way that minimizes raw material costs and maximizes output of the most profitable components of the mix. The corporate task is to make the combined whole more valuable than the sum of the independent parts.

COMBINED SERVICES

Combined services or products for the consumer are often suggested as a source of synergy. Thus in the household appliance industry the volume leaders have found synergies in selling and servicing a full line (refrigerators, freezers, dishwashers, disposers, ranges, washing machines, and dryers). Each product has its competitors—for example, Maytag in washing machines and Tappan in gas ranges—and its special design issues, but one way to compete in this mature industry is for a corporation to promote full-line service to consumers.

Such synergies are difficult to achieve. The corporate task of coordinating the actions of several business-units is burdensome, and consumers may just not care about the joint effort. Combinations of sewing machines and television sets, for instance, are rare. Fast-food restaurants don't sell groceries. Thus this kind of corporate strategy must be cautiously designed.

An area currently in flux is financial services. Insurance companies are buying investment-banking firms; brokerage houses are offering checking accounts; and so on. Any corporation that hopes to benefit from such combinations needs a well-conceived strategy. One possibility is to focus on investment services for selected markets, for example, life insurance, mutual funds, stockbrokerage, commodities, and other futures contracts for the middle-income individual. Although it is doubtful that a single "counselor" could provide expert advice in each kind of investment, he or she could at least draw on expert skills in the corporation, and then balance the assets and risks for a particular client. An alternative strategy might be to give full cash management and accounting service for professionals: checking accounts, credit cards, payment of bills, income records, preparation of income and other tax returns, personal loans on autos, and the like.

A set of combined services—one of the examples above or many other sets—normally must be backed up by a series of specialized business-units, each with its own technological and institutional constraints. If these supplying organizations take the limelight or pursue strictly parochial interest, little merging of service will occur. In contrast, if the corporation manages the synchronizing of the services, the strategy has a much better chance of success.

In summary, portfolio selection of compatible business-units may make synergy possible. Realization of that synergy, however, depends on a corporate strategy that requires the separate units to integrate their activities on a few selected fronts. The synergy may be possible in vertical buy/sell relationships, in full utilization of a common raw material, in providing a synchronized set of services, or in some other reinforcing actions. But it is the corporate strategy that sets the priority to be attached to such integrated action. It stipulates the thrusts (such as further acquisitions to enhance joint efforts) that are designed to generate differential advantage in serving stakeholders. It sets the targets for coordinated effort. Such a strategy turns independent enterprises ("states") into a "federal" organization—"a more perfect union."

BEYOND THE PORTFOLIO

Corporate portfolio strategy is comparable to the domain in a business-unit strategy. In selecting its portfolio, a diversified corporation is picking a group of domains in which to operate. In effect, the corporation is placing, and then readjusting, its bets on attractive niches in attractive industries.

Domain, however, is just one of four parts of a business-unit strategy—as outlined in Chapter 2. Sources of differential advantage, strategic thrusts, and target results are added elements—elements that are necessary to convert business-unit strategy from selection of a battleground into a more focused, action-prompting directive. Similarly, corporate strategy should push beyond the selection of a portfolio.

The present chapter has focused on corporate inputs—that is, ways corporations can help make their business-units more effective. The development of select resources is one approach. Here, the strategy of a corporation may center on low-cost capital, outstanding managers, corporate R&D, centralized marketing, or other resources that will be especially beneficial to its assemblage of businesses. As a second approach, a corporation may foster particular synergies. Like the development of select resources, fostering synergies adds potency to that of the various business-units acting independently. With imagination, corporate managers can undoubtedly devise still other inputs that will give their business-units unusual strengths.

The corporate inputs help the business-units build a differential advantage over their competitors. They add to the power the business-units acting separately can develop. And, occasionally, a corporate input is so potent that the prospect of its further use governs the selection of businesses to add to the portfolio.

Moreover, when we think of the actions a diversified corporation should take to develop its desired portfolio and to marshal its strategic inputs, a four-part corporate strategy emerges. This four-part strategy, which parallels business-unit strategy in nature, is outlined in Figure 4–3.

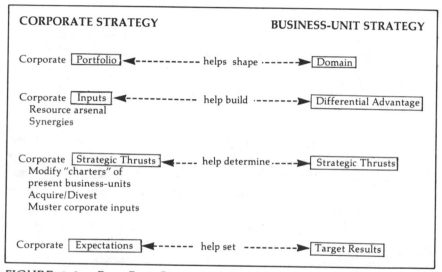

FIGURE 4–3. Four-Part Concept of Corporate Strategy Compared with Business-Unit Strategy

Just as a good business-unit strategy includes strategic thrusts and target results, so, too, does a good corporate strategy. The corporate strategic thrusts deal with (a) modifying the charters of existing business-units, (b) making acquisitions and divestments of business-units, and (c) mustering corporate inputs.

The corporate target results, or expectations, should normally include both financial and nonfinancial goals. Nonfinancial targets are often suggested by a review of the corporation's standing relative to key stakeholders. Milestone targets for specific dates will help to convert the strategy into operating plans.

Clearly, such a four-part strategy goes well beyond portfolio selection. It includes the elements necessary for a trajectory for the corporation.

Shaping External Alignments

HOSTILE VERSUS PASSIVE ENVIRONMENTS

The feasibility of every strategy depends upon the cooperation—or opposing countermoves—by an array of people outside our own organization. No strategy is ready for implementation until the likely responses of at least the key external actors are fully anticipated.

Thus this chapter focuses on two issues: How are key actors likely to respond to our thrusts? In light of that predicted response, what kind of alignments among actors should we try to establish?

PASSIVE ENVIRONMENT

Our pioneer heritage creates a bias about strategy. In the traditional Western scenario, the physical obstacles may be great, but customers will like the new services we provide, employees will welcome new and better jobs, and supporting organizations such as railroads will cooperate. Despite a few hostile Indians in the background and occasional feuds between the cattlemen and settlers, the environment is basically friendly and benevolent. Our task in that setting is to provide the vision, mobilize resources, and share in the hard, systematic work of turning opportunity into achievement.

Note that in this view a series of well-planned moves will overcome the obstacles and that the response of people affected is preset. Occasionally, such a relatively simple situation exists, but most strategy today runs into other people's strategy and must deal with their countermoves.

Hostile Environment

In a "hostile" environment several key groups will resist the moves called for in our strategy. In fact, they probably will be aggressively pursuing their own objectives, which may include our fitting into their plans. How much direct conflict arises will depend, of course, on the strategy we elect. Perhaps some arrangement can be found that will be at least acceptable to two or more groups. But negotiations will be necessary, and in that process our strategy may have to be modified. Everyone is pushing; our aim in this game is to position ourselves so that we are not pushed way off course—or, if we are lucky and smart, that occasionally we get pulled along toward our goal by their efforts (like riding the surf).

The scramble for production of wide-bodied, medium-range jet airplanes—at the end of the 1970s—illustrates this kind of process. Airbus Industries, a joint French-German venture, was several years ahead in the market with its 240-seat model. Boeing countered with a proposed new line of planes (B757, B767, B777) focused on a similar market segment. The physical characteristics of both Airbus and Boeing lines were sharply competitive: lower fuel consumption; less noise; wide-body; medium-range; around 200-passenger size. But much more than plane design was involved in making sales in the important international market.

Foreign airlines need the financial backing of their local governments, and that backing could be secured only by recognizing other concerns of the respective governments. To help deal with local employment and nationalism, Boeing negotiated subcontracts for components in Italy and Japan and for Rolls-Royce engines in England. Airbus, via the French government, courted Spain with support for entry into the Common Market, and India with broad trade benefits. Clearly, the groups vitally concerned extend beyond the plane producers and airline customers, and an array of interlocking strategies on issues far removed from plane production are involved.

Key parts of the environment are busily pursuing their own objectives, and our strategy must be linked to theirs. Directly or indirectly, we try to manipulate this environment. In the process our strategy may be modified, especially because the various actions and reactions of other actors are hard to predict.

In a "hostile" environment, strategy must be adroit and adaptive.

RANGE OF OPTIONS

Relationships with key actors vary widely. We may elect to fight with a competitor head-on, as Avis does with Hertz. Or the competition may be mixed with cooperation—even to the point where competition is publicly denied, as is the usual relation among universities and among hospitals.

Sometimes a desired result is so expensive or so risky that no one firm wants to seek it alone; so a joint venture focused on a particular outcome is created. The pipeline bringing crude oil from the north slope of Alaska is such a venture. Several pilot plants experimenting with gasification of coal also are jointly sponsored by companies that compete on most other fronts.

In many other relationships mutual dependence is pervasive and continuing. Professional football and the television networks, for instance, have a durable marriage; clearly, the football teams could not operate in their present manner without the broadcast income. Automobile manufacturers and their dealer organizations are likewise dependent on each other.

Coalitions and alliances may be multifaceted. For example, a company in the specialized business of insuring real estate titles is valuable to—and also dependent on the goodwill of—mortgage lenders, surveyors, real estate brokers, and in some areas, local lawyers who make the title search. In this arena exchange of favors and mutual trust are vital to success. Similarly, in the growing field of solid-waste disposal strategy must recognize the interaction between equipment manufacturers (and their maintenance organizations), trash collectors, environmental control agencies, bond underwriters, and users of the output such as steam for utility generators.

Society is increasingly complex and interdependent—in terms of technology, trade, regulation, and geographic scope. External alignments must fit these trends and change with them. And as just illustrated, there are a variety of choices in the way the relationships will be structured.

ANALYSIS OF KEY ACTORS

Success and, indeed, survival of every business depends on either obtaining the support or neutralizing the attacks of key actors in its environment. We live in a highly interdependent world. To steer a course through this ever-changing structure, we need a keen insight into the behavior of those actors who affect our fate.

Who Must Be Considered?

Resource suppliers and customers provide direct interaction with the business. As suggested in the discussion of the resource converter model in Chapter 1, included here are employees, material suppliers, bankers, stockholders, governmental agencies, other community groups, and the like. Because all these contributors are more or less dependent on our company, they are often called *stakeholders.* Typically, an exchange relationship exists—a trading of inducements for inputs; so for actors in these groups we are concerned with both what we give up and what we get in return.

    Competitors are also important—competitors for resources and competitors for customers. Unless we are careful, the actions of these people can upset our best-laid plans. The analysis can be extended to a third level—to the resource suppliers, customers, and competitors of our competitors—but this extension is necessary only in special cases.

    As a practical matter, only key actors in the above groups warrant close analysis—see Figure 5-1. A *key* actor is a stakeholder or competitor who in relation to us has a lot of power. A customer who buys over twenty-five percent of our output, the only available supplier of fuel for our plant, a competitor who has the capability of hiring away our engineering staff, a regulatory agency that approves the quality of our new products—all are examples of key actors.

What Are the Motivations of Each Key Actor?

Because we want to predict what each key actor is likely to do if left alone, how each of them will respond to our initiatives, and often how we can modify each's behavior, it behooves us to know what makes all of them tick. How do they normally behave, and what might cause them to change?

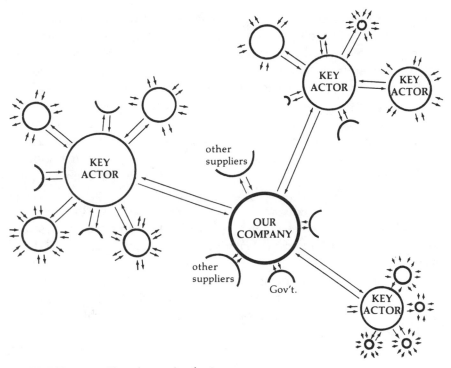

FIGURE 5-1. *Key Actor Analysis*

Key actors, like any of us, operate in their own social/economic system. Each key actor has a going enterprise with its particular resources and established relationships with external groups. (We should know what these are.) Inevitably there will be *patterns of behavior*—normal responses to normal pressures. This established flow gives us a baseline for predicting future behavior. To understand it we should do our best to look at the world as each one sees it.

Just as we appraise our own relative strengths and weaknesses in estimating our own outlook, so too should we size up the strengths and weaknesses of each key actor. Such a *capability profile* of our competitors is especially valuable. This assessment will tell us what is *possible* for key actors to do and where their limitations lie.

Next, we take an empathetic look at the future. For each actor, what *new pressures and opportunities* are likely to arise (shifts in markets, cost changes, new technology, and the like), and how is each likely to react? In particular, what will be absorbing most of each actor's attention? What internal or external resource limitations will each confront? What commitments restricting options is each likely to make? What are each's chief risks? What could upset each's plans?

Experience indicates that a surprising amount of information about any organization operating in the public sphere can be assembled by systematic observation. Speeches, press releases, published data, announced plans, positions taken on controversial issues—when regularly pulled together and analyzed—give a broad picture. And many kinds of alignments with key actors provide personal contacts that are an additional source of data. More subtle is assessing the personalities of important executives, and the values they cherish. But even here, insights can be picked up directly and indirectly.

Such a key-actor assessment serves several purposes: (a) The predicted behavior indicates what the actor is likely to try to impose on other actors—including us. (b) From the assessment, events or actions that will appeal to the actor can be surmised, as can weaknesses and vulnerabilities. These conclusions can be very useful in negotiating a desired alignment with that actor. (c) More specifically, the likely reaction of the actor to particular strategic moves that we might initiate can be predicted.

What Is the Relative Power of Each Key Actor?

Power, in the present context, is the ability of an actor to modify the conduct of others, and on the other hand, the ability to prevent someone else modifying his or her conduct. Obviously, relative power will affect which actor can pursue a chosen strategy with the least concession to others.

In relationships between business organizations, power is based largely on an ability to restrict the flow of desired inputs on attractive terms. Thus if OPEC can withhold needed crude oil, it has a lot of power over petroleum refineries, or if a bank can withdraw necessary loans, it has power over the borrower. To simplify the discussion, we consider a large customer withholding an order or a governmental agency withholding approval as other examples of restriction of a desired input.

When we start analyzing power relationships, we soon see that there are degrees of power, costs of exercising power, and all sorts of countervailing power. For example, the degree of power I have over you depends on the number of good alternative sources you can turn to for the input I am providing. The fewer and less attractive the alternatives you have, the greater is my power. Thus one consideration in designing strategy is its effect on the number of alternatives that will remain open to you and to me. For instance, you may be a large and prestigious customer, but I will hesitate to sell you a third of my output if there are few ways to replace this volume in the event you threaten to withdraw.

Of course, the other side of the coin is that I have power over you if you lack alternative sources of supply. If through the help of my friends, the Teamsters, I can delay your use of alternative sources, the impact is similar. Coalitions gain strength when their membership can, directly or indirectly, narrow the number of options various actors have.

The kind of power we are discussing is potential; only rarely is it actually exercised. In fact, most people are reluctant to use their power—for several reasons. The person being pressured may call up countervailing power; that person will start to develop new alternatives (coal, solar energy, and the like as alternatives for crude oil); future friendship and trust will be lost; a reputation for harsh dealings may spoil relationships with other suppliers. On the other hand, total reluctance to use power can undercut a person's influence; he or she will soon be regarded as a paper tiger. Consequently, in assessing power we have to consider willingness to use it as well as capability.

In summary, the analytical approach just outlined gives a basis for setting up external alignments. First, key actors are identified—the external organizations or persons whose continuing cooperation is vital to our strategic moves. Second, for each key actor an assessment is made of each one's motivations, strengths and weaknesses, probable future behavior, and likely response to our actions. Third, the relative power of each key actor to pursue his or her own course is estimated. This analysis provides insights about present and probable future behavior of the human forces in our environment; these are the dynamic elements from which a realistic interaction strategy must be forged.

CHOICE OF ALIGNMENTS

As when a nation designs its international strategy, a look first at the simpler one-to-one relationships shows the varying colored pieces that then must be fitted into the overall mosaic.

One-to-One Relationships

A business-unit's relations with its diverse resource suppliers, customers, and competitors are sure to take different forms. They range from close cooperation to sharp conflict. The matrix in Figure 5–2 suggests a way to deal with this array.

When Cooperation Is Likely To Pay Off.   On one axis of the matrix we show the benefits to us of cooperating with a specific key actor. Our interests may be highly interdependent, as between Pratt & Whitney and Boeing in designing engines for the new wide-bodied jets, or, at the other extreme, the interest may be as contrary as NBC and CBS—what one wins in the number of viewers, the other loses. (Even in this latter example, cooperation in dealing with other media or regulatory agencies may be beneficial.)

The other axis reflects relative power—our ability to impose our will on the other actor compared with that person's capacity to make us conform to his or her will. Availability of alternatives and backup resources are the usual sources of such power. Sears, Roebuck and a small South Carolina manufacturer of dungarees are a classical example of the range on this scale.

The words in the quadrants merely suggest the kind of relationship with a key supplier or customer that we can readily achieve under the different conditions. Of course, each actor will view the situation from

FIGURE 5–2.   *An Approach to One-to-One Relationships with a Key Supplier or Customer*

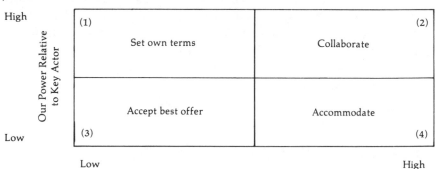

Note: If the key actor is a *competitor* instead of a supplier, the horizontal scale ranges from high to *negative* on the left end, and the suggestive terms change to "Fight aggressively" in quadrant 1 and "Defend" in quadrant 3.

his or her own perspective, and that person's preferred course of action may differ from ours. So some negotiation and testing of power may be necessary.

The matrix has to be modified if it is applied to relations with competitors. As already noted, cooperation with a competitor can have a negative impact for us; consequently, behavior in the first and third quadrant may be direct conflict rather than cooperation.

Open warfare, the Avis-versus-Hertz syndrome, is implied for competitors finding themselves on the left side of the matrix. Rarely, in fact, is a fight to the death selected as a strategy. Besides being illegal if done deliberately in restraint of trade, competition is usually tempered by common interests that call for joint action on some fronts while competing on others. And clearly the business-unit whose relative power is weak will try to stall and look for new alternatives (e.g., a special market niche) where the big competitor will not follow. So the strategy choices for firms finding themselves in this kind of environment focuses more on selecting the basis (or bases) on which to compete and determining the extent of joint action that will be acceptable on other dimensions.

Where the benefits of working together predominate—the right-hand side of the matrix—cooperative alignments are called for. The more dynamic and uncertain the environment, the more attractive will be joint efforts with financiers, equipment suppliers, customers, regulatory agencies, and the like. The electronics and computer industries grew rapidly partly because collaboration has been the prevailing relationship between suppliers and users. In contrast, the energy program in the late 1970s moved at a snail's pace in part because collaboration between interested parties proved very hard to sustain. (Governmental and public concern dealt more with who would get what than with pooling resources to confront the monumental task.)

Relative power obviously affects the kind of joint action it is wise to seek. Two comparatively strong actors—for instance, Texas Instruments and General Motors approaching computerization of automobiles—can work as roughly equal partners. However, if one firm is weak relative to the other, it will probably have to accommodate—that is, fit into the changing situation as best it can, accepting the dictates of the stronger actor as constraints while trying to develop some capabilities that will be attractive to the dominant partner.

Although these two considerations—relative power and potential benefits of cooperation—provide insight on desirable one-to-one alignments, other factors deserve careful attention. Are the stakes high or low? If low, perhaps a modification of the traditional relationship does not warrant the expense. Legislation may prohibit certain kinds of joint effort. Past experience with either fighting or collaborating sets the stage for future alignments. Because all such factors are likely to vary from actor to actor, the optimum path to pursue in each relationship calls for particular attention.

Use of Supplier Analysis. A specific case will illustrate how the type of analysis just outlined clearly shaped the strategy of one company—Ethicon Sutures—at a critical stage in its development. Ethicon manufactures surgical sutures for stitching up operations ranging from delicate eye repair to leg amputations. For years, surgeons threaded sutures through an eye in the needle used. (The needles, of course, vary greatly in size and shape.) Then a new kind of needle was invented that could be crimped at the factory onto the end of a piece of suture. This arrangement saved the trouble of threading the needle, but much more important, it reduced the hole that was pierced to draw the suture through the tissue.

Ethicon adopted a strategy of featuring the new needle-suture combination, each encased in a sterile container, but it ran into difficulty obtaining needles. Its primary needle supplier dealt chiefly in textile needles; surgical needles were a sideline. So when Ethicon asked this supplier to devise a technology to make the new type of needle, the supplier expressed reluctance and insisted on large volumes of each size and shape. Moreover, to increase volume the supplier reserved the right to sell needles to other suture companies. A second supplier, also focusing on textile needles, was even less interested; a third, much smaller manufacturer lacked capital to tool up for the full line and also lacked the quality control so important for the surgical market.

In terms of the matrix, the primary supplier had substantial power over Ethicon but did not see much benefit in close collaboration. From its view, its relations with Ethicon fell in the first quadrant. Ethicon was in a weak bargaining position, yet the outcome of negotiations was vital to its new strategy. Further analysis of the R&D activity of the primary supplier indicated that this company intended to move away from the needle business. So Ethicon predicted that long-run prospects were poor for getting the relationship into quadrant 4, let alone quadrant 2.

Consequently, Ethicon decided it could not risk staying so dependent on a disinterested supplier. It first explored a joint venture with the smaller company to make one or two sizes of the new needle, but it soon worked out an arrangement to acquire a stockholder position in the company. That enabled Ethicon to establish a collaborative relation with the company—quadrant 2. Several years were needed to develop the capability of this company to make the various kinds of needles with the necessary quality. As Ethicon cut back on purchases of traditional needles, its old suppliers became even less interested in maintaining prompt delivery and quality. All this slowed Ethicon's growth and delayed pushing its new product across the total market. But in the end Ethicon escaped from its dependent and therefore weak position.

DEGREES OF COLLABORATION

Economic theory and much of the business literature is preoccupied with competition. We are conditioned to think in terms of zero-sum games. A broader view of society, however, highlights the mechanisms by which people cooperate. The miracle of modern civilization is the way specialized outputs are combined, traded, and combined again to generate sophisticated services and goods. So when we talk of collaboration as one form of external alignment, we are dealing with a fundamental phenomenon.

Collaboration between key actors varies in degree.

1. *Informal mutual aid* is the most common. You help me as a neighborly act; later I probably return the favor. Sociologist Peter Blau observes that this sort of cooperation permeates social relations; it differs from economic exchanges in the unspecified nature of the return help, and it requires a high amount of trust that mutually supportive actions will be continued.* This is the foundation of good-will with employees, suppliers, customers, bankers, and a host of other points in the environment.

2. *Formal agreements* covering the scope and nature of cooperation become necessary when advance commitments are large and when many individuals must have a consistent understanding about the relationship.

3. *Joint ventures* break out a particular area for intense collaborative activity and provide for a pooling of knowledge and resources related to that activity. The joint venture may be a temporary consortium for a large project such as the construction of a dam, or it may be a corporation with indefinite life.

* See *Exchange and Power in Social Life* (New York: Wiley, 1964).

4. *Mergers* carry collaboration to the extreme, in which separate identity is sacrificed for the benefits of central direction of the combined activities.*

Many other variations are possible. Nevertheless, these four degrees of collaboration clearly indicate the profound impact that external alignments can have on the process of strategy formulation.

Collaboration implies some sharing of decision making. When American Motors undertakes selling Renault automobiles in the United States and probably using some Renault parts in its own production, clearly American Motors' strategy in the United States will include Renault inputs and vice versa. And under accommodation the adjustment of initial plans is likely to be even greater. In other words, strategic planning involves dynamic give and take, in which more than our own interests must be considered.

Of course, managers of a business-unit may choose to limit the extent of collaboration. Crown Cork & Seal, for instance, as a point of strategy, rarely installs can-making equipment in customers' plants— as do its leading competitors—because it wishes to retain greater flexibility. This successful company builds strong informal ties to its suppliers and customers but minimizes formal agreements.

The alignment with each key actor is a separate, unique relationship. The approach to shaping these relations outlined thus far stresses a one-to-one analysis—because each key actor is important to us and each presents a distinct set of factors and opportunities. Nevertheless, a *collective view* of all of a company's external alignments is also desirable.

A company develops a reputation for aggressiveness, for fair dealings, for consistency, and the like—so the way one actor is treated raises expectations in other dealings. For example, in its early history Sears, Roebuck had a reputation of squeezing its suppliers once they become highly dependent on Sears' purchase orders. Later, Sears adopted a strategy of assuring its efficient suppliers that they could earn reasonable profits, and to carry out this strategy close collaboration in product design and production scheduling is often undertaken. Not every one of Sears' thousands of suppliers agrees with the application, but the policy is clear—not to use its power for short-run benefits, rather to build a reputation as an attractive customer.

*The economist, Oliver E. Williamson, has argued in *Markets and Hierarchies* (New York: Free Press, 1975), that merged operations are more effective than competitive markets for handling exchange when mutual trust is vital. Mutual trust is necessary, he says, when uncertainty is high and key actors are few (two features of a hostile environment we listed at the opening of this chapter).

It is entirely possible to be ruthless in some spheres and cooperative in others—say, purchasing and labor relations—but some public rationalization of such behavior is desirable to create an aura of reliability, even integrity.

The combined set of alignments must also be weighed in terms of the total demands on resources. Few business-units have the personnel and capital to support several aggressive fights at the same time. In fact, even close collaboration simultaneously in several different areas may create severe problems of internal coordination. Thus although the very essence of strategy deals with change, it is often advisable to ration or stagger the volatility.

COALITIONS

The careful analysis of each key actor recommended early in this chapter provides the underlying data base on which the various relationships are built. That same bank of data may suggest desirable alliances or coalitions. A coalition is an agreement among at least three actors on joint action; often some of the actors have only indirect relationships with each other.

Circumstances Leading to Coalitions. Often a business-unit discovers that by itself it cannot bring about the changes it desires. It lacks the necessary power. To reach its objectives it rallies allies. In practice, this use of allies in coalitions is much more common than generally realized.

Quite diverse organizations may form a coalition around a common cause. For example, the gun lobby that opposes restrictions on private ownership and use of guns is supported by strange bedfellows: hunters, people who want guns to protect their homes, criminals, and firms with a commercial interest in the sale of guns and ammunition. Acting separately, they would have limited impact on Congress, but their united strength has been remarkably potent.

In the gun lobby example, each participant has a direct concern with the outcome. A variation is found in the support of tariff barriers. Here, trading of support is common—I will support your protection if you will support mine. Such mutual helping of friends is found in all sorts of business situations, from the sale of consulting services to professional courtesy among doctors. We are not suggesting that participants in such coalitions are cavalier about giving their support, although some may be; considerable effort may be devoted to deserving the support. Rather, the point is that coalitions are necessary to achieve the desired impact.

As already noted, the allies may embrace people who are only indirectly involved. Thus in the aircraft example cited at the beginning of this chapter, airframe manufacturers, engine manufacturers, airlines, finance companies, and governments are all included in the coalition. All are required to make the international sale of aircraft a workable business, and each actor has to adopt a strategy regarding the coalitions each will join.

Basically, when coalitions are formed, one or more business-units recognize that they cannot passively wait until the people with whom they have direct dealings are all set to act. Instead, they actively sponsor a whole chain of interrelated events by several different agencies. Consider a grain dealer wishing to sell feed to catfish raisers. Taking a cue from the way frying chickens are now raised and marketed by the millions, the grain dealer has to interest farmers in mass production of catfish in artificial lakes. This is appealing, because catfish are very efficient converters of grain feed into meat. But to market the output, local "factories" are necessary to clean, cut, package, and freeze the meat. Refrigerated trucks must take the frozen fish to wholesale distribution points, and a marketing company has to sell the product either to fish-and-chips and other restaurants or to a slowly emerging retail-store market. These are the main actors, although cooperation of zoologists, government inspectors, and others is also essential.

The way such a new industry is developed and the successful entrepreneurs establish themselves is through a coalition. Perhaps one enterprise will undertake two or more steps, but complete vertical integration is unlikely. Thus someone has to appreciate what conditions are necessary to attract collaborators into each step and then must induce related actors to adjust their activities in a way that will create these conditions. The leading and profitable firms in this new business will be those who have mastered the art of forming and guiding coalitions.

Coalition in the Health Field. Coalitions may be vital in all sorts of settings. For example, an old hospital located in the downtown section of a typical city faced a dismal outlook. Its leading doctors and full-paying patients were moving to the suburbs; a proud history carried with it outmoded facilities; Medicaid patients could not provide or attract resources for rebuilding. A bold new strategy was to become a teaching hospital focusing on specialities; this would attract a high-quality staff, and full-paying patients would be sent for special treatment on referral from suburban hospitals. However, a wide array of allies were needed. The state medical authorities had to bow to local political pressure for a teaching hospital in that part of the state. The Veterans Administration had to locate one of its new health centers on an adjacent site, providing an additional volume of use for the specialty capabilities. The city had to clear land for new buildings and help finance a closed (safe) parking garage. The trustees had to raise additional funds for upgrading the plant. And this hospital complex had to be a significant part of a broad plan for revitalizing the downtown section of the city.

Throughout several years of planning and development, the critical job of the hospital administrators was to keep all contributing elements back of the plan. This proved to be predominantly a political task. Alternative suggestions kept appearing, usually with sponsorship from competing locations. To meet these challenges some modifications in the original strategy were negotiated. A continuing promotional effort has been necessary to sustain commitment to the venture at national, state, and local levels. Withdrawal of support at any one of these levels would probably kill the plan.

Coalitions may be necessary for survival, as the above examples indicate. We suggest that they be approached as elaborations of the simpler direct alignments every enterprise must cultivate. A coalition network is indeed more complicated, because more actors are involved and inducements to cooperate may come from third parties, but the analysis of motivations and options of each key actor is still the starting point.

MAINTAINING OPTIMUM ALIGNMENTS

Shaping external alignments is a never-ending task. Even with the most thorough analysis of each key actor and the wisest choice of relationship, tomorrow will present new problems. Personal relations require nurturing, and the external world keeps changing. Because of interdependence, changes in one sector or alliance tend to make ripples in others.

Moving Target

The world as seen by the people with whom we deal is as full of turbulence as our own world. Consequently, it is unrealistic to assume that a satisfactory arrangement today will remain as attractive tomorrow.

Perhaps it will. Nevertheless, prudence requires that we frequently re-assess the opportunities and threats each key actor perceives. External developments, the success and pressures from each actor's resource suppliers, as well as changes in our own aspirations and resources lead to change.

If we seek to shape the relationship rather than merely react to someone else's initiative, then we should detect early the need for adjustment. We may elect to stand pat, but that should be a deliberate choice. Or we may wish to generate counterpressure or draw a new actor into the coalition. The underlying presumption is that each alignment will evolve.

Considering the full set of external relationships that every business has, several of which are sure to be interdependent, a moving target is normal and inevitable.

INTERNAL UNDERSTANDING AND SUPPORT

Virtually all external alignments call for some kind of internal reactions. Schedules are developed on the basis of expected inputs. Personnel is trained to fulfill service commitments. Defenses are practiced, loyalties created, values established. Then when an external alignment bearing on such internal activities is modified, a corresponding inside adjustment is expected.

But the internal system may not be eager to change. Aside from social inertia, sudden change adds uncertainty and often anxiety, so managers have to take time to explain new alignments and to arrange the necessary support.

Experience shows that obvious though the need for this coordination may be, it does not always happen. Our emissaries in the external world may promise revised actions that the internal bureaucracy is unable or unwilling to deliver. The more dynamic the external alignments—which we have argued in the preceding section is desirable—the more likely is the slippage in actual performance.

Here, then, is a realistic constraint on external commitments.

Two other constraints on frequent changes in external alignments have already been mentioned. One is the capacity of a business-unit to do several things at the same time. A social system and managers personally have limits on the number of shifts they can master concurrently, so there may be a strategic question of what to do first and what to postpone. The second point is the need for enough consistency in actions to be perceived as having "character" and dependability. Much action internally and externally is based on inferred values and predicted reactions. If a firm vacillates so much in its external alignments that no one knows what values and reactions to predict, continuing relationships are hard to develop.

CONTINGENCY PLANS

Careful analysis of external actors whose behavior could upset a narrowly focused strategy may lead to contingency planning. When predicting the behavior of external actors, especially those more powerful than we are, often several possibilities emerge. Consider, for instance, the plight of the Acme Shoe Store which features Florsheim shoes. Acme's analysis indicates that Florsheim will probably continue to rely on independent retailers. But national sales have failed to grow, and perhaps Florsheim will decide to open more of its own retail outlets to replace stores like Acme. Faced with that possibility, should Acme's strategy include a *contingency plan* to pursue in case Florsheim threatens to stop supplying Acme?

Continuing the example, Acme has several alternatives. It can add other lines, so that the loss of Florsheim shoes would not be catastrophic. It can reduce its long-term obligations (on its building and the like), so that liquidation with minimum loss would be possible. It can form a coalition with other Florsheim retailers, which would bring joint pressure on Florsheim if any new company-owned stores were opened. Or, it could try to build such a large volume of sales of Florsheim shoes that Florsheim would be loath to replace that outlet (or offer to buy it). Note that any one of these moves has a significant qualifying effect on the main strategy of Acme and that modification of strategy results from Acme's analysis of Florsheim's situation and its possible moves.

How much attention should be given to contingency plans is usually debatable. The answer depends on (a) how serious is the threat—the magnitude of the results and the likelihood, (b) the number of alternatives and the ease and lead-times of using them, and (c) the need to start action now to keep an alternative open and the cost of doing so reasonably. The unknowns are many. Consequently, many companies do little or no contingency planning. Nevertheless, as the Acme Shoe Store example suggests, careful study of potential behavior of key actors does highlight major risks—and for such risks often contingency planning may be wise indeed.

A course of action related to contingency planning is systematic monitoring of the situation of key actors to detect when significant changes are brewing. Such monitoring is examined in Chapter 12 as a significant feature of control.

CONCLUSION

External alignments are crucial, integral parts of every company strategy. In shaping strategy these alignments warrant fully as much consideration as internal integration—yet in many strategy studies internal analysis is pursued more diligently than external analysis. Of course, external relations are considered, but too often we assume that other actors will remain passive—changing only in response to our initiatives. Too often we make an inadequate study of the pressures on and likely responses of key cooperators that occur quite independently of the interaction in which we are a party. As a consequence of this oversimplified, self-centered view, our strategy is in danger of being static.

An approach to the design of external alignments has been outlined in this chapter. First comes careful analysis of key actors—*who* must be considered, *what motivates* each one, what is the *relative power* of each. Then with this background, alignments are negotiated. Among the possible arrangements that should be considered are (a) simple, one-to-one relationships, (b) various forms of alliances and coalitions, and (c) within either kind of structure, varying degrees of collaboration.

Examples have been noted but, of course, each alignment must be tailored to fit the specific interests of two or more participants. Moreover, evolutionary changes in these relationships should be expected and, if possible, anticipated in dependencies and commitments made. A lot of skillful navigation is necessary, both with and against currents and around snags, and the strategy may be modified as events unfold.

This recommended close attention to external alignment makes several contributions to the strategy formulation process:

1. Important thrusts may emerge—ranging from lining up alternative sources of supply to campaigns to influence legislation.

2. Danger of blockages arising from outsiders responding to other pressures in their environment may be spotted and systematic monitoring of such developments undertaken. If risks are high, contingency plans may be developed.

3. Third parties whose support is valuable may be identified and explicit steps taken to cultivate this support.

4. Negotiating strength is increased, and thus the chances that an external actor will force an unwelcome modification in our strategy is reduced.

5. If a battle appears unavoidable on one front, a safe posture on other fronts may be called for; an overcommitment of executive time and other scarce resources should be avoided.

6. A more reliable assessment is likely of risks entailed in various strategic alternatives, and this may alter basic choices.

Any or all of these contributions will make a strategy more realistic and doable.

Birth and Nourishment of a New Strategy

How is a clear, forceful strategy established? How do changes in strategy arise? Preceding chapters have explored the role and scope of strategies, but it has been left to this one to review the process for formulating a strategy within an organization.

We are concerned about the way strategies come into existence for two reasons. First, the process is likely to determine the quality of the strategy adopted—its astuteness, its foresightedness, its level of risk, and the like. Second, the formulation process affects significantly the commitments of those who execute the strategy and also the instruments best suited to implement it—as we shall see in Part II.

Strategy formulation has several dimensions, and in our discussion we shall move from the easily recognized, explicit steps to more subtle considerations. The broad issues are these:

- What formal strategic planning system will be most helpful?
- Where will the impetus to get that system moving come from?
- How can we achieve internal acceptance and commitment to new strategies as they unfold?
- How should we deal with the uncertain, and often lengthy, development that may be necessary?

DESIGN OF A STRATEGIC PLANNING SYSTEM

REASONS FOR EXPLICIT SYSTEM

Many a company has become successful without systematic attention to strategy. Typically, its founder had the vision and/or luck to select a favorable domain plus the capability to exploit this growing market. The less-fortunate entrepreneurs dropped by the wayside; a sort of Darwinian competition sifted out the fittest. And years later managers of the favored enterprises had to muster the wisdom to adjust to a new environment. Many companies die at this stage, because successors to the founder lack his insights and luck. The process usually centers in one or two persons in command of the business who subjectively plot the course. A few geniuses in this art of being in the right place at the right time have made great fortunes.

For several reasons complete reliance on a "great leader" to formulate strategy is unwise in today's turbulent world. It involves high and unnecessary risk. There are too many potential changes for one person to perceive them all. Rarely can a single person comprehend upsets in social, political, technological, as well as economic areas. Moreover, a shift in strategy usually requires adjustments by several departments of a company, and predicting the likely impacts of these adjustments calls for specialized technical judgments. The interaction between departments under various alternatives has to be explored. Possible external coalitions either supporting or opposing a proposed strategic move should be anticipated. Seldom can a single individual (or a close partnership of two or three) give attention to and carefully assess all these angles. To rely on his or her hunch or intuition is risky indeed.

Inspired, creative ideas are still fed into the system. (Some may get lost, but others will be stirred up.) Thus the introduction of orderliness and more people is not a replacement for a person with great ideas. Rather, in a strategic planning system those ideas are subjected to examination from diverse viewpoints—and the risk is thereby reduced.

The "great-leader" approach to strategy also builds little understanding and commitment. Key executives who will have to interpret and execute the new strategy are merely confronted with a tough assignment that undercuts in at least some respects a pattern of activities they have struggled to create. In contrast, all good strategic planning systems insist that these key executives take part early and intensely in the thinking and the shaping of the new strategy. As a result, they usually feel that the strategy is partly their own creation. They may not concur in all the estimates, but they do know why various decisions were made and what outcomes are intended. These feelings and insights will have an important bearing on how the strategy is executed—as we note in later chapters.

To illustrate what we mean by a strategic planning system, three systems—of increasing complexity—are very briefly reviewed. Detailed description of procedures, forms, and the like would distract from the focus of this book, but the basic characteristics of such formal systems should be clearly in mind.

PLANNING FOR A SINGLE-LINE BUSINESS

The primary steps in strategic planning within a single-line company or a business-unit of a diversified company are sketched in Figure 6–1. In this particular system the total cycle from environmental forecasts to

FIGURE 6–1. Strategic Planning Cycle of a Single-Line Company

PRIMARY STAGES	OUTPUT	COMPLETION AND APPROVAL DATE	MAIN PARTICIPANTS
Basic guidelines	Environmental forecasts: Opportunities & treats Key assumptions Projected results of present strategy Planning gaps to meet objectives	June 1	Senior management
Tentative strategy	Domain Differential advantage Thrusts Approximate results	August 1	Senior management
Three-Year Program	Action programs for thrusts Resource requirements Confirmed strategy Target results	October 1	Functional managers, then Senior management
Next-Year Plan	Departmental plans: Inputs and Outputs Milestones for strategic thrusts Financial and capital budgets	December 1	Functional managers, then Senior management

approved budgets is separated into four stages: basic guidelines, tentative strategy, three-year program, and next-year plan. Main participants and completion deadlines are also indicated for each step.

In practice, much more two-way interaction occurs than this chart depicts, and each company will tailor the sequencing, spacing of deadlines, total planning horizon, and similar matters to fit its particular needs. Nevertheless, several features of the system shown here deserve emphasis.

1. Strategy formulation is separated from day-to-day (or tactical) decisions and is given explicit attention. This is a deliberate attempt to foster objective, imaginative, long-range thinking. Broad analysis need not be pushed aside to resolve today's pressing problems.

2. Then, the longer-run strategic directions are translated into increasingly specific plans through a formal sequence of programming and budgeting. Linkages such as strategy thrusts, action programs, shorter-range goals (milestones), and target results tie together broad concepts and monthly financial budgets.

3. The temptation to prolong analysis of external forces and possible responses is held in check by deadlines. Strategic planning requires give-and-take of ideas and information. No person sees the total picture at first; what to communicate and why is ambiguous; mindsets of various individuals have to be adjusted. But this iterative process cannot continue indefinitely. There must be conclusions—decisions—so detailed planning and action can proceed. The planning system stipulates when and where each kind of question should be raised—resolved—reopened—and who normally participates.

4. Line managers are major participants and are responsible for conclusions. It is *their* plan. Staff people may help, but this is not a task that can be fully delegated to them.

PLANNING FOR A DIVERSIFIED COMPANY

When a company diversifies, it adds to the strategy questions faced by each business-unit the portfolio and input issues explored in Chapters 3 and 4. Typically, it also inserts another layer of management to handle company-wide directions and allocations. One way to fit these additional elements into a strategic planning system is diagrammed in Figure 6–2.

This particular diagram, based on extensive research by R. F. Vancil and P. Lorange, emphasizes the flow of planning requests, pro-

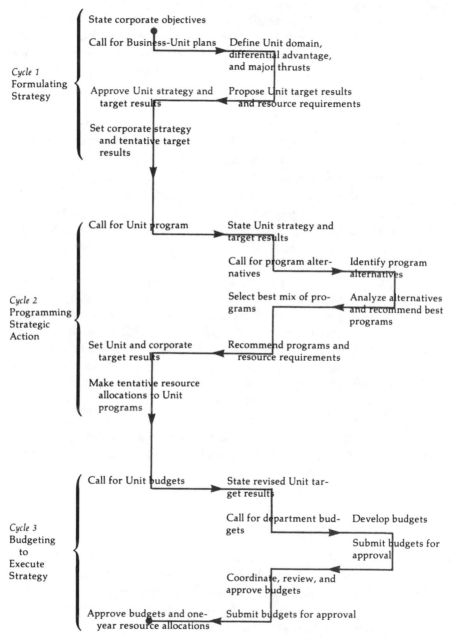

CHIEF EXECUTIVE	BUSINESS-UNIT MANAGERS	FUNCTIONAL DEPARTMENT MANAGERS

Cycle 1 Formulating Strategy

State corporate objectives

Call for Business-Unit plans → Define Unit domain, differential advantage, and major thrusts

Approve Unit strategy and target results ← Propose Unit target results and resource requirements

Set corporate strategy and tentative target results

Cycle 2 Programming Strategic Action

Call for Unit program → State Unit strategy and target results

Call for program alternatives → Identify program alternatives

Select best mix of programs ← Analyze alternatives and recommend best programs

Set Unit and corporate target results ← Recommend programs and resource requirements

Make tentative resource allocations to Unit programs

Cycle 3 Budgeting to Execute Strategy

Call for Unit budgets → State revised Unit target results

Call for department budgets → Develop budgets

Submit budgets for approval

Coordinate, review, and approve budgets

Approve budgets and one-year resource allocations ← Submit budgets for approval

FIGURE 6–2. *Vancil and Lorange System for Strategic Planning in Diversified Companies.* Adapted from article in *Harvard Business Review*, Vol. 53, No. 1 (January 1975), pp. 84–85. Terminology has been adjusted to usage in this book.

94

posals, and decisions throughout the organization. Key points to note include:

1. Different kinds of issues are assigned to different levels in the organization. The total planning process is divided into steps, and each step is performed by that level where the needed knowledge and perspective is likely to exist. Neither the CEO nor the lower-level managers can prepare an effective strategic plan alone. Ideas flow both from the top down and from the bottom up.

2. Allocations of scarce resources (capital, key personnel, R&D facilities, and the like) require more attention. When a single-line company needs more resources it negotiates with outsiders, but in a diversified company decisions about which specific ventures to back are made internally.

A Highly Sophisticated System

Texas Instruments (TI), a diversified electronics company, is highly dependent on new-product development for its continuing success. To aid in dealing with its rapidly changing technology, this company has a unique strategic planning system. While utilizing all the concepts sketched above, the TI system is further elaborated to meet special needs. The company may be pushing forward on a dozen or more distinct opportunities concurrently, and it wants positive action on each of them. Progress toward the different opportunities does not fit neatly into the annual planning cycle; some advance faster than others, and competitive pressure varies. For this strategic planning, the company wants to draw heavily on its management and technical personnel who are already responding to a control and incentive system which stresses profitable operation of existing businesses.

Distinctive features of the system TI has designed to meet these needs include: *

1. Planning for each new opportunity is organized as a distinct program. It has its own manager, budget, deadlines, and review. Necessary chunks of technical competence, market data, financial estimates, and the like are identified and organized as special projects. At milestones in this planning effort the opportunity is reassessed and decisions made on how many more resources to allocate to pushing

---

*For a more complete description of the TI system see: P. Lorange and R. F. Vancil, *Strategic Planning Systems* (Englewood Cliffs, N.J.: Prentice-Hall, 1977), pp. 338–361.

ahead. Each program is closely supervised and moves along at its own pace.

2. This focus on each program separately provides better opportunities to identify uncertainties, assess risks, and request special studies (R&D, market analysis, resource availability, and the like) that may reduce these. Although killing the project or sharply altering it may be unpleasant, a forum is created in which such issues can be openly addressed.

3. Managerial and technical personnel to staff these separate programs are drawn largely from operating departments. Most of these people retain their operating responsibilities and devote only part of their time to the temporary planning assignment. Such dual assignments are feasible in TI because: (a) time devoted to planning assignments is charged to the program budget so that the operating programs will not be "footing the bill" for unrelated research; and (b) each person is evaluated and rewarded for contributions to the strategy programs as well as contributions to operating programs.

4. A subsystem has been devised for comparison of the various strategy programs with respect to progress, risks, and revised estimates of long-run results. Scarce resources are then allocated on the basis of these comparisons. At least quarterly, and more often if necessary, senior executives assess progress and may adjust emphasis—or abort—any program.

This system enables TI to maintain very strong efforts on new business development while also pushing for profitable current operations. Moreover, the system has an unusual degree of flexibility. On the other hand, it is expensive, and only a company with a background of sophisticated management practices could live with the inherent complexities.

The strategic planning system for a specific company should, of course, be tailored to its particular needs, traditions, and resources. Nevertheless, the three examples outlined above suggest that the plan will be more effective if the following features are incorporated:

- Separate, explicit attention to strategic planning.
- Close linkages between environmental forecasts, selected domain, and differential advantages, programs to develop needed strengths, and financial budgets and other operating plans.
- Deadlines when at least tentative conclusions about one stage in planning cycle become planning premises for the next stage.

○ Participation and responsibility for strategic planning placed primarily on line executives who will carry out the strategy.

Especially in diversified companies:

○ Clear distinction in the roles to be performed by different levels in the organization.
○ Opportunity for objective, informed assessment of uncertainties and risks.
○ Provision for resource allocation that supports the selected strategy.
○ When exploring several distinct opportunities, a separate program for developing each with flexibility for different rates of progress.
○ Adjustment of performance measurements and incentives so that good strategic planning is rewarded as well as good short-term results.

A planning system with these features helps get strategic thinking into the mainstream of management. It is a way of working together—a known social system—that increases the odds that wise, timely decisions will be made.

PLANNING CORPORATE STRATEGY

Business-units, we have argued, provide the underlying strength of every diversified corporation, and the strategic planning systems just outlined focus on strategy for these vital operating units. In addition, corporate managers always face two other strategic issues—what business-units to own and what advantages to seek as a corporation in providing resources to these units. Planning for these two issues—called portfolio strategy and corporate input strategy in Chapters 3 and 4—must be included in the overall system.

Corporate strategy can be easily fused into any of the planning systems, as summarized in the previous two sections of this chapter. The existence of a good system for business-units provides a natural avenue for linking corporate and business-unit strategies.

Corporations with a strategic planning system like the one diagrammed in Figure 6–2 will usually have a (corporate) strategy planning staff that provides the following inputs:
For Cycle 1–formulating strategy:

○ Prepares a tentative portfolio strategy that will fulfill known corporate objectives and communicates to each business-unit its expected role in the portfolio.

○ Prepares corresponding tentative mission assignments for corporate resource departments.

○ Provides the overall corporate perspective in the review of strategies proposed by business-units and by corporate resource departments.

○ Identifies acquisitions and divestments needed to round out the corporation's portfolio. (The staff may also participate in making acquisitions—an activity beyond the planning stage.)

For Cycle 2–programming strategic action:

○ Calls attention to impact on overall corporate strategy of proposed program targets and resource allocations.

The corporate strategy actually adopted is, of course, strongly influenced by the inputs of the operating units. They inject realism and alternatives to the proposals of the corporate planning staff. Much negotiation may take place before the chief executive makes the official decisions.

Good corporate strategy is rarely an accident. It requires nurturing. If a diversified corporation seeks benefits from its size, then some mechanism for astute attention—such as a corporate planning staff—should be built into the planning system.

The TI system is more flexible. As with TI's business-unit planning, separate corporate questions can be studied intensively when they are "hot"; decisions and actions are not anchored to a fixed annual cycle. In the TI approach a planning program—with its own mission, resources, and deadlines—may study a new domain or ways to build a unique corporate resource. The pace can be geared to the attractiveness of the opportunity and to competitors' actions.

In this multiple and varied thrust system the portfolio strategy develops as missions, and scarce resources are assigned to business-units. To keep total operations in balance TI uses computer models of financial results. The likely financial effect of changes in strategy can be quickly examined at any time. Also, with the aid of the models, the incremental impact of resource allocations can be foreseen. In fact, many elements of TI's corporate strategy remain stable for long periods. But the system helps managers make refinements and additions in a timely and studied manner.

IMPETUS TO CHALLENGE
THE STATUS QUO

The strategic planning system just discussed provides a mechanism for change. It introduces order and a procedure for moving from dreams to practice. But the system alone can be sterile. Without some person or event triggering a major challenge, the scheduled planning can merely refine and adjust current operations. To break new ground, which in today's world is often necessary, a provocative push is needed.

This impetus to challenge the status quo comes primarily from individuals, not a system. Four potential sources deserve careful attention.

External Pressure Groups

External groups may bring sufficient pressure on a company to force a reexamination of its strategy. For example, dissatisfied stockholders or worried creditors may insist on a critical review; reform groups concerned about the natural environment or consumer safety may undercut the company's good reputation; labor unions have their own elected officers who stay in office partly by challenging management. Many such groups press for a change in company practice because, unlike most customers or suppliers, they cannot walk away from company activities; if their lot is to be improved, a change in company behavior is the source.

Pressure from such special-interest groups is an unsatisfactory way to get strategic planning started. By its very nature, a pressure group has a parochial viewpoint. It wants its concerns met first and gives only secondary weight to other resource contributors. Rarely is a request of "more for me" accompanied by constructive suggestions of how the company can modify its strategy to make this possible without wresting their gain from other stakeholders. Third, pressures of this sort usually come late, after plans are completed and often after operations are well established.

Nevertheless, prods, or potential prods, from these outside sources should not be disregarded. They may trigger a more general review of existing strategy. Of course, as pointed out frequently in preceding chapters, the whole adaptation process will be much easier if the external pressure can be anticipated. This requires forecasts of sufficient credibility to jar complacency with the status quo.

INTERNAL ENTREPRENEURS

Every company has at least a few employees who develop strong convictions about how "we can do it better." Sometimes these beliefs deal with basic directions—opportunities—that the company should pursue. For example, the personnel director of a clothing firm became convinced that his company had to move into sportswear and other informal attire if it was to maintain its strong national distribution system. He became a missionary within the organization on this move (even though it fell outside his function) and staked his professional reputation and job on it. Eventually, he won a full hearing, and the firm adopted some, though not all, of his proposals.

Inertia is an inevitable, indeed desirable, characteristic of any established organization. Members are busy getting today's work done; they have policies and routines to simplify action, and they have learned how to depend on each other. Change, especially a major upsetting change, is not welcome. Consequently, new ideas are filtered in terms of how easily they can be fitted into the existing patterns. Threatening ideas tend to be suppressed; they don't bubble up through the hierarchy as serious proposals. In such a setting, vigorous, persistent advocacy by a missionary is needed to propel a novel proposal into the strategic planning system. Of course, if and when the novel proposal promises to lighten some recognized external pressure, it may emerge as an "idea whose time has come."

Close study of the process of strategic change in many companies reveals that an internal entrepreneur is often the catalyst who wins serious attention to a major switch in domain or differential advantage. The challenge for strategic management is how a tolerable number of internal entrepreneurs can be nourished and identified.

DEVELOPMENT STAFF

A third way to activate the strategic planning system is simply to hire someone to blow the whistle at the appropriate times. Often that flagging of new opportunities and threats is part of the assignment of an R&D director, a product planning director, a new ventures manager, a corporate planner, or similar senior staff.

Such a solution seems so easy we had better review the drawbacks. (a) Experience shows that individuals adept at substantive corporate planning soon move to line jobs. The turnover is high, and credibility for a succession of people is difficult to maintain. (b) In any one technical area the need for major strategy shifts is intermittent; a single organization cannot digest frequent changes of this sort. Because most staff people are really knowledgeable about only a few industries, they have long lulls in creative activity. (This contributes to the turnover noted above.) (c) It is easier to organize and administer staff seeking alternatives for recognized problems than to predict and diagnose those problems in the first place. Discontinuities in the environment, shifts in values and objectives, unanticipated behavior of competitors, and the like make the task of flagging opportunities quite nebulous. Thus neither the boss nor staff subordinate knows when the job is well done. (d) Judgment about when to speak up is required—a watchdog, growling all day will be ignored; going to sleep can be disastrous. (e) Staff, like the line, can get trapped in tradition or involved in supporting previous recommendations. (f) This kind of staff is expensive, and smaller firms cannot afford it.

These drawbacks are substantial but not overwhelming. Larger companies may well decide to have staff monitor external developments and internal successes, and be active participants in guiding the strategic planning system to the major opportunities. However, effective use of staff in this kind of role has proved to be elusive. Just the right people and skill in using them is required. (Because of the difficulties cited, companies occasionally call in outside consultants to take a fresh look at existing strategy.)

SENIOR MANAGERS

The impetus to challenge the status quo may come from pressure groups, internal entrepreneurs, or planning staff, as just noted. Nevertheless, it is senior managers who really call the shot. They can recognize or suppress these challenges, and they personally can play a pivotal role in detecting the need for a change. Signals come to them from all sorts of sources—suppliers, trade-association committees, acquisition brokers, university seminars, actions of competitors, and many other channels. Internally, poor results or high turnover of the best people or disappearance of a major obstacle (a person, technological block, financial constraint, or the like) may prompt a strategy shift.

A decision to sponsor serious study of new strategies is made subjectively. It springs from some mysterious combination of "an ear to the ground," sifting out crucial and persistent developments, constructive imagination, and an attitude that welcomes change.

ACCEPTANCE AND COMMITMENT

The strategic planning systems and the impetus that prompts them into action, which we have been discussing in this chapter, imply dedicated, unified behavior. There is a presumption that the best ideas will be presented for review, that any disagreements will be resolved objectively by designated executives in the hierarchy, and that once a course has been selected, subordinates will accept the choice and work diligently on the next step. The external environment may be cantankerous and uncertainties bothersome, but internally, harmony prevails.

That approach to strategy formulation is deliberately simplified so that we can focus on important aspects one at a time. Now in this section we want to confront some of those simplified assumptions—notably the way diversity of personal values and internal politics complicate the process.

Personal Values

Recently a medium-sized petroleum company that needed additional sources of crude oil received a "feeler" about a joint venture in one of the Middle Eastern countries. The company president dismissed the possibility with, "I just don't want to be in bed with those bandits." The managing partner of a prestigious law firm, to cite a similar situation, turned down a participation in a real estate venture because, "Our professional objectivity is a precious asset. Even though this venture is a straightforward business risk on which we probably would make a good profit, our involvement might be misinterpreted. I don't want to spend time explaining our behavior."

A potential change in strategy in both these examples was shaped by the personal values of a key executive. The aspirations, preferences, moral standards, and other values of individual managers differ. Important variations relate to the degree of acceptable risk, sensitivity to inconvenience of other people, yen for growth, willingness to defy entrenched custom, feelings about reliability, and integrity. Each of us has likes and dislikes for internationalism, horse racing, television soap operas, bargaining, or living in Sioux Falls.

Inevitably these personal values affect managers' perceptions, what they communicate, their enthusiasm for particular proposals, and their commitment to any strategy they are asked to execute. Consequently, which strategic opportunities receive the most attention and which proposals are screened out depends to some extent on strongly held beliefs and values.

Personal values are influenced by prevailing company norms—the company's local culture. Typically, one or a few strong, respected senior executives set the tone. Their values become widely known, mostly through their actions. Risks that should be taken, attention to the environment, the precedence of the bottom line over customer or employee relations, and similar matters are likely to be treated in a manner congruent with values endorsed by the tone-setters. More specific values may likewise reign supreme. A classic example is Baldwin Locomotive—a blue-chip company in virtually all respects fifty years ago. The senior managers had intense loyalty to coal-powered steam locomotives; advocating diesels was like preaching Mohammedism in the Baptist Church. To its dying day, Baldwin claimed the best steam locomotives in the world.

This close tie between personal values and company strategy has great potential advantages. A good fit of personal beliefs and a selected strategy leads to emotional commitment and dedication. If Avis managers are really going to "try harder," they must endorse the norms of that company.

But granting the desirability of fit, how can we also be assured that company strategy will be kept in tune with environmental changes? Basically, there are three options:

1. Accept the dominant values of senior leaders and look for an attractive strategy that fits within this set of goals and constraints. There may be a niche these leaders can enthusiastically support that also wins the continuing cooperation of resource suppliers.

2. Try to change the values held to ones congruent with the strategic opportunities in the environment. For instance, if one of the conditions for future success in the company's setting is stable employment, then try to convince key executives that stable employment would be a great company achievement. Or, in a dying industry in which only a few relatively small firms can survive, try to convince key executives that laying off extra people (including old friends) is socially sound.

3. Transfer personnel so that executives are working in a business-unit in which the values they already hold are compatible with a strategy that is workable in the environment. Thus when Seagram Corporation directors concluded that an aggressive sales promotion posture was essential, they hired a new president who believed whole-heartedly in strong sales promotion; as expected, the strategy he

recommended included heavy advertising. To a significant extent, the strategy was largely shaped by the personnel selection process.

Assuring a good fit of farsighted strategy and the personal values of senior executives is obviously a delicate matter. Who is to decide whether present top executives are the right people to set and execute a well-conceived strategy? For a business-unit within a diversified company this crucial task rests with top corporate managers. For a single-line company, and for the top level in a diversified concern, only the board of directors has even the nominal power. If the board is unable or unwilling to take action when a misfit arises, then the rigors of competition will exact its toll.

In addition to senior executives, a fit between strategy and other key personnel is vital to effective execution of a strategy. This matching is discussed in Chapter 10.

INTERNAL POLITICS

Intertwined with personal values of individuals is company politics. Every organization requires cooperative efforts, and in this process of helping each other favors are received and returned. Often the mutual help clusters around support (or opposition) for a rallying "cause" such as advocating (or blocking) the transfer of field warehousing from the manufacturing department to the marketing department.

Much of what was said about external alignments in Chapter 5 can be applied to internal politics. Key actors, sources of power, coalitions, all have their counterpart within a firm. Of course, within a company a manager has more clout to check political action that is clearly harmful to the enterprise. Nevertheless, on the borderline and if company good is not yet clearly defined—as is often true during the strategy development stage—supporting one's friends is an inevitable practice.

Proposed strategy changes invite internal political maneuvering. For example, phasing out one product while expanding another, building for growth in Europe instead of trying to expand in an already saturated United States market, more subcontracting and less self-manufacture—all are upsetting to some parts of the existing business. Such changes would lead to a shift in the relative power of key actors within the company; some reallocation of resources is likely; pockets of specialized knowledge and friendly relations with outside suppliers—often cultivated over a period of years—would decrease in importance; uncertainty and insecurity about one's future worth would increase. These are deep concerns to those affected. Understandably, they will seek out their friends and try to devise ways to reduce the threat.

Note that the change in strategy would also have favorable outcomes for other people. They pick up what the former group loses. In an expanding situation a whole series of new job opportunities might be envisaged. Thus Xerox could expect a better reception to a proposed strategy change than, say, the Union Pacific Railroad.

A wise manager should anticipate and analyze these likely reactions. They will affect the information received, counterproposals, cooperation in exploring effects of the move, and perhaps power plays if the system is sufficiently "democratic." The questions to ask oneself are similar to those already posed on pages 74 to 77 in Chapter 5. Stated another way, a manager sponsoring a new strategy should make an early identification of:

1. Who will benefit from such a change and know it? (Explain and enlist their help.)
2. Who will suffer and know it? (Identify offsetting factors, or "defang.")
3. Who could benefit and not realize it? (Convert them.)
4. Who could suffer but not realize it? (Soft-pedal—low communication.)

Such an analysis provides a basis for interpreting reactions to a proposal and for planning its implementation when and if it receives official endorsement.

Clearly, divergence in personal values and company politics complicate the functioning of a strategic planning system, but these complications increase the need for some such system. Knowing when and where key issues in strategy formulation should be resolved increases the chances that something useful will emerge from what is inherently a sensitive complex process. Conversely, personal values and internal politics running unchecked by any strategic direction give birth to splattered, zigzag courses and close to chaos.

INCREMENTALISM

Strategic planning and its execution typically advances at an irregular pace. In this respect the neat schedules of when key decisions will be made, such as that shown in Figure 6–1, are misleading. Thus in this section we take a closer look at timing.

Unpredictable Time Lags

The total span between recognition that a change in strategy should be seriously explored and having the resulting new strategy in operation is long—ranging from two to over ten years. A thorough study of threats and opportunities may take several months. Then, following a search for alternatives, feasibility studies are made of the most attractive ones. Perhaps R&D work on a new product or process is vital, and a constructive finding may take years. For instance, one company has been researching for a low-cost way to convert coal into gasoline for eleven years. Market tests for some ideas take a year. To shorten the time on any of these steps increases the uncertainty.

Moreover, the time required for each step is hard to predict. For instance, no one knows when a breakthrough in research will occur. If an acquisition is contemplated, finding the right firm that is willing to join forces is chancy indeed. The duration of legal roadblocks vacillates widely—as people dealing with pharmaceuticals or casinos frequently testify, and the development of political coalitions—internal and external—is quite uncertain.

In strategy formulation there are no regular summer heat and autumn wind that assure the crop will be ready to harvest in October.

Recycling: Sequential Learning

Strategy is crisscrossed with uncertainty. As a result, new facts and unexpected situations keep popping up that force reexamination of earlier assumptions. The drop in the value of the United States dollar in 1978, for example, sent the planners in a rubber company "back to the drawing boards." Entry into the European adhesive market via a Belgian plant no longer looked attractive. However, in negotiations relating to the proposed plant a possible joint venture emerged that is keyed to a plant in a less developed country. If this thrust is pursued, the United States company's export strategy must be modified. Thus the new learning calls for recycling the previous analysis.

Learning may start anywhere in the planning cycle. Sugar refineries, for instance, had to dispose of large quantities of a fibrous by-product called bagasse. One possibility was to use the bagasse as fuel to generate electric power, and this steered the sugar refineries into a world analysis of competing fuels for steam power plants. Here the potential use led to market analysis rather than a known market need leading to product development. Then, what was learned about fuel requirements was recycled back to the refinery engineers.

Taking Each Step when the Time is Ripe

In addition to reasons already noted, the pace of strategic planning depends on urgency. Factors affecting urgency of action include:

1. *Competitors' actual or anticipated behavior.* For instance, IBM speeded up its decision to market its 360 series because Honeywell had announced a new computer that would challenge IBM's existing lead in design.

2. *Importance of a head start.* The premature entry of several companies into the videotape market shows the importance they attached to a head start; they launched their marketing campaign before engineering problems of hooking into existing television sets were solved.

3. *Transient opportunity to acquire resources, merge, or enter coalitions.* Thus when the Franklin National Bank (with assets of over two billion dollars) became insolvent and was suddenly available for acquisition, the European-American Bank faced a unique opportunity to greatly expand its United States operations. Somebody had to take over Franklin National within a period of a few weeks. In fact, Franklin National's heavy orientation with retail banking on Long Island did not exactly fit European-American's strategy for expansion in the United States, but the ailing bank did represent a large foothold in United States banking that would take years to acquire through internal growth alone. Thus European-American altered its strategy to fit the opportunity—and negotiated the takeover.

4. *Other internal or external commitments.* To continue the preceding example, at least one New York City bank wanted very much to absorb Franklin National. The fit into *its* growth strategy would have been excellent. But this bank was still digesting its previous merger and had neither the capital structure nor executive personnel to handle the overgrown Franklin National. For it, the time was not ripe.

5. *Recognition by key executives that some action is needed.* The classic example here is the Ford Motor Company's tardy move away from the Model T. The much-needed modification could not be made until Henry Ford, Sr. finally accepted the need for a change. Over thirty years later, George Romney had difficulty getting American Motors executives to recognize the opportunity for a small car—the Rambler—in the United States market. In this instance, as in the Ford

case, external financial pressure and a dwindling market position were necessary to induce action. A common problem with the readiness of key executives for a change in strategy is that all of them do not "see the light" at the same time. This can be serious, because strategy development usually requires inputs from different departments, and foot-dragging in any one department hinders the entire program. Thus part of the timing issue is when sufficient power has been mobilized back of a change to pull a reluctant minority into line.

For any of these reasons, the timing of a particular strategic move may be speeded up or slowed down. Instead of a neat, logical sequence, for example, a resource may be acquired before the market is clearly established, or an antitrust charge may delay the public sale of securities, which slows down the construction of a new plant. Each shift in pace or sequence calls for a new assessment of risks. And, once committed to even part of a program, the remaining options are narrowed (as already noted, availability of alternatives often affects relative power). Progress is made by irregular increments.

Such unexpected developments give strategy formulation its "dynamic" quality. As external cooperation becomes increasingly unmanageable, a company finds itself in a hostile environment—as noted at the beginning of Chapter 5.

CONCLUSION

The preceding discussion of the birth of a new strategy separated parts of the general process to highlight the nature and influence of each part. Strategic planning systems, sources of pressure to activate such a system, gaining acceptance and commitment while the strategy is being shaped, and recognition of the irregular and incremental path new strategies often follow—all are features that deserve attention.

In practice, these features are much more intertwined than our discussion implies. The following interactions are important for the total process to function effectively:

1. *A strategic planning system must be treated only as a framework within which the more irregular, less formal, and subtle aspects of strategy formulation can be brought into focus.* The system establishes some of the basic groundrules: how and where proposals will be examined; who will be consulted on various inputs; who makes authoritative decisions; and how such decisions are related to shorter-range planning. Being known and understood by executives through-

out the organization, this orderliness is a significant aid when someone gets a hot, urgent idea to exploit.

For reasons sketched in the section on incrementalism—unpredictable time lags, recycling, and shifts in the urgency of action—few strategies emerge neatly from a prescheduled sequence. Instead, the planning cycle can be speeded up or slowed down and missing pieces fitted into the puzzle out of sequence. (The Texas Instruments scheme has the most flexibility in this respect.) Nevertheless, the process is understood, and participants can recognize where a particular input fits and what else is needed.

Deadlines still serve a useful purpose. They flag the need for some sort of guidance to short-term planning—even if it is "no change yet." Also, they call for a review of progress that rekindles interest and prevents long-run thinking from languishing.

In the hectic life of most companies, some sort of attention-directing, pace-setting mechanism is needed to help busy executives to work together constructively. That's what planning systems are for.

2. *The system will not run itself.* Some powerful executive(s) has to keep the players on track. He or she makes sure that internal entrepreneurs are not smothered, that development staff is perceptive and creative, and that senior managers take their strategy roles seriously. Indeed, this powerful executive—often the CEO—may have his or her own views on future directions for the business; but more important is his or her motivating other contributors to vigorous, provocative participation. Also, someone must orchestrate who occupies key positions. As noted earlier, the directions a business takes—or does *not* take—and the enthusiastic commitment to that cause are conditioned by the personal values and energies of the individuals in influential jobs. Thus a necessary feature in getting a new strategy launched is having executive personnel who are willing, perhaps eager, to make a change.

A related task is keeping internal politics within bounds. Give-and-take accommodations and diplomatic trade-offs are a normal part of cooperative effort; they help build esprit de corps. The lurking danger that may hurt strategy formulation is informal understandings among important executives not to rock the boat because existing comfortable status might be upset. When personal convenience takes precedence over long-run company strength, someone has to blow the whistle.

3. In a dynamic company, *this whole process of strategy formulation should become the normal, traditional way of confronting and resolving strategy issues.* The process should be "institutionalized."

Both the way planning systems are used and the roles and relationships between people can become so accepted and expected that executives give little thought to who does what. Then, the company develops skill in pursuing the process. The know-how becomes part of the group's behavior pattern; some expertise grows out of experience; confidence develops from past successes. And with such institutionalized skill, a company can promptly deal with unexpected opportunities or threats. Temporary deviations from the established pattern may be allowed and acknowledged, and occasionally modifications in the process may be explicitly discussed. But a way to do strategic planning has become part of the company's basic repertoire.

One aspect of skill in formulating strategy is focusing on important subjects. In Chapters 1 and 2, the selective nature of strategy was stressed; strategy centers on a relatively few distinctive characteristics and assumes that other features of company activities can be performed "satisfactorily." Also, in moving from missions to programs, strategy concentrates on only crucial thrusts. Care must be exercised that neither the planning system nor the executives using it inject so many dimensions that this selectivity gets buried. For business-units, strategy typically can be confined to (a) selecting an attractive domain, (b) picking a basis for differential advantage in that domain, (c) deciding what major thrusts are necessary to move from the present position to the desired position, and (d) establishing target results that can be expected from following the course outlined in (a), (b), and (c). Even within this framework, substantial judgment is needed in deciding what to cover.

The formal planning systems sketched in the beginning of this chapter provide for each of these four strategic elements as an embryo strategy progresses through the cycle. Although that progress may be halting—to overcome a major uncertainty or to develop commitment—the eventual outcome can and should be a dominant guiding mission for the business.

PART II

PROPULSION
Translating Strategy into Action

Programming—Too Much or Too Little

INTRODUCTION TO PART II

"If wishes were horses, beggars might ride." So, too, with strategy. The design of strategy is not enough. Even the wisest strategy will come to naught unless a whole series of supporting moves puts that plan into effect.

Inertia is inevitable (and desirable) in every company. Policies are known, ties with customers and resource suppliers are established, employees have learned to depend on each other. Such behavior norms help execute the old strategy. A new strategy, in contrast, calls for a break in some of these patterns—at the appropriate time—and the building of different commitments and behavior. A revised management structure specifically fitted to the new strategy must be created.

If strategy is thought of as a trajectory or flight plan for an enterprise, then we must now consider propulsion—the set of forces that will enable the enterprise to follow that course.

In Part II we look at six mechanisms that managers can use to promote this transition:

- Programming—Too Much or Too Little (Chapter 7)
- Building Revised Patterns of Behavior (Chapter 8)
- Organizing to Execute Strategy (Chapter 9)
- The Right Person and The Right Carrot (Chapter 10)
- Resource Allocation—Power of the Purse Strings (Chapter 11)
- Controlling the Dynamic Process (Chapter 12)

Each of these tools has strengths and weaknesses. When improperly used, they can become serious stumbling blocks, but when employed in the right place at the right time, each is powerful. When used in a balanced combination, as urged in Part III, the impact is even more potent.

As in Part I, the analysis aims at action in business-units (single-line companies)—because that is where rededication is crucial. The same tools for change, however, can be easily adapted to corporate redirection. Understanding what is necessary for business-unit action is key to corporate staff's ability to provide tools and climate that will help to bring about change.

Lure of Programming

Programming has great appeal as an instrument to execute strategy. The series of stipulated steps promises results. Thus we yearn for a national energy program or, within a company, an employee productivity program. Unfortunately, we can have too much or too little programming. The scope, degree of detail, timespan, and adaptability all must be weighed.

Possible differences in programming are illustrated in the following classics.

1. A Cook's Tour, in which each move is laid out from start to finish—with each day and perhaps hour specified as to place and activity. Even the dinner menus may be set in advance.
2. The Lewis & Clark expedition in 1804–1806 from what is now St. Louis to the mouth of the Columbia River on the Pacific Ocean. Here, only the objective was clear; moves had to be decided from day to day amid staggering uncertainty and precarious resources.
3. Frontier homesteading—consisting of relatively small, incremental advances. Each highly decentralized move had its own targets, and the success or failure at one point strongly influenced the next moves.

A basic question in programming the execution of any strategy is where in the range suggested by the above examples to concentrate. A Cook's Tour is too rigid; a Lewis & Clark expedition is unstructured and risky; homesteading offers only halting and often unpredictable advance.

To develop guides for using programs in strategy execution we will consider three basic types of programming:

Comprehensive programs: the man-on-the-moon approach.
Incrementalism: feeling your way.
Selective programming.

MAN–ON–THE–MOON APPROACH

Preparing Comprehensive Programs

Clearly, one way to put a new strategy into effect is to build a comprehensive program. The successful landing of a man on the moon is eloquent argument for this approach. Starting with a sharp objective, we then design a series of steps that will move the business-unit (or company) from our starting position to that goal.

Almost always each of these major steps will require subprograms, and a further spelling out calls for subsubprograms. To land a man on the moon and bring him home, for example, required a spaceship; the spaceship needed, among other features, a guidance system; the guidance system needed small rockets, and so on. There was a program for each successive step, and many projects within each program. Company programs are not so complex, but launching a new product does call for programs in R&D, production, marketing, and service functions—and each of these typically have subprograms. Theoretically, every step is carefully laid out.

Although finding reliable input data may be very difficult, the basic process of building any program is clear: (a) Divide the total project into steps. (b) Note any necessary sequences among the steps, such as legal approval before public announcement of a bond issue, or assembling a product before painting it to avoid scratching during assembly. (c) Decide who will be accountable for each step. (d) Determine resources needed and their availability for each step. (e) Estimate the elapsed time required to complete each step. (f) Assign definite dates for the beginning and ending of each step, based on (b), (d), and (e).

The scope and detail to which such programming is pushed in advance will depend on how the resulting estimates are to be used. When the primary purpose is future planning, rather than control, a convenient rule of thumb is to extend the programs and subprograms down to a level at which the manager responsible for carrying out a particular part of the action is confident that he or she will be able to fulfill the mission within the scheduled timeframe with the assigned resources.

These comprehensive programs can be summarized in several ways. (a) The *timing* of interrelated moves can be laid out. The program(s) reveals which events must precede others and how long the respective steps will take. By combining this information together, we can prepare a PERT network or master schedule. Such a picture of the total set of related moves gives the strategy managers a handle on where to try to speed up action and where to make readjustments if one subelement is off target. The so-called *critical path* (that necessary sequence of moves which will take the longest total time) deserves continuing attention.

(b) *Resource requirements*—people with particular skills, production capacity, materials, energy, services, and the cash flows necessary to provide these inputs—can also be summarized from the comprehensive programs. Both the total requirements of each kind of resources and—even more valuable for managerial purpose—the time and place where the resources will be used can be spelled out. Such information is especially useful in dealing with outside groups, because the strategy managers now know when a new supply of a particular resource must be obtained quickly from the most convenient supplier or when time is available to negotiate with alternative sources.

P.P.B. Experience

The most ambitious attempt to use comprehensive programming was launched in the federal government over a decade ago. *Planning-programming-budgeting*, or what is widely known as P.P.B., developed in the Department of Defense and was later extended to all executive branches. It tried in a single vehicle to deal with issues of timing, resource allocation, control mechanisms, and detailed coordination. The trials and tribulations of this experiment throw light on what business executives can expect from comprehensive programming.

Under P.P.B., planning leads to the adoption of what in this book we call strategy. The selected strategy is then elaborated in a comprehensive program, and the resources required for that program become the justification for the annual budget requests submitted by each department and agency. This scheme permits centralized review of objectives and strategy, which prior to P.P.B. had been very sporadic; on the other hand, budgets cannot be merely continuation of the status quo except as they are tied—through programs—to approved strategy. For example, if United States defense strategy drops large naval aircraft carriers, such ships would not appear in programs (except for disposing of those already on hand), and budget requests for the operation of aircraft carriers would not be approved because of lack of support in a program.

In practice, P.P.B. did not work. The reasons for this failure include several lessons bearing on comprehensive programming in business.

1. The new programs stressed by P.P.B. gave too little attention to large, ongoing operations. The bulk of activities in most government departments have developed over the years; both internal and external groups have learned to depend on such agencies as the Bureau of Labor Statistics, Social Security, Postal Service, and the like. Predictability, inertia, and repetitiveness are positive features in such services. Traditional budgeting suited these established organizations better than the program concept that focuses on a series of one-time moves. For business, the lesson is that *strategic change is likely to call for different management techniques than continuous running of well-established business-units.*

2. Most of the departments lacked a suitable data base and analysts skilled in estimating how alternative strategies might be carried out. Preparing realistic programs for various strategic alternatives— which the P.P.B. system called for—was beyond the existing capability of almost every department except the military, where tremendous resources are devoted to exploring various strategies. Such program estimates that were passed up and down the hierarchy typically were prepared by newly recruited personnel and did not incorporate the judgment and commitment of line managers. The more qualitative the program—say, auto safety—the more serious lack of experience became. *Good strategic programming, then, takes the time of well-trained, busy executives.* It cannot be done well over a couple of weekends.

3. The P.P.B. scheme forced the preparation of detailed programs for all branches and sections that would eventually be affected by a strategy, because such programs were needed for budget estimates. This tended to create rigidity and premature commitments. Especially for innovative programs dealing with such problems as hard-core un-

employment and ghetto housing, more experimentation and read-justments based on new learning were needed. These successive revisions were hindered by the complete, though perhaps ill-conceived, package required for the initial approach. And where various parts of a program were assigned to different organizational units, bureaucracy interfered with revision. Here, the P.P.B. lesson is that *detailed programming tends to reduce adaptation.* When confronted by dynamic, uncertain situations, the trade-off favors postponing the specific planning until very close to when action must begin (even though this does complicate resource planning).

4. During P.P.B.'s heyday, there was a lot of unrealistic talk about balancing cost/benefit results of different programs. The central planners assumed that resources could easily be shifted from one activity to another—and perhaps back again a year or two later. Often these were not small shifts. Instead, the changes contemplated would require reassignment of many people, reorganization, revised policies, and a new set of personal commitments. In reality, government offices (and companies) cannot be turned around that fast. Morale slumps; foot-dragging stalls much change until a new set of planners concoct yet another program. The P.P.B. enthusiasts were overly impressed with the power of programming. They failed to recognize that redirecting a social organization calls for modification of policies and traditions, shifts in roles and personal power, perhaps switching personnel—in addition to the program—and all this takes time. The lesson here is that *programs calling for major internal change usually need reinforcement* from organizational and personnel shifts—and *time to digest.*

For these reasons, at least, the P.P.B. experience raises doubts about reliance on comprehensive programming to execute strategy.

Comprehensive programming is wise for a business firm only when several tough requirements are met. (a) The strategic goal must be clear and sharp and commitment to it high. (b) Achievement of that goal must be of great importance to the company, and completion "on time" (ahead of competitors or while the environment is still favorable) must be urgent. (c) Resources, including able managers, should be available—and not too deeply immersed in existing operations. (d) Uncertainties should be "manageable"—that is, of a sort and size that able managers can cope with.

In practice, these requirements are rarely present. Boeing's move into commercial jets and IBM's shift to its 360 line of compatible computers are classic examples, but such situations are unusual.

The arguments for adopting an incremental approach to programming, summarized in the next section, flag a variety of circumstances when comprehensive programming is *not* appropriate.

INCREMENTALISM—FEELING YOUR WAY

Some executives believe that programming should be short-range and narrow in scope. Next year's programs can then be built on the outcomes of what we do today and on the actual conditions prevailing next year. Progress, under this approach, is achieved by a series of increments, each building on the preceding ones. Most department stores grew in this way. So did downtown shopping centers (in contrast to the construction of suburban centers, which usually are fully planned).

Although specific planning is restricted to small changes and short timespans, broad strategic and longer-run objectives may exist. Senior managers can keep stressing these objectives and related values so that the programmed increments do move in a general direction. The objectives are sufficiently broad and far enough out, however, to permit flexibility in picking subjects and deadlines for each programmed step. Over thirty years ago Lindblom reported that this bit-by-bit approach was the way most strategies evolve, and more recently Quinn argues that incrementalism is good management.*

The reasons a company may take the incremental approach include the following.

PROGRAM UNCERTAINTIES

Rarely is a company able to lay out a practical, workable program for the full installation of a new strategy. A new strategy typically involves time-consuming moves, each with a degree of uncertainty in its outcome—R&D explorations, developing a new set of customers in a new market, opening a mine, building a favorable reputation in a foreign country are examples. From two to ten or more years are normally required for the complete transition.

Uncertainties abound. Even the initial estimates of outcomes, costs, and adequacy of resources contain guesses and probabilities that open the way for deviations from plans. Then, during the long span

* See C. E. Lindblom, "The Science of Muddling Through," *Public Administration Review*, Spring 1959; and J. B. Quinn, "Strategic Change: 'Logical Incrementalism,' " *Sloan Management Review*, Fall 1978.

when work is being carried out, unexpected changes are sure to occur. Changes in the environment, surprises by competitors, improvements or losses in our own resources, shifts in the health and desires of key individuals, sudden growth in other business-units which deflects executive attention—some or all such factors will create operating situations that differ significantly from those originally predicted.

Cross-impacts of relatively minor surprises can radically change the outcome of the program as a whole.

If we try to program in detail over, say, a three- to five-year period, much of that program will have to be revised to fit the conditions that actually emerge. Such revisions take executive effort and therefore are costly. The people who devoted themselves to the initial program usually have some reluctance to change. The existence of the original program invites the making of commitments earlier than really necessary, thereby sacrificing flexibility.

This combination of inevitable uncertainties during the time-span involved, coupled with costs of adjusting an early program to the unpredicted conditions, argues for postponing detailed programming as long as lead times will allow.

Strategy Modifications

A further reason for postponing and restricting detailed programming is that the strategy itself is subject to change. If the strategy is modified, then a detailed program for activities several years hence may be aimed in the wrong direction.

An adaptable strategy has several advantages:

1. Environmental changes, including competitors' actions, which occur during the implementation period may make a revision of our strategy highly desirable. We modify our strategy as unexpected opportunities or threats arise.

2. Sometimes the strategy is deliberately unspecific. When faced with several major contingencies, instead of betting on a single one we may adopt a course of action that permits us to decide later which way to jump. For example, with a strategy to move into solar heating we may program the designing and manufacturing of the equipment but postpone a decision on channels of distribution. Prepared opportunism is the extreme form of such intentionally vague strategies.

3. Typically, strategies have multiple objectives and multiple dimensions or degrees of each objective. Senior executives differ in the importance they attach to security, fame, short-run profits, and the

like. The trade-offs between these objectives usually have not been—and probably cannot be—thought through when a strategy is adopted. Too many possibilities would have to have been explored, and in trying to resolve hypothetical problems needless acrimony can develop. Thus the strategy is deliberately left vague on such matters, postponing clarification until the actual choices that must be made can be seen more sharply.

4. External political pressures also may make adjustment of strategy wise. As noted in Chapter 5, few companies are in such a dominant position that they can impose their strategy on all resource contributors. Instead, periodic negotiations occur about the way cooperative action will be carried forward. In this process revisions of some features of our strategy may be a necessary concession. If our bargaining position unexpectedly improves, we may be able to pursue our objectives more aggressively.

For these reasons it may be desirable to keep strategy pliable. Adjustment is to be expected. If the strategy itself is unsettled, then a detailed program to carry it out has limited value. A single comprehensive program conveys a misleading certainty, and it will probably have to be completely redone at a later date. Theoretically, a company might follow two or more programs, each suited to a different scenario, and at a later date select the best one; but maintaining several detailed programs is so complex and expensive that few companies could even consider the possibility.

Incrementalism does, indeed, provide flexibility. However, a danger in embracing the incremental approach is that action will be too timid. Today's problems always loom large. If our efforts to carry out strategy focuses only on the hurdles just ahead, we may be perpetually getting ready to start. The drive necessary for a big change can too easily get lost.

SELECTIVE PROGRAMMING

Grand-scale programming, such as that used to put a man on the moon, rarely fits the execution of company strategy. At the other extreme, incrementalism often lacks the positive push required to get a fresh strategy in place on time. For most companies most of the time, selective programming provides the concentrated effort needed. It can be used to great advantage to reach short-term and intermediate goals.

When Short-Term Programming Is Desirable

During the short term—a year or two in the framework of this book—uncertainty is less of a hazard to programming. Also, the need to prepare for and take action soon increases the benefits of a well-conceived program. Broadly speaking, then, the shorter the planning horizon, the more useful programming becomes. This suggests that programs be used selectively within a longer-range strategy.

For the execution of strategy, several guides can be stated.

Program the Major Thrusts Singled Out in Strategy.   An important element in business-unit strategy is identifying major moves that are especially adroit in advancing toward the domain and differential advantage sought (see Figure 7–1). Because these thrusts are so important, programming effort is warranted. These thrusts should be given priority, and one way to assure this preferred attention is to spell out who should do what and when. Even though some revisions of the program may be likely, the cardinal importance of pursuing these ends justifies the effort involved in planning and replanning.

Sometimes thrusts are stated in a timeless mode, such as "build a reputation for quality (or new design) leadership," or the horizon may be very long, such as "at least 80% of production coming from developing nations by the year 2000." In such cases, *intermediate objectives* as to the progress expected within, say, two and five years should be established. Then the programming focuses on this shorter period.

Program Other Critical Short-Term Moves.   Here the trick is to decide where a prompt start is critical for the strategy to succeed. Among the possible moves to investigate in this connection are:

1. Projects with such long lead times that they must be started now if they are to be completed when the end result is needed. Power plants with likely delays on equipment and environmental approvals are a classic example.

2. A necessary first step in a sequence. For instance, R&D on a new product must be almost complete before detailed marketing or production plans can be started.

3. Development of a capability that will be used in a prepared-opportunism strategy. Access to large financial resources, for example, may be needed for any of several scenarios that have been predicted.

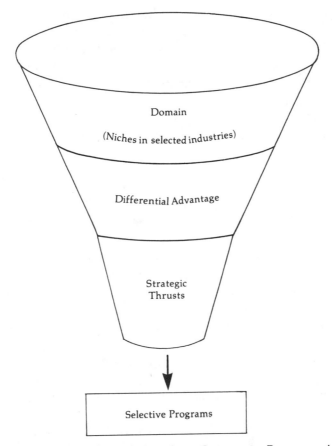

Domain

(Niches in selected industries)

Differential Advantage

Strategic
Thrusts

Selective Programs

FIGURE 7-1.   *Normal Flow from Strategy to Programming*

4. An exceptional opportunity that will soon lapse. An illustration is when the Air Force is about to award a contract for a new fighter plane that will be the standard for perhaps a decade.

Program To Protect a Future Resource Allocation.   In diversified companies in which business-units compete for scarce resources, it may be necessary to stake out a claim before those resources are fully committed to other business-units. Partial use of a sales force or distribution system, key executive talent, exclusive use of a patent or a market niche—any or all may be ingredients in a strategy. Only by building a program showing their future importance can a strong case be presented for reserving the resource that is not yet needed.

Program with an Eye on Public Relations. The existence of well-developed programs usually becomes known beyond the programmers themselves, and those who hear about it wonder "how that will affect me." Occasionally, programming will be undertaken to boost employee morale; it is an indication that the company is "on the move." Or, planning expansion in plant capacity might discourage a potential competitor from doing likewise. Rarely will such public relations effects by themselves warrant a programming effort, but they can tip the decision in marginal cases.

When To Shun Specific Programming

Our strong endorsement of selective short-run programming should be coupled with a few cautions. These warnings relate to detailed programming, not to the much simpler mapping of broad steps.

There is little point in designing programs now for moves that can be deferred without damage. At a later date, when the time to start that move has arrived, we will face fewer uncertainties and can build a more reliable, doable program. For detailed programming, the rule of thumb is "never do today what can just as well be done tomorrow."

When a large investment is surrounded by high uncertainty, the prudent maneuver is to seek some way to delay the big commitment. Options or subcontracts are among the ways to "buy time." Similarly, a pharmaceutical firm paid a stiff tariff to a developing country for five years because of uncertainties about its market; no local production program was considered until the size of the market was clear.

Public relations may be a factor. A manager may want to avoid controversy about location, jurisdiction, or resource allocation that would surface in the process of programming, or may be anxious not to show his or her hand to equipment suppliers or other outsiders. Thus detailed programming is postponed as long as possible.

Broad-Stroke Programming

There is a kind of strategic planning that uses several programming concepts but does not pretend to any refinement in its estimates. For lack of a better term, we call it *broad-stroke programming.*

When formulating a business strategy, one or more senior executives must give some thought to the steps that will be necessary to reach the desired domain with the chosen differential advantages. Relying heavily on subjective judgment, the major moves, the sequences, and even the timing are mapped out in broad strokes. This kind of thinking is one test of feasibility of the proposed strategy. Also, it serves as a basis for selecting major thrusts.

A similar analysis is useful in executing strategy. Although it lacks the factual foundation and group judgment normally included in programming, it does give a first approximation of actions that will have to be taken sooner or later. Then, as new opportunities arise or unexpected threats emerge, executives have at least a rough framework for gauging their impact.

For example, when AEC—an auto equipment firm—decided to start its own production in Brazil, the top executives worked with a broad-stroke program involving plant location, building, equipment, labor training, local managers, and financing. The initial program, which called for employing a Brazilian general manager as the first step, was revised when a very attractive plant became available in Belo Horizonte. Nevertheless, the existence of the broad-stroke program had a marked effect on AEC's decisions on when to take occupancy of the plant and what commitments to make to the local government on hiring and training local labor.

Note that although a PERT network is unwarranted, the concept of a critical path can be applied to the broad-stroke program. For intermediate steps, at least, the major events can be listed in sequence. This sequence guides executives on where next to focus attention so that the implementation of the strategy will keep advancing.

STRATEGY PROGRAMS VERSUS CONTINUING OPERATIONS

The preceding analysis treats strategy programming as a separate activity, more or less independent of other managerial duties. In practice, the clash with running today's business is probably the main foe of a well-planned execution of a new strategy.

Where To Place Priorities?

In an established business the execution of a new strategy normally is entwined with existing operations. The burden of changing is superimposed on getting today's work done well. This double, overlapping task creates conflicts that may—and often do—undermine even the wisest programs. Common trouble spots include:

1. Line managers not only help prepare programs, they also are assigned specific tasks in the new program. Such involvement of line managers in new thrusts has large benefits—in better planning and in capable execution. The catch is that the programmed change is an added burden. Typically, no relief from previous assignments is provided. Unless slack exists in the organization, managers are forced to scrimp on either their regular jobs or on the new assignments.

2. Usually, expense allowances for programmed steps in strategy execution are merged into the annual budget of the departments that will do the work. If existing personnel is expected to do the added work, there may be no allowance at all. Then, if pressure to cut expenses arises it is the extra, special task that gets squeezed down.

3. Control standards and reporting schemes are typically well established for continuing operations. The whistle blows even for small deviations. In contrast, special programs with difficult-to-measure outputs often are loosely controlled. It is an old maxim that "watched results get priority in attention."

4. Rewards—bonuses, salary increases, and even promotions—in most companies are tied to results in current operations. The payoff comes from the bottom line or some other quantitative output. Meeting strategy targets typically is considered desirable but secondary to today's business. Thus rewards give managers a clear message of where priorities lie.

5. More fundamental than the four problems just noted is the very nature of strategic change. Strategic change is a routine-disrupting, unique experience. It calls for initiative and imagination to overcome natural protection of the status quo. It has a mission of its own that differs sharply from the tasks of managing established operations effectively and efficiently. Both are necessary, but their inherent differences stir up trouble when we try to merge them together.

Ways to deal with each of these clashes are discussed in following chapters. The point being made here is that even well-conceived programs may have rough sledding. The existing system tends to push the strategy implementing programs advocated above into second place. The structure we carefully nurtured to carry out our present operations has momentum—a momentum that is likely to override new, unusual, and somewhat fragile programs. If there is deliberate sabotage of the programs, as can happen, the arguments for taking care of current need become even louder.

Consequently, any approved programs must be given high priority. Without committed support from people in powerful positions, the programmed phases of a new strategy may get lost in the swirl of busyness. Some way must be devised to keep the new as well as the old on course.

DEGREES OF CONFLICT

The task of reconciling strategy programs with continuing operations varies widely. When the new strategy is basically an extension of existing strategy—for example, expansion into the West Coast area or acquisition of a firm that makes materials which were previously purchased—the degree of conflict should be low. Present jobs are not threatened; a basis for expanding budgets is known. But when a company decides to change, for example, from basic chemicals to specialty chemicals—or a savings bank shifts into commercial banking—customers, conversion technology, control systems, capital investment, organization and other features must be altered. In such situations both the number of new activities and their difference from present ones are large. Here program priorities become difficult.

The status of a business-unit in a corporation portfolio also makes a difference. Stars in high-growth industries are more accustomed to change and are prepared to allocate resources to bring it about. They tend to take strategy programs in their stride. Cash cows usually are more stable, and they operate under tighter financial controls. For them even an extension of existing strategy will require prodding, and a sharp shift will be like major surgery—acceptable only on the threat of death.

The welcome that strategy programs will receive in a specific company should be carefully studied, as the above examples indicate. For the programs to produce the intended action they must be reinforced with matching resource allocations, organization, and controls. The amount of such support that will be needed in a specific setting depends on the nature of the clashing—as sketched in the last few pages.

CONCLUSION

Programming has a vital role in putting a new strategy into action. It should be used to focus attention on strategic thrusts and to lay out a series of steps on these selected fronts that can then be monitored and strongly supported. Such programs are a key device available to central managers for assuring that their desired strategy is being launched.

Special programs also can be forged to obtain resources that have long lead times. Such moves are often necessary to keep strategic options open. Other potential uses include the first step in a necessary sequence, dealing with an exceptional opportunity, protecting a resource allocation, and taking a public relations posture.

This spelling out of *who* is to do *what, when* harnesses effort. It guides cooperative action to spots that are critical for carrying out the strategy. No major strategy change can be achieved without programmed moves.

Note this strong endorsement does not include comprehensive, detailed programs that try to cover an entire implementation. Rarely will the future be clear enough and a company powerful enough to follow a set of blueprints. Instead, detailed planning of some moves is delayed until the results of thrusts are known (or can be forecast with tolerable accuracy). Judgment must be exercised in selecting which fronts—markets, resources, R&D, internal organization, government support, and so on—to attack next. Within the programmed areas considerable adjustment may be necessary.

The complexity and dynamic character of the total scene, however, raise the value of selective programming. In the turbulence, selected moves are achieved because of the disciplined effort induced by the programs.

Programming alone is not enough. It needs support. Support from reshaped behavior, revised organization, key personnel, resource allocations, and constructive control is also necessary. These elements of strategic action are examined in the next five chapters.

Building Revised Patterns of Behavior

Strategy execution does not just happen. Many university presidents, for example, have decided to place heavy emphasis on continuing (adult) education—but a close look at the courses offered and the students in classrooms reveals very little change. The behavior patterns of professors change at glacial speeds. Even when strategic thrusts are carefully programmed, managers often discover that activities on the firing line are slow to adjust.

Such sluggish response to new strategy is the subject of this chapter. First, reasons for the inertia are reviewed, then a series of steps that can help narrow the gap between strategy and actual behavior are outlined.

Inertia Is Normal

Every successful organization develops much customary behavior. There are standard ways to buy materials, bill customers, pay for overtime, call a directors' meeting, and perform many other activities. Work has a normal pace; communication channels are known; an array of standards and values become accepted norms.

These normal behavior patterns are essential to survival. In fact, many behavioral scientists describe these repetitive work patterns as *the* organization. Managers deliberately design many policies and procedures to assure that work is done in a desired manner. Customs grow up to fill in where actions are not prescribed, and over time a whole set of relationships, both inside and outside the organization, become normal patterns. This social structure makes cooperative joint action possible. Dependability promotes coordination; predictability aids efficiency.

Nevertheless, the stable, reliable, often finely tuned ways of working together may become roadblocks to new endeavors. For instance, a commercial bank nurtured over the years to deal with large accounts fumbled with a strategy to enter retail banking. Several obstacles arose: (a) Past policies and procedures were not suited to deal with large volumes of small transactions. (b) Standards for granting credit, for expenses, and so on no longer fit. (c) New customers were strangers and responded in unpredictable ways. (d) More subtly, many employees felt that most of the new customers were not worthy to be clients of their bank. The employees had a haughty pride—and commitment—in serving prestige depositors; serving the "little guy" clashed with cherished values.

All enterprises—steel mills, hospitals, insurance companies—have a similar inertia, much like the momentum of an ocean ship. Managers cultivate these habits and values; they are a significant part of the so-called experience curve that gives established businesses an edge over newcomers. However, when we wish to change the direction, a great deal of effort may be necessary to revise the previously encouraged patterns.

Unless steps are taken to deal with entrenched behavior patterns, the execution of a strategy is likely to be diverted and twisted from its basic aim.

DIAGNOSE NEED FOR CHANGES IN BEHAVIOR PATTERNS

The momentum of our present operations is a valuable asset. Any new strategy must build on this base. Thus an early task in strategy execution is to decide just what to modify—and what to leave alone.

Determine Which Existing Policies and Customs Should Be Revised

An obvious first step is to consider systematically all prevailing policies, standard operating procedures, customary methods, and other current practices in light of the new strategy. Does each one give maximum support to the strategy? Where must revisions be made?

Both formally approved action guides and informal practices should be included in this review. The norms that shape actual behavior do matter.

Each department should participate—to assure full coverage. This cross-checking may become tedious, but it has by-product benefits. During discussion of whether the new strategy does or does not have an impact on prevailing behavior in a department or section, (a) the strategy is explained to many key people, and (b) unanticipated difficulties in execution may be discovered.

In a clash between current practice and a logical interpretation of the new strategy, the strategy view does not always win. Reasons for current practice may be compelling. For example, expansion strategy of a metal-refining company pointed to use of a new process in its Grand Rapids plant. However, local review of these plans turned up environmental restraints on drainage that prevented a shift to the new process in that location.

Misfits between new strategy and prevailing behavior may not be as clear as in the preceding example. Local people who prefer not to change may be less than candid about their actual practice, and in some instances long-run implications of the strategy itself may not be fully revealed. Thus the confrontation is deferred.

These practical difficulties in fully detecting misfits between a new mission and current behavior patterns do not diminish the desirability of a systematic search. Knowing where misfits exist greatly improves a manager's ability to overcome them.

Decide When To Press for Change

Not all misfits should be revised immediately. Strategy spans a long period, and some moves must be deferred until the groundwork for them is laid. During that ensuing period, perhaps the strategy itself will be altered. Thus behavioral changes can be made too soon. For instance, eventually one of the leading life insurance companies plans to withdraw entirely from writing industrial debit insurance, but to start retraining debit salespersons now would clearly be premature.

On the other hand, new habits take time to establish. Even when people want to adopt a new mode, learning requires practice. Underground coal miners can't become dragline operators overnight.

The need for simultaneous conversion throughout a company varies. For instance, an advertising agency adopted a strategy to go worldwide in serving its clients. An affiliate in Latin America, in fact, continued to focus on purely local business—with only vague statements about the multinational hookup. Actually, this delay in joining the new thrust did no serious damage, because the revised pattern of work was far more critical in Europe and Japan. In contrast, when Honda decided to manufacture cars in Ohio, foot-dragging could not be tolerated in either Japan or the United States.

Programs for strategy execution, of the sort recommended in the preceding chapter, help managers decide *when* to push specific behavioral changes. Also, learning time factors discussed below bear on the optimum *rate* of change. In our observations, however, the overriding diagnostic issue is simply for managers to thoughtfully weigh what adjustments are required and when to initiate them. Perceptive attention is crucial.

CAREFULLY RESHAPE SELECTED BEHAVIORS

Altering a well-established practice calls for both formal and informal action. At least four kinds of measures are practical in a business setting.

REVISE STATED POLICIES AND PROCEDURES

When a misfit has been spotted, the natural reaction is for the appropriate manager to state explicitly a revised policy or procedure. This new statement of desired behavior—reflecting the new strategy—becomes part of the official doctrine of the organization.

Official statements do matter. As Chester Barnard observed years ago, most employees have a wide zone of acceptance. Within this zone they do what the organization asks. The least a manager should do is make clear what desired behavior is.

The likelihood that not all employees will follow newly announced policies all the time is no reason for leaving the issue confused. Just because limitations exist on the impact of official statements does not mean that their use should be abandoned. Instead, the lesson is that managers have to be sophisticated in the way they use policies and standard procedures.

A policy may (a) be specific or general in its instruction, (b) deal with one or many aspects of a problem, (c) place limits within which action is to be taken, or (d) specify the steps in making a decision. Procedures deal with a sequence of steps often involving several persons, and usually they leave less discretion to those doing the work. Now, when a new strategy requires a change in such existing standing plans, a manager tends to stress what is different. Skill is needed to be clear about the desired change but at the same time keep the total instruction in balance.

ENCOURAGE INFORMAL ADJUSTMENTS

Anyone who has tried to ski—or drive a bulldozer—solely on the basis of written instructions knows that even the best manual deals with only selected aspects of the total activity. A period of personal interpreting, experimenting, practicing, and improvising always is necessary.

Group behavior is more complex than individual skills. Even with some policies and procedures spelled out, change in cooperative activities requires a long adjustment period. When an international watch company, for instance, shifted from jobber distribution to direct sales to retailers, plans for contacting retailers, handling orders, extending credit, and the like were carefully prepared. Nevertheless, at least a year was required before the new system ran smoothly. People were not sure what the new plans meant until several cycles had been completed. New personal relationships had to be formed. Plans were elaborated informally. Confidence in what other people would do gradually emerged. Some disagreements had to be mediated. The official policies and procedures did, indeed, fix part of the system, but many of the norms for collaboration developed informally.

New strategy typically calls for revised policies and procedures, and revised policies and procedures always call for mutual adjustments in behavior patterns. A strategy change will not be fully effective until this adjustment has had time to work itself out.

Relations with outsiders are part of the adjustment. Although policies and procedures apply directly to internal actions, often the total behavior pattern includes customers or vendors or other resource suppliers. As in the watch-company example just cited, execution of the new strategy requires a new set of external relationships. These, too, must be molded into a customary, continuing relationship. In practice, the independent status of outsiders significantly complicates this process of shaping a revised system. Yet usually a strategy rests on assumptions that revised internal-external cooperative systems will be established.

Provide Time To Learn the New System

The process of changing a behavioral system—to fit a new strategy—is more than an intellectual exercise. Both adjustment in the social structure and modification of personal values are required.

To work together effectively, people need to know what to expect of others, what their role is, where they can get help, who has power, and what sources of information are available. A major strategy change upsets many of these established relationships. Workers need to relearn what is "good" and "bad" in the new system.

Individual values and behavior must also change to fit the new system. When the prestigious New York bank mentioned earlier in this chapter entered retail banking, a host of modifications were made in procedures, branch-office organization, lending authority, and the like. The basic problem, however, was to modify the attitudes of employees toward the blue-collar depositor. Genuine interest in such people had to replace crisp politeness.

Conversion to a new behavioral system takes time. Social structure and personal beliefs cannot be altered overnight. Managers can assist in the transition, however, by dealing with three psychological factors: learning, anxiety, and confidence (see Figure 8–1).

Learning new relationships and attitudes—like other learning—is aided by clear explanations, opportunity to try the new way, further questions and explanations, more trials and adjustment, and then practice. If a manager helps everyone involved recognize that this kind of process may be tedious at first but will avoid confusion later, the total transformation will be expedited. But mature and successful people will not always willingly accept the need for learning.

Any change that alters a person's primary source of satisfaction for security, social, and self-expression needs is sure to create anxiety. Just the uncertainty about how the new system will affect each personally is unsettling. Such anxiety often causes odd behavior—irritability, resistance, lack of enthusiasm. Managers should do all they can to relieve

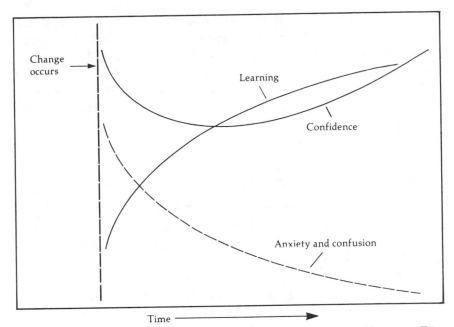

FIGURE 8-1. Psychological Factors Involved in a Change of Systems. Diagram Indicates How Response to Change Shifts over Time. From W. H. Newman, et al., *The Process of Management,* 5th ed. (Englewood Cliffs, N. J.: Prentice-Hall, 1982), p. 576. Reprinted by permission of Prentice-Hall, Inc.

anxiety during a transition period. Stating facts, explaining future plans, stressing future benefits, having people meet new associates, scotching rumors, showing awareness of a person's personal problems—all help allay anxiety. With rare exceptions, bad news faced promptly is better than extended worry. If answers to specific questions cannot be given, assurance of when and how the information will become available is helpful.

Both learning and relief of anxiety help to rebuild confidence. In addition, managers can bolster confidence by reinforcing desired behavior. Public recognition and reward to persons who successfully utilize the new design will transfer attention from old ways to the new pattern; continuing acknowledgement of success will restore a sense of competence that had been placed in doubt when familiar behavior had to be altered.

These personal and social adjustments take time. Experience indicates that major reorganizations require at least a year to digest, even with strenuous efforts to speed the conversion. Because of this required investment in time and energy, we naturally hope that a new system can be used for several years. Like research for a new medicine or tooling up for a new airplane model, we want a period of stability when we can recoup our investment. Similarly, most people need a spell of stable productivity following a siege of readjustment. Although we anticipate recurring need for change in the behavioral system, the wise manager knows that there are personal and economic tolerance limits to the frequency of change.

Reinforce Desired Behavior with Rewards

"Money talks" is an oversimplification. Nevertheless, the idea of rewarding desired behavior is very sound. The reward may take the form of personal praise, public recognition, promotion or other improvement in status, or indeed a pay increase.

Such rewards provide direct incentive for the extra effort that adopting new behavior entails; fully as important is the message. They all communicate to the person rewarded and to many other members of the organization what management desires and the importance management attaches to new modes of behavior.

Although the use of rewards to alter behavior is considered commonplace, in practice managers frequently fail to make full use of them. Too often managers talk about actions that will support a new strategy, but then they continue to treat good old Bill the same regardless of how well he responds. Such a practice actually has a negative effect on the carrying out of a new strategy.

CREATING A FOCUSED CLIMATE: SENIOR EXECUTIVE ROLE

Two ways to translate strategy into plans for day-to-day action have been recommended. The preceding chapter discussed *short-run programs* focused on immediate steps necessary to move from the present to a new, desired position. In this chapter we have stressed *revised policies and procedures* that help structure new patterns of behavior. Both are necessary.

But formulating and stating such plans is not enough. Also needed is psychological acceptance—and preferably commitment. Many factors help build this commitment to a new strategy, including what has been aptly called a *focused climate*. The focused climate adds motivation behind the short-term programs and revised policies.

Every established organization has its own climate—or culture. There are traditional values about customer services, spending money, accepting risks, taking the initiative, and many other matters. This climate obviously affects the ease or difficulty of carrying out a specific strategy. The prevailing values may make that strategy popular (or unpopular), and they shape local interpretations.

Careful Use of Executive Influence

Executives, especially senior executives, help form the climate within their bailiwicks. They cannot escape being public figures. Their behavior is closely watched for cues. The vice-president who jokingly said, "Guess I'll walk through the office in my shirt-sleeves just to start a rumor," was well aware that many people would try to infer meaning from even his casual actions.

Because they are inevitably in the local spotlight, senior managers should behave in a way that creates a climate favorable to the execution of company strategy. It is actions and decisions, more than words, that convey the message. The president who is lavish with a personal expense account will have difficulty securing strong support for a cost reduction program. Likewise, the promotion of a product manager who uncovered a new market for a product will send signals throughout the organization. Specific decisions are magnified because they help generate widespread feelings and attitudes.

The importance of climate is highlighted in a recent study by McKinsey & Company. These management consultants carefully compared the senior management practices in a set of companies with excellent performance records against a comparable set of companies whose performance has been "not outstanding." Differences in climate are closely associated with differences in results. Among their findings are the following.

Stress Selected, Simple Goals

The excellent companies all had a few well-recognized goals or themes. "Our company is built around customer service. . . ." "Growth is essential. We expect to be the largest company in our industry within five years. . . ." "Pioneers in banking. . . ." Such terse statements as these illustrate an overriding goal. Usually the less successful companies did not have clear-cut, integrating concepts of mission.

To an outsider these goals seem almost naive. However, they have taken on real meaning within the companies that use them, and somewhat like a religious creed, they call forth emotional commitment.

Obviously, these overriding goal statements should be linked to company strategy. Strategy—as used in this book—has more facets, but often a tersely stated mission does capture the essence of the strategy.

As suggested in Chapter 7, a second type of goal typically found in the successful companies are more immediate short-run objectives. These are the thrusts in our definition of strategy. For example, "a mini-size car ready to market in 1985," or "current, error-free, computerized subscription lists by the end of the year." At any one time a successful company singles out only a few such themes for prime attention. Usually they are simple to understand, achievable, and have a strong action focus.

Of course, the thrusts or themes change as old ones are achieved and new ones are added. The more successful climate is one that avoids a complex array of themes with varying priorities. Instead, the normal pattern is focus on a few carefully selected thrusts. The evidence suggests that the excellent companies somehow sift through a great diversity of influences and alternatives and select for emphasis in operations a simplified set of goals. On major issues, at least, a clear-cut value system replaces uncertainty and ambiguity.

BUILD ACCEPTANCE THROUGH SYMBOLIC BEHAVIOR

These goals and thrusts become powerful values in the company climate only when they are strongly supported by the senior managers. The McKinsey study shows that the chief executive alone can set the tone. The way that person allocates time and attention tells what he or she considers important. But because the chief executive cannot be in many places at once and personally participate in many decisions, the more effective CEO takes actions that become symbols of the values he or she is advocating. Here are four kinds of useful symbols.

Hands-on participation by the key executive. Calling on customers to get their reaction to products and service, attending the closing of an important sale, personal review of affirmative action moves, participation in new-product meetings, conducting discussions or having dinner with executive trainees are examples. Perhaps the CEO gets involved only on a sampling basis, to avoid being a bottleneck, but there is no doubt about the genuine concern being shown.

Positive reinforcement of actions that are consistent with the overriding goal or selected thrusts. This includes field visits to locations where positive action has occurred, with praise to participating workers; special awards for outstanding performance; on-the-spot granting of additional assistance to people already moving in approved directions. Some executives give such reinforcement again and again over a sustained period to drive home the central message.

Pointing out *role models* of desired behavior. An example of successful performance makes a goal seem real and doable. Just as the four-minute mile is no longer a fantasy, so can a pilot's on-time record or branch manager's inventory turnover be singled out for others to follow.

Support of *myths*. Every company has its stories of exceptional actions: the president who personally delivered a bicycle on Christmas Eve so as not to disappoint a customer, the power-line repairman who kept electricity flowing to a hospital during an ice storm, the liquor-company executive who dumped an entire batch of whiskey down the drain because the taste was not up to quality standards, the manager who was fired the day it was discovered that he lied to a Congressional committee, and so on. Over time the details of the stories may get distorted, but they are part of the company lore. Such stories that support the overriding goal can be repeated to help establish the mystique of the company.

Through such well-worn methods as these, the senior managers of excellent-performance companies make clear the selected company values. By creating such a climate, people throughout the organization are more likely to execute their various assignments correctly and enthusiastically.

This repeated emphasis on a few selected themes builds focused behavior. By clarifying priorities, it improves performance. However, the analysis and testing that precede the execution stage may be complex, prolonged, and sophisticated. Part of the skill in creating an effective, uncluttered climate is being most careful in selecting those goals and thrusts that are paramount.

SHIFT FOCUS AS STRATEGY EVOLVES

The focused climate just described may become outdated by new opportunities, or as a strategy unfolds a new product, energy-saving technology, or a new organization may be necessary. Senior managers especially must be active in bringing about these additional, second-generation changes.

Evolving strategies sooner or later call for shifts in company climate. The focused emphasis appropriate several years ago no longer is top priority. A new theme should be created. This means that the support built for the previous thrust now must be redirected, and this is a delicate transition. Normally such a change is appropriate only after several years, and most employees are well aware that the external world creates new demands over that length of time.

T. J. Peters, who has done pioneering work on focused climates, suggests a cycle pictured in Figure 8-2.

During the early stage, the new strategy and the accompanying policy and programs are still being worked out. Some people will be involved in this new planning, and through this participation they will understand and probably endorse the change in direction. Other people will necessarily be "minding the store," because previous activities must be continued to maintain company momentum while modified activities are being planned and tested. (The 1983 model automobiles must be made and sold while the 1984 and 1985 models are being developed.) Then comes a phasing-out of the old and building support for the new. It is during this transition and throughout middle stage that

FIGURE 8-2.   *Five-to Nine-Year Cycle of Strategic Transition.* Reprinted by permission of the publisher, from T. J. Peters, "Symbols, Patterns, and Settings: An Optimistic Case for Getting Things Done," *Organizational Dynamics,* Autumn 1978, © 1978 by AMACOM, a division of American Management Associations, p. 21. All rights reserved.

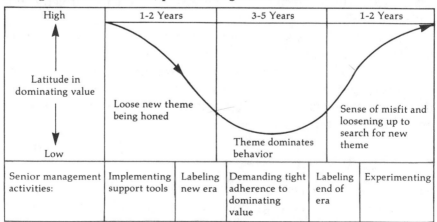

High	1-2 Years		3-5 Years	1-2 Years	
↑ Latitude in dominating value ↓ Low	Loose new theme being honed		Theme dominates behavior	Sense of misfit and loosening up to search for new theme	
Senior management activities:	Implementing support tools	Labeling new era	Demanding tight adherence to dominating value	Labeling end of era	Experimenting

senior managers build acceptance through symbolic behavior—as described above. Finally, pressure builds for another task, and senior managers must start preparing people psychologically for fresh leaps forward.

CONCLUSION

Execution of strategy always involves numerous modifications in the customary work habits and values of many different people—both employees and people working for customers and suppliers. Resistance is natural, because these changes upset the existing social structure and threaten personal feelings of security. However, no new strategy can be carried out until these behavior patterns are revised.

To implement a strategy, then, managers should systematically diagnose which prevailing policies and customs need to be altered. Also, they should weigh when such modifications should be initiated. This mapping of the task is important, because literally thousands of adjustments of standards and habits will be necessary.

Two broad approaches to achieving the required behavioral changes are useful. One approach involves painstaking attention to each of the required adjustments flagged in the diagnosis. Stated policies and procedures often must be revised and corresponding informal practices brought into line. Time should be allowed for employees to grasp and practice their new behavior, and the reward structure should be tailored to encourage the transition. Many strategic planners fail to recognize how widespread and tedious this adjustment process is, and consequently they underestimate the difficulty of successfully carrying through a strategy change.

The second approach is more concerned with general motivation and values. Senior executives should help create a focused climate that strongly supports the major thrusts of the strategy. They provide this leadership by carefully targeting their personal influence, stressing selected simple goals, and using symbols to popularize basic themes. Of course, the focused climate must be associated with the more specific adjustments noted in the preceding paragraph.

The linkage between such strategic concepts as domain or earnings per share may seem obscure, but it must be forged if a strategy is to succeed.

Organizing to Execute Strategy

C HANGING THE ORGANIZATION, along with firing the apparent culprit, is a popular response by managers under stress. Perhaps frustrated, the manager feels that he or she is at least "taking action." Such a shift in organization may, indeed, be called for, but it is a remedy that should be used with prudence and foresight.

Surprisingly, organization design tends to lag behind strategy formulation. It is employed only sporadically as a tool for promoting strategic change, and too often existing organization actually holds back the execution of new strategy.

This chapter explores ways organization can aid in carrying out strategy. The following issues are discussed:

1. Creating operating divisions that match strategy.
2. When to combine or split off business-units.
3. Organizing corporate headquarters to support strategy.
4. Timing changes in organization.

This sequence permits us to look first at a simple, clean structure and then consider added complexities and refinements. Because organizing diversified corporations is more difficult than realigning single-

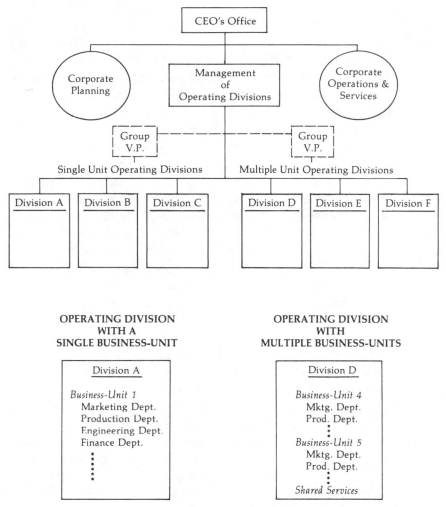

FIGURE 9-1   Schematic Organization of a Multiproduct Corporation

line companies, our discussion focuses on larger corporations. Figure 9-1 gives a schematic picture of the organization we will be discussing.

CREATING OPERATING DIVISIONS THAT MATCH STRATEGY

The simplest organization form that aids the execution of strategy is a series of operating divisions—one for each strategic business-unit. Each of these *business divisions* is semiautonomous—making almost all its own operating decisions—and also largely self-contained—

having direct supervision over most of the activities necessary to carry out its mission. Thus, a business division is like a single-line company, except that it operates with the guidance, constraints, and assistance of its corporate owner. (Of course, in a company with only one strategic business-unit, the distinction between a division and the corporation disappears. They function as an integrated whole.)

Before exploring the practical difficulties in setting up business divisions in this simplified form, let us note why such an operating group is so attractive from a strategic management viewpoint. A semiautonomous, self-contained business division has the following advantages.

1. The management of each division can be suited to *its* strategy. Even a small portfolio of business-units will include variation in targeted growth rates, acceptable risk, customer sophistication, sensitivity to costs and inflation, technology, and other critical factors. By creating each division with a relatively narrow focus, its total management design can be *tailored* to that particular purpose. Also, the possibility of staffing each division with executives committed to its mission is improved.

2. The narrower focus prompts *adequate attention* to external and internal threats and opportunities. In contrast, executives with multiproduct responsibilities are likely to overlook new developments in some industries and brush some problems under the rug.

3. *Prompt, integrated response* to threats and opportunities is more probable. Fewer managers have to exchange information and judgments, and they can communicate with one another swiftly and clearly. Bureaucratic attitudes are less likely to interfere with voluntary cooperation. The strategic programs and focused climate, discussed in the two previous chapters, are easier to achieve.

4. The *morale* of key people can be more easily tied to division accomplishments. Executives are able to see the results of their own efforts, to take actions they believe are best, and to feel that they are playing an important role. The resulting enthusiasm and devotion to the success of their particular division tend to spread to employees at all levels in the division.

5. *Control* is more direct. The people accountable for achieving strategy targets are few and clearly defined. Although measurement of intangibles remains elusive, short-run profit results for the division are available. Buck-passing, so common in large, multiproduct, functional departments, is minimized.

These benefits of decentralized business divisions should be kept in mind, because in most corporations a divisionalized structure is subject to frequent attack. A decentralized, divisional structure breaks up large, powerful, functional departments for marketing, production, engineering, and the like—and puts the pieces into the business divisions. Functional specialists and corporate staffs are often unhappy with such a dispersion—at least in situations in which functional departments have in the past reported directly to the top of the pyramid. Also, we shall soon note reasons for modifying structures with a single business-unit per division. When weighing various modifications versus an unsullied single unit per division setup, we must not underestimate the potent advantages listed above.

WHEN TO COMBINE OR SPLIT OFF BUSINESS-UNITS

For strategic planning it is convenient to establish a separate business-unit when three conditions are met: (a) a distinct cluster of products or services are sold (b) to an identifiable group of customers (c) in competition with a well-defined set of competitors. These guidelines seek units that can and should have distinct *marketing* strategies.

For purposes of formulating total business strategy, however, and even more for organizing operating divisions, the marketing considerations alone are inadequate. Here are several common difficulties and ways of dealing with them.

INCLUDE ALL MAJOR FUNCTIONS IN BUSINESS-UNIT CONCEPT

Business-unit strategy is built on a synthesis of resource procurement, engineering, production, and marketing considerations. Differential advantage may arise from any one or more functional areas, and strategic thrusts typically require synchronization of moves on several fronts. To be effective, the strategy manager should be able to harness these diverse elements into a unified program.

With respect to organization, the simplest way to make this united strategic effort doable is to place all the main operating activities involved under the supervision of the manager who is also responsible for devising and executing the strategy. Thus the business-unit manager would have his or her own engineering, production, marketing, and so on. This is the self-sufficient concept that we noted in the preceding section. In General Foods Corporation, for example, the

Maxwell House Coffee Division has its own bean-purchasing operation, its own roasting plants, its own sales force, and so on; although
not completely self-sufficient, the division does direct the major operations.

Trouble arises when—as often happens—it is impractical to divide
up functional operations and assign the parts to the various business-
units. For instance, it would be very costly for an automobile tire corporation to have separate plants for "original equipment" sold to auto
manufacturers and for replacement tires sold to a dealer network.
Similarly, book publishers may have separate marketing organizations for trade books and textbooks, but few firms can afford to further
subdivide the textbook field force into separate crews for, say, accounting texts or economics texts.

A possible resolution of this *indivisible-operation* problem is to
place two or more related business-units in a single operating division.
The indivisible operation (plant, sales force, computer, or the like) is
run by the division as a *shared service* for its business-units. Except for
the shared service(s), each business-unit supervises its own operations.
The key to this arrangement is the responsiveness of the shared service
to the needs of the business-units. If the shared service decides on the
nature and quality of its output and makes allocations to the business-
units, then the ability of the business-units to pursue their own strategies is undermined. In contrast, if each business-unit decides what services will be provided, then each unit retains control over its own
destiny.

Note that a shared service cannot be held to minimum cost or maximum efficiency if its activities respond to the convenience of several
business-units. Fortunately, in many situations the factors of strategic
importance to the business-units do not dominate the cost structure of
the shared service. For example, the size and message on General
Foods' boxes can be changed without seriously affecting the costs at the
box plant. If they do, a charge-back of costs should be arranged. But
the business-unit continues to decide on subjects vital to its strategic action.

In the divisional organization just described, each division is
substantially self-contained. Functional operations are divided and
assigned at least to divisions if not all the way to business-units.
Because only two or three business-units place calls on the shared services, the division management can anticipate their requirements, ar-
bitrate scheduling conflicts, and allocate costs fairly. The organizational distance between the service and the business-units served is still

relatively short. The aim, of course, is to find an economical way to give each business-unit direct power over operations necessary to carry out its strategy.

COMBINE VERY SMALL BUSINESS-UNITS INTO A RELATED OPERATING DIVISION

A different, relatively minor, reason for placing two or more business-units in an operating division relates to size. A business-unit may be so small that it cannot afford a full roster of functional executives. For example, a breakfast-food company sells its scraps and seconds as cattle feed. This by-product activity is profitable, but it does not need many high-powered managers. Because cattle feed is so different than the rest of the company, it is treated as a separate business-unit; nevertheless, it needs an organizational home.

Occasionally, a new product falling out of R&D work or utilizing some unusual capability of the company requires business-unit attention if it is to survive. Yet in the product's early life it cannot support full-time functional specialists.

Practical treatment of such small business-units is to place them in divisions where they can find sympathetic help. The division serves as a nursery for hatching new businesses and raising them to viable size. The business-unit manager makes the decisions, but he or she relies on advice and assistance provided by people whose main activity lies in another business-unit. Although such dependence on "rich relatives" is not ideal, it does establish a focal point for strategic direction of a distinctive piece of the company.

USE PRODUCT MANAGERS, NOT BUSINESS-UNITS, WHEN A CLEAN BREAK IS NOT FEASIBLE

The creation of a whole series of operating divisions, each largely self-contained and semiautonomous, has been urged in the preceding discussion. The goal in such organizing is to secure concentrated attention on a whole but narrow segment of the business. A word of caution is now in order.

Some operations just do not divide up neatly. There are no clean breaks. In IBM, for instance, typewriters can be separated from computers without much trouble, but dividing up the huge data-processing activities is very difficult. The selling of various kinds of equipment overlaps; the designing of products is interrelated; customer service cuts across both product and customer classification. Possible dividing lines in one function, such as industry markets in marketing, make little sense in other functions. Consequently, the sensible business-unit for most of IBM's data-processing equipment in the United States is a complex multi-billion-dollar operation. That size is too large for simple, concentrated organization—yet a forced splitting up would only complicate matters.

Pharmaceutical companies face a similar situation. Here the instability of product-line sales, because of new discoveries and unpredictable government regulation, would give product divisions a short and uncertain life. Also, production facilities are scrambled, and a single sales force promotes almost all the pharmaceutical products. Although some activities such as veterinary sales can be placed in separate business-units, the central core is hard to untangle.

Strategy execution is not aided by trying to split off divisions in which no consistent and enduring separation can be found. Instead of tearing symbiotic relationships apart, other ways must be found to encourage strategic action.

One widely useful device is a *product manager*. Like the manager of a business-unit, a product manager focuses on the success of a particular product line. However, this manager works predominantly in a staff capacity—relying on managers of production, marketing, and other operations to take actions necessary to make the product line a success. The product manager watches for opportunities and threats to his or her product, proposes strategic moves and programs, monitors current operations, urges action when necessary. He or she relies on voluntary cooperation, with an occasional appeal to senior executives when the stakes are high.

The specific role and authority assigned to product managers varies from one organization to another. Occasionally, they make binding decisions on a few subjects such as inventory levels or prices. Such variations are not the subject of our immediate discussion. Rather, the point is that product managers can be injected as partial substitutes for separate business-units when circumstances prevent creating such units. Many of the benefits of business-units listed at the opening of this chapter will be lost, but attention to strategy at the vital product-line level is provided. (If the critical focus centers on serving particular types of customers or on resource supply, rather than on product lines, staff positions concerned with these issues can be established.)

Summarizing: Strategy execution will be significantly aided by establishing separate, self-contained operating divisions for each business-unit. The manager of such a division has the flexibility of action and the motivation to make that particular business succeed.

Opportunities for economies, however, may call for placing two or perhaps three related business-units in one division. Very small businesses may be unable to support experts in all functions, and even medium-sized business-units may find a particular shared service a distinct advantage. Nevertheless, the manager of each business can pursue the distinct strategy for that unit, because the shared service is organizationally close and subservient.

More troublesome are extremely large business-units, in which a possible basis for dividing one function is impractical in other functions. Technology prevents ideal organization. To obtain at least some strategic attention to parts of the large whole, product managers can be added. Although they lack clout, they can beat the drum for strategic action at the operating level.

ORGANIZING CORPORATE HEADQUARTERS TO SUPPORT STRATEGY

Business-units and operating divisions are the locations where most strategic action takes place. Because they are on the firing line, that is where sound organization is crucial. Nevertheless, supporting organization at the corporate level is also necessary. Thus we now turn to arrangements above the operating divisions that buttress these primary action centers.

The organization at corporate headquarters can either aid or hinder the execution of corporate strategy. The critical issues are not particular job titles nor the existence of sections with special names—such as strategic planning. Rather, it is important that provision be made for several vital activities—and also that work which should be performed in the operating divisions not be usurped by headquarters staff.

The vital corporate activities often include:

1. Serving as *outside directors* for existing divisions.
2. Planning the future corporate portfolio and supporting moves.
3. Making acquisitions and divestments of businesses.
4. Developing new ventures internally.
5. Reinforcing corporate input strategies.

In a small, diversified corporation two or three senior executives may personally perform such of these activities as their strategy requires. Very large corporations, on the other hand, may have separate officials or even *offices* for each. A closer look at what is involved will help in deciding how much superstructure is appropriate for a specific corporation.

BOARD OF DIRECTORS FUNCTION FOR EXISTING DIVISIONS

The first concern of a diversified corporation is helping its existing divisions run well. The quandary is how to help. Being highly decentralized (as just recommended), the divisions tend to be independent and self-sufficient. Yet the corporation has a vital interest in their achievements.

A useful approach is to think of the corporation serving as an *outside director* of each division. Such directors have broad responsibility but do not mix into daily affairs. Their role includes the following duties:

1. Ensuring that a sound strategy has been formulated, and that the strategy is consistent with corporate guides for that division as to domain, risk levels, target results, and the like.
2. Selecting capable executives qualified to execute the approved strategy.
3. Insisting that tough actions be taken when necessary, even though such actions may be personally unpleasant for the division executives.
4. Rewarding key people for outstanding performance, and if necessary removing key people for poor performance.
5. Making sure the internal control system will provide early warning of major detectable problems.
6. Giving final approval to very large transactions that will significantly affect the future of the division (for example, ten percent of assets).
7. Serving as a sounding board; asking discerning questions; providing objective advice.

All these functions need to be performed in relation to each business-unit—whether it is legally a separate corporation or a division within a company. If well performed, they provide outside pressure on managers of the business-unit to develop its full potential.

A diversified corporation is in a unique position to provide individuals to perform this outside director role. At least one senior official, who is not an operating executive within the unit, should be designated for each business-unit. The difficulty faced by separate enterprises of obtaining good outside directors is thereby avoided. The person appointed can be given the time and resources necessary to be well informed; he or she is concerned about the unit as a total undertaking; contacts with other units and with external developments give the person broad perspective; at the same time, the "director" is not protecting a particular department within the business-unit, nor is the person beholden to its general manager for his or her job.

In fact, one of the relative advantages of a diversified company compared with a series of smaller firms lies in its ability to find, give staff support, motivate and adequately compensate *outside directors.*

The number of business-units in a corporation may increase to the point where the corporate CEO cannot personally perform this outside director role for all of them. If this occurs, the usual remedy is to appoint an executive vice-president, or if necessary, several group vice-presidents. These executives are extensions of the CEO's capacity to supervise; each works with about five or six business-units. Good organization practice is for all of them to rely on a single set of corporate staff and service units, *not* to build their own empires. In this way the guidance given to each business-unit will reflect the objectives and the portfolio and input strategy of the corporation as a whole.

PLANNING FUTURE CORPORATE PORTFOLIO AND SUPPORTING MOVES

A second essential activity at the corporate level is planning future actions of the corporation. As discussed in Chapters 3 and 4, corporate strategy involves (a) the choice of businesses to operate, (b) the corporate input strategy, and (c) the moves necessary to attain that preferred position.

The existing business-units make significant contributions to this overall planning through their own searching for new opportunities. Nevertheless, broader integrated planning has to be done at corporate headquarters. Decisions are needed with respect to:

Expansion or contraction of existing businesses.
New businesses to enter.
Charters for existing and new business-units, including the objectives, values, and planning assumptions communicated early enough to aid lower-level planning.

Resource allocations—long- and short-term capital, perhaps key
personnel or critical materials, permissible high technological or
political risks.
Results targets for both long-run and intermediate stages.

Because this planning involves at least the consideration of "milk-
ing," curtailing, or even liquidating some business-units, it is unrealistic to expect business-unit managers to supply data on all alternatives.
Also, these managers are rarely in a position to appraise expansion
possibilities in unrelated areas. Consequently, some of the detailed fact
gathering and analysis must be performed centrally. The challenge is to
be realistic and practical while, at the same time, being farsighted and
creative.

Making Acquisitions and Divestments of Businesses

If a corporation decides to change its portfolio of business-units, acquisitions or divestments are likely. Someone has to identify good prospects for acquisition—or buyers for businesses to be sold—and someone has to engage in that often time-consuming and specialized process
of negotiating a "deal."

Organizing for these tasks is difficult, because in most corporations
the purchase or sale of a business-unit occurs at irregular intervals—
often with an inactive spell of several years—even though the existing
portfolio is reviewed each year. Because of this irregularity and the
need for specialized skills, outside assistance from investment bankers
and corporate lawyers is commonly used. Nonetheless, at the time of
acquisition substantial blocks of managerial time are required. If compatibility of personalities, traditions, and operations are carefully
assessed in advance—as is usually desirable—key corporate executives
must take part.

Corporate strategy will determine the importance of acquisition or
divestment activity. Corporations rapidly diversifying, as was popular in the early 1970s, may need separate staff devoted exclusively to
this kind of work. In contrast, corporations planning to build on businesses already within its portfolio will probably make only temporary
arrangements for the occasional acquisition or divestment they en-
counter.

Developing New Ventures Internally

An alternative path to diversification is developing new businesses
within the corporation. Instead of acquiring an established business,

the corporation supports *internal entrepreneurs*. These entrepreneurs may take a new product idea from the research lab or get the concept for a new type of business from the outside. With resources supplied by the corporation, they explore, test, and develop the concept until it either flops or becomes a workable business-unit.

New business concepts closely related to existing business-units normally will be placed in the operating divisions that contain the established activity. The corporation merely supports the localized outreach. If the new concept has no natural home, or if the corporate executives believe that home will not provide the necessary attention and drive, then some special corporate organization becomes necessary.

No generally satisfactory organization for internal entrepreneurs has yet emerged. A few large corporations, including DuPont, have created a separate division for new ventures. The results have been mixed—partly because the personnel, traditions, attitudes, and procedures transferred from other parts of the corporation don't suit the fledgling ventures. The 3-M Corporation, which is recognized for its launching of successful new products, encourages internal entrepreneurs to set up shop almost anywhere in the organization they can find an executive sponsor. However, even in this case the success apparently results from a larger number of attempts rather than from an unusually favorable organizational form.

Texas Instruments has a unique system for developing new products that may become the base for a new business-unit. A new-product concept is set up under the Corporate Development Committee as a separate project—with a project manager, subprojects, resource allocations, time schedules, milestone reviews, and other sophisticated project management techniques. The most distinctive aspect in TI is the organization. Responsibility for various pieces of such a project is assigned to managers who concurrently have operating jobs. Almost everyone wears two hats—one for some chunk of the development of a new product and one for running a tightly budgeted part of this year's output. Such dual assignments are feasible because of TI's well-designed planning and control systems. Few other corporations have this degree of managerial sophistication coupled with a tradition to be thinking about future business and current achievements at the same time.

For most corporations, then, providing an organizational home for new ventures is a ticklish task. Ventures that are based on simple extensions of an existing skill can be placed in an operating division in which that skill is well developed. But really distinct ventures need freedom to move along unfamiliar paths. A small independent unit is usually necessary, and this unit should be highly selective in the resources and ideas it borrows from other divisions of the corporation. Moreover, there must be recognition that the appropriate organization will change as the venture grows and matures. The tempo of change will rarely synchronize with that of larger, better-established divisions.

Reinforcing Corporate Input Strategy

One other way a multidivision corporation may elect to gain a differential advantage is via better access to resources. By obtaining capital, energy, raw materials, or perhaps people in a manner not available to its divisions separately, the corporation gains some leverage. Possible corporate resource strategies have been discussed in Chapter 4. They include backward integration into raw materials, foreign manufacture of components, coordinated labor relations, corporate financing based on total assets and earnings, and the like.

Of course, each division is vitally concerned with obtaining its resources, and—consistent with our emphasis on decentralizing to operating divisions—we assume that ninety-nine and forty-four one hundredths percent of the contacts with resource suppliers will take place at the division level. However, if a corporation seeks major synergetic benefits from a strategic corporate approach to a particular resource, then some reinforcing organization above the division level may be desirable.

Vertically integrated oil corporations, for example, typically have a supply-and-distribution office. This office directs movements of crude oil from various sources to the corporation's refineries (sometimes swapping crude oil with other corporations to reduce transportation costs) and likewise directs movements of refined products to bulk distribution centers. The aim is to capture the maximum advantage from being vertically integrated.

Other corporate resource strategies may not require as frequent coordination of interdivision relations as in the preceding example, or, once a procedure is established, the divisions may be able to coordinate directly. However, some oversight is desirable if the synergy is an important strategy. Each corporate input strategy should have some kind of an office responsible for its execution and revision.

More than the initial planning is involved. The projection of the strategy into daily operations requires interpretation and monitoring. Changing opportunities, threats, and achievements call for adjustments. Perhaps only one or two persons can do the work. Nonetheless, explicit assignment of the task is a useful step in smooth execution of the strategy.

Two points of clarification are important. At this point we are not talking about operating services that are sometimes set up to perform a specialized task for the entire corporation. For example, centralized warehousing or computer facilities may be established. The purpose of such central services is to obtain economies. Rarely, however, are they of sufficient importance to be called a corporate strategy—which will affect the destiny of the corporation. Instead, we are saying that if a corporation does seek distinction through one or more input strategies, a small office aiding and monitoring each strategy will increase the odds of its success.

Any such strategy-coordination office should be kept small. There is always a tendency for headquarters offices to withdraw activities from operating divisions and to formalize details. To discourage this bureaucratic tendency, give each office only enough people to do its important tasks.

Summarizing: The headquarters organization of a diversified corporation should always provide (a) senior executives who can fill the outside director roles for each of the business-units, and (b) executives plus a staff assistant who formulate the *corporate strategic plan*. These provisions are necessary regardless of the specific strategy that the corporation adopts. If the strategy also stresses (c) further diversification, (d) internal entrepreneurship, or (e) corporate input synergies, then additional provisions will be needed. The scope of such additional offices will depend on the nature and size of corporate strategic thrusts. At this level for these activities just a few very able people—not a large number of unimaginative operators—can provide the essential spark.

Of course, the corporate headquarters will also perform other activities such as legal, treasurer, financial accounting, stockholder relations, and the like. These are important, normal corporate operations. Our preceding discussion, however, focuses on corporate-level functions that are indispensable to the best strategy execution.

ORGANIZATION IN TRANSITION

Wise managers seeks a synergistic fit between their selected strategy and their organization design. As we have done in this chapter, attention centers on the organization as it will be after any necessary modifications have been completed. While conceiving of this design, we set aside for the moment the transition problems of moving from where we now are to where we would like to be. In simplest terms, if we know where we *want* to be in a few years, then as organization issues arise we can resolve them in the direction of that future structure rather than by whims of the moment.

However, the conversion process presents both obstacles and opportunities. These are too varied to discuss systematically in this book, but three issues do arise often enough to call for at least brief comment.

Matrix Organization as a Temporary Compromise

Matrix organization is a seductive idea. It can be helpful, but should be used with caution.

Of course, within some kinds of business-units a matrix setup is the normal—and often optimum—organization design. For a construction firm, advertising agency, or engineering consultant—for example—there is repeated need for at least two strong viewpoints. Coordinating the efforts of specialists on the unique features of a new chemical plant, advertising campaign, or jet-engine design calls for a strong *project* manager. At the same time, department managers must be sure that each specialized *function* is performed with skill and efficiency. Thus we create a matrix in which persons on the job are directed by two bosses, a project manager and a functional department manager. Generalizing this kind of arrangement, when two (or more) viewpoints are important (such as customer, product line, geographic region, or function), we create an organization in which a representative of each gives directions. The burden of mediating conflicts is offset by the benefit of two-pronged guidance.

This matrix concept is appealing when a new strategy suggests a reorganization. Suppose, for example, that a new operating division concentrating on video disks is established and that logic calls for transferring pieces of the long-established manufacturing department to the new division. Why not create a matrix with both the video-disk division and the manufacturing department giving directions for the production of disks? Temporarily at least, the new division needs technical help from manufacturing, and disruption of established relationships within manufacturing would be minimized. Then when sufficient volume or specialization occurs, we can give the disk division its own manufacturing facility.

Drawbacks of a matrix in this example include the possible reluctant responsiveness of manufacturing to the frequently changing needs of the new division, and vague accountability for failure to achieve production deadlines and cost estimates. On the other hand, if the outlook for video disks is quite uncertain, perhaps some short-run compromise arrangement is preferable to making large investments immediately in a separate production capability.

A further consideration is that there might be long-run cost benefits from using the manufacturing department as a source of disks on a continuing basis. As long as this possibility is alive, a shift of production to the new division should be postponed.

The argument for withholding an activity from the operating divisions need not center on production—as occurred in the preceding example. Corporations often maintain a centralized field sales organization, like General Foods did in its early history. Centralized research is common, and centralized obtaining of capital is almost universal.

These examples of centralized operations do not justify a leap to matrix organization. More restrained compromise with the concept of self-contained divisions are preferable in most corporations: (a) Typically, most functions can be assigned to the operating divisions. Usually, only one or two functions are on the borderline, and we do not have to complicate the entire structure to accommodate these exceptions. (b) If the advantages of a large-scale department servicing all (or most) operating divisions are compelling, this corporate department can be treated like a *shared service*. The strategic initiative still lies within the divisions. (c) Even in those exceptional cases in which the actions of such corporate departments become part of the corporate input strategy, coordination with the divisions can be obtained through periodic negotiations of schedules, transfer prices, and the like. (The "outside director" at the corporate level can be helpful in coordinating such activities.)

Matrix organization at the corporate level may be justified as a transition device, but usually its use reflects fence-sitting—an attempt to have a new organization without dismantling the old one. It is a sure way to double the already staggering load of meetings senior executives must attend.

Using Organization as a Tool for Management Chance

Organization can and should aid the carrying out of strategy—as we have been discussing throughout this chapter. But not all organization changes are aimed at that purpose. Sometimes the changes are merely a convenient way to deal with other kinds of problems.

Not uncommon is a change in organization to resolve an unpleasant personnel problem. Bill Blow, for example, was a long-service executive; he had lots of friends but clearly had outlived his usefulness. Rather than fire or retire Bill, duties were reassigned so that, in fact, Bill was out of a job. In another case, a job was split in half because the incumbent was unable to do the total task satisfactorily. A different company created a new position of marketing director because the sales vice-president devoted most of his time to selling. This list could go on and on.

Another tactic is to create a new position as a means of emphasizing a policy or procedure. When the CEO establishes a new director for operations research, human resources, strategic planning, or cost control, the message is clear. However, if the response is languid, then the injection of local representatives in each operating division provide frequent local interpretations. After the desired practice becomes normal behavior, the extra organization can be dismantled. Similarly, a few executives use matrix organization for a year or two as a way of raising the status of one of the viewpoints, then move on to a simpler structure.

There may be occasions when such expedient use of organization is the only effective path. However, it is expensive—in two ways. Organization change soaks up a lot of energy of busy people, as we note in the next section. Also, each time organization reshuffling is employed for a purpose that could be accomplished by simpler, more direct means, the significance employees attach to formal organization is undermined. They wonder, "What devious scheme are the big shots up to now?"

Clearly, the support organization can give strategy will be stronger if these expedient moves are avoided.

TIMING ORGANIZATION CHANGES

A good fit between strategy and organization structure boosts the probability that the strategy will be vigorously carried out. Ideally, then, insofar as the organization needs adjustment to reinforce a new strategy, the organization should be changed as soon as a new strategy is officially endorsed. Prompt action provides the help from the new setup when it is most needed to overcome resistance to change. Also, revising the organization conveys a message that senior executives are ready to shift the strength of the enterprise to support the fresh direction.

Corresponding adjustments in the entire management system should also be made rapidly. Revised information flows, adjusted measurements and controls, realigned incentives, all should match the new organization. Each bolsters the other.

In practice, such prompt integrated action is difficult to achieve. An early obstacle is that new strategy rarely bursts forth complete and settled. Instead, the strategy unfolds. Key elements are implemented first, others later. The early thrusts provide information about, say, production feasibility or market acceptance that helps shape subsequent moves. The environment may be either more or less favorable than predicted. Thus there is a question of when in this formulation process the final strategy is sufficiently clear and stable to justify strong commitments to a new management design. Such a commitment both expedites the outcome and tends to freeze its dimensions.

Sometimes the equivalent of market tests or pilot plants can be tried in a corner of the organization, but the moment for decision arrives before many uncertainties can be removed. At this point timid managers postpone reorganization, even though doing so hinders exploitation of the new strategy. Bold managers move forward with the new structure, taking a significant risk that the changes may turn out to be ill-advised.

In addition to this question of when, for organizational purposes, to treat a new strategy as settled, timing is affected by the length and cost of transition. Reorganization requires many personal adjustments. Duties change. Sources of formal and informal information have to be relearned. Who has power and who should be consulted need to be tested. Values are modified. Knowing what behavior to expect from associates and bosses has to be experienced. Confidence in oneself and in the team has to be reconfirmed. All this takes time. Even for small changes six months may be required to regain effectiveness. In major reorganizations often two years are needed to develop a smooth-working social structure. Meanwhile, there are tensions and anxieties.

Because reorganizing takes time and drains emotional energy of many people, frequent reorganizations are undesirable. Each major shift is an investment we hope will yield a benefit over a period of years.

With respect to strategy, this cost of reorganization is a factor in deciding how often and when to launch new initiatives. If a company is still learning to operate under a recent realignment, yet another shift will cause confusion and upset morale. In contrast, a staid company may need the tonic of a new thrust and the reorganization that goes with it.

These brief observations about the timing of reorganizations, the use of organization for indirect purposes, and the tempting recourse to matrix organization illustrate social aspects of organizing. There is always danger that such issues will overshadow the structure we wish to achieve. If allowed to occur, such muddying can cause serious loss. The design of operating divisions and of corporate structure, discussed in the opening sections of this chapter, has a profound and long-lasting impact on strategy execution. The pushes and pulls involved in modifying organization should not undercut this design that will serve strategy best.

CONCLUSION

Three basic themes run through this chapter:

1. *Build the primary organization around business-units*—the same units that are singled out in formulating strategy. Try to make them self-contained, and decentralize authority to their managers. This arrangement puts power where competition is keenest, builds morale, assists control, aids prompt response to changing conditions, and facilitates coordinated action. The organization, then, reinforces the business-unit strategy.

Some compromise may be necessary because of optimum size of operations in a few functions. Thus very small business-units may be merged into a multiple-unit division, and shared services may complicate the self-contained ideal. The unfavorable impact of such exceptions on strategy execution should be reduced by insisting that it is the business-unit manager who stipulates what services will be received.

Note that the organization structure within the various operating divisions should not be uniform. Each division faces a different environment, has its own strategy and technology, and probably is in a different stage of development. Consequently, its needs will be distinct, and its organization should fit these needs. A uniform structure would inevitably cheat some divisions.

2. *Organize the headquarters of diversified corporations to help their business-units.* A prime aid is the appointment of well-qualified "outside directors." Providing good "outside directors" to guide and assist the various business-units is a unique advantage of diversified

corporations. In addition, typically corporations should furnish financial, legal, and other specialized services to their operating divisions. However, the high decentralization to operating divisions implies a small size for corporate staff. Most of the "horsepower" should be placed within the divisions close to where most decisions are made and action is taken.

3. Finally, after the two preceding requirements have been met, *provide for distinctly corporate activities.* Corporate activities important for strategic management are (a) portfolio planning, (b) making acquisitions and divestments, (c) developing new ventures internally, and (d) managing corporate resource departments. The size and importance of these activities will vary widely among corporations—depending on the corporate strategy being pursued.

A properly designed organization can be a powerful tool for expediting strategic action. Conversely, poor organization can be a serious obstacle. But time and effort are required to reshape an organization. Thus wise managers think through what future structure will best support their strategies and then move in that direction as rapidly as related strategic developments permit.

10

The Right Person and the Right Carrot

KEY EXECUTIVES ARE crucial; they make strategy come alive. All the measures for implementing strategy that are discussed in other chapters of Part II will be ineffective unless properly qualified and motivated persons are in the pivotal positions in the organization. Just as the personalities of Alfred P. Sloan and Thomas J. Watson were entwined with the strategies they advocated, every new strategy needs its champions.

Moreover, because modification and elaboration of strategy are significantly influenced by people in key positions, placing individuals with *known preferences* (biases, predilections, managerial habits, capabilities, and the like) in these positions is one way to shape the strategy that is likely to be executed.

Three issues are always involved. What kinds of people are best suited to carry out the selected strategy for our specific company? Do present executives fit these needs, or can they change enough to fit, or should fresh executives be brought in? How can company incentives be designed so that the reformed executive team will be motivated to promote the strategy? These issues are the focus of this chapter.

MATCHING DESIRED EXECUTIVE ABILITIES WITH STRATEGY

Each company strategy calls for a unique set of executive talents. For example, a strategy to fully integrate American Motors with Renault requires different abilities in the United States operation than would a Chrysler strategy merely to import foreign-made autos. Still another set of talents will be needed when a book-publishing firm decides to launch a pioneering programmed-teaching division. Much more than differences in product knowledge is involved.

General Manager Types

A first step in clarifying the executive abilities desired to carry out a new strategy is to think about the chief executive of the business-unit. (The actual title may be general manager, president, executive officer, or the like). Here, we assume that it is the chief executive who calls the shots and sets the tone. He or she decides the emphasis to be placed on new processes, market position, mechanization, cash flow, or other goals—the degree of risk to take—the amount of disruption with its as-sociated costs—the pressure to meet targets placed on subordinates—the attention given to social impacts—as well as the major thrusts to outsmart competitors. Thus, under this approach, priority goes to de-scribing a chief executive best suited to implement the strategy.

These specifications of the desired chief executive will, of course, be fitted to the particular strategy and the local situation. Nevertheless, sensitivity to the way diverse strategies affect the kind of managers needed is helpful. For this purpose, Table 10–1 is highly suggestive. The particular behavioral characteristics covered in this table have been selected to distinguish between what the Dutch authors call *archetypes*. They are not intended to be comprehensive. Instead, the aim is to highlight variations in personal qualities that seem to match differences in strategic direction.

In addition to the highly personal talents suggested by Table 10–1, a chief executive needs qualities more closely tied to the strategy selected for the business. These include: relevant technical knowledge, strength in crucial factors for success in the selected business niche, skills suited to the role the business-unit has in the corporate portfolio strategy, and strong commitment to any new elements in the business strategy.

TABLE 10-1. Strategic Management Archetypes

Strategic Direction Type of Manager	Explosive Growth Pioneer	Expansion Conqueror	Continuous Growth Level-Headed
Behavioral Characteristics:			
Conformity	Very flexible, very creative, divergent	Appropriately non-conformist, creatively structured toward anything new	Strongly structured, according to the timetable, security
Sociability	Very extrovert, much flair and glamour but driven by circumstances, mistrustful	Selectively extrovert, forms small groups of chosen individuals	Amicable, team-worker, maintains grip, well-regarded
Activity	Hyperactive, restless, anticipatory, uncontrolled	Energetic, reacts to weak signals, nervous with great self-control	Directed to objective, stable, according to agreement
Pressure to achieve	Stormy, daredevil, seeking challenges, motivate by anything unique	Increasing sphere of influence, calculated risks	Level-headed growth, satisfaction through control of the situation
Style of thinking	Intuitive-irrational, thinking disconnectedly, original, divergent	Capable of seeing beyond limits, generalist, rational	Solid, systematic, penetrating, specialist

| STRATEGIC DIRECTION | CONSOLIDATION | HARVEST | RETREAT-REPOSITION |
Type of Manager	Administrator	Economizer	Insistent diplomat
Conformity	Reproducible, routine, docile	Bureaucratic, dogmatic, rigid	Maximal flexibility within a fixed objective, accepted restrictions
Sociability	Introvert, training	Procedural	Considerate/human, decisive/inspiring confidence, allays emotion
Activity	Stable-static, via procedures, waits and sees, "yes, but"	Laissez-faire, doing what has to be done, little initiative	Steady, retentive but flexible
Pressure to achieve	Maintaining of status quo, defending of territory	Reactive behavior, stimuli from outside	More strategic-directed than tactical-directed, carefully measured input
Style of thinking	Solid and conformist vision, connection with earlier situations	Legalistic, everything according to precedent	Broad, relativistic, manysided

Source: J. G. Wissema, H. W. VanderPol, and H. M. Messer, "Strategic Management Archetypes," Strategic Management Journal, January 1980, p. 43, Tables 1–4. Reprinted by permission of John Wiley & Sons, Ltd.

Rarely will an actual chief executive fulfill all the ideal specifications for the job, but seeking to match capabilities with mission requirements boosts the chances of a reasonably good fit. Conversely, it is useful to identify what qualities would be fatal doors to disaster! This concept of focusing on the personality of the chief executive is widely recognized. Especially in published news stories, replacement of a top executive is often associated with reaching for a person qualified to carry out the new strategy. The main lesson behind most of these stories, however, is that at a much earlier date senior management failed to think through the match between sound strategy and a chief executive suited to that strategy.

Diverse Qualities Needed in the Team

A more complete and realistic approach for staffing to carry out a new strategy is to look at the capabilities needed in the total management team. This broader scope has two advantages. (a) As just noted, a chief executive rarely possesses all the qualities that are desired. Consequently, we select associates (vice-presidents and the like) who have strength where the chief executive is weak. Within the total team all the desired top-management talents should be present. (b) The chief executive must be supported by an array of functional specialists and by managers able to deal with different constituencies (the simplest example is Mr. Inside and Ms. Outside). Although they are not expected to be generalists, their diverse inputs are nonetheless important to the execution of a new strategy.

Job descriptions—both written and implied—are the primary guides to qualities needed in various members of the top team. However, these must be thoughtfully revised to reflect the new strategy and also to provide the complementary strengths discussed in the preceding paragraph. Strength lies in the total team. The aim is a portfolio of managerial capability in the same sense as a diversified corporation seeks a portfolio of businesses.

A provocative way to analyze capabilities of a management team has been devised by Ichak Adizes.* He argues that varying proportions of the following kinds of abilities will always be needed: P—technical ability to *produce* the service or product; A—*administrative* skill to plan, organize, and control group activity; E—*entrepreneurial* flair

---

* See *How to Solve the Mismanagement Crisis* (Homewood: Dow Jones–Irwin, 1979).

to adapt to turbulent conditions, create new services, and accept risks; and I—*integration* talent to reconcile, balance, and unify group activities and goals.

Two further features are critical parts of the Adizes model. (a) It is so unlikely that a single individual will be able to provide the deserved mixture of the four capabilities P, A, E, and I that the composite should be sought in the management team. (b) The optimum proportion or emphasis on P, A, E, and I varies from company to company and from time to time. The relative emphasis depends on company strategy, which in turn is strongly influenced by the stage of the company in its life cycle.

A fledgling firm, for instance, first requires the heavy weighting of E—entrepreneurship, but once launched must give primary attention to P—production. As the firm grows, A—administration also grows in importance. When the firm becomes a cash cow, the need for E—entrepreneurship is very low, whereas P—productivity, A—administration, and I—integration should all be strong. Figure 10–1 suggests how the need for P, A, E, and I might shift during a full life cycle for a company.

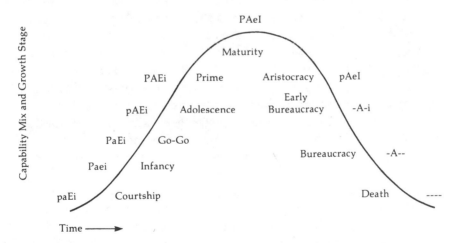

Note: Capital letters indicate strong emphasis.
      Small letters indicate secondary emphasis.

FIGURE 10–1.   Changes in Kind of Managerial Capabilities Needed at Various Stages in Company Life Cycle. Reprinted by permission of publisher, from Ichak Adizes, "Organizational Passages—Diagnosing and Treating Lifecycle Problems of Organizations," *Organizational Dynamics,* Summer 1979, © 1979 by AMACOM, a division of American Management Associations. All rights reserved.

Of course, in practice a company may choose to describe the managerial talent it needs in terms that differ from Adizes' P,A,E, and I. The important point is to base the specifications on the new strategy and to revise these specifications when the strategy is revised. This is not the place to compromise. Gaps between the kind of managers called for by an updated strategy and the present roster should be flagged.* Unless the human resources needed are clearly recognized, the likelihood that individuals suited to the task will be in key posts is extremely low.

Functional departments can be analyzed in the same way as just suggested for overall management. Strategy changes will upset the status quo of some departments more than others. Thus in each area a new set of desired managerial capabilities should be formulated. Evasion of adjustments to a new strategy at this level will block or slow down execution of revised strategies.

Effect of Magnitude of Change

Future talent needed is stressed in the preceding paragraphs. An additional dimension considers what the company is now doing and the magnitude and direction of the leap to a new target. Most change is incremental; it builds on what is already being done. Consequently, managers directing a switch can rely heavily on the existing social structure and can nudge or expand without major disruption.

In contrast, some strategic changes are more drastic—reversing direction or sharply altering the character and volume of work. For instance, when a decision was made to stop expanding the automobile tire business of Firestone, to close six plants permanently, and to slash United States production for private-label customers, a very tough manager was required. Likewise, when a small state bank in New Jersey was acquired by a statewide chain and revamped (personnel rose seventy-five percent) to be an important regional office, a dynamic manager was needed. Thus in drawing up executive specifications, the scope and speed of change are factors, in addition to the destination.

---

*As discussed later, unavailability of particular kinds of managers may force a revision of strategy. However, we cannot be sure that such a lack of human resources exists until both needs and availability have been fully explored. Meanwhile, we proceed on the presumption that managerial personnel is an adaptable variable.

USING PRESENT EXECUTIVES TO CARRY OUT A NEW STRATEGY

Key personnel who will execute a new strategy can be the existing staff of the organization unit charged with the new mission (although they may be in different positions), or newcomers can be brought in. Specifications of the kind of executives best suited for the revised mission, which we discussed in the preceding section, are essential in making this choice.

ADVANTAGES OF RELYING ON PRESENT TEAM

Using executives already in place is an alternative that should always be weighed. It has several distinct advantages.

- The old hands already know many key actors, the local conditions, customary practices—roles—values. Consequently, the initial learning time is short, and the chances of inadvertent mistakes are low.
- Their own qualities (both good and bad) are better known and more deeply understood by their associates. Outsiders can be known only superficially at first.
- Insiders often, though not always, have a loyal following among subordinates and peers. Their participation in a new program ensures a high degree of cooperation.
- By calling on people who have served well in the past, the company enhances its reputation for continuing and considerate employment.

If existing personnel also possess specific capabilities needed on the new team, then these carry-over advantages quickly resolve executive selection. However, such carry-over advantages alone are rarely sufficient.

INDIVIDUAL ADAPTABILITY

Last year's team, no matter how great, will have to change to meet next year's challenge. Every new strategy requires that at least some members change their behavior. Thus we must predict how well specific individuals will adapt to the revised needs.

Adaptability has several dimensions. The most obvious is acquiring new *knowledge*—for example, understanding a switch in technology, the needs of a different customer group, newly minted government regulation and regulators, fresh international competitors, or the like. Able executives can often learn to "play in a new ballgame," unless the technical discipline or the complexities of culture and language call for years of training. However, individuals differ in their openness to unfamiliar ideas and their speed of absorption.

More difficult than acquiring knowledge is changing one's *attitudes, values, and commitment.* A company's strategic shift, for instance, from being the quality leader—the Cadillac of the industry—to seeking volume on the basis of past reputation is no mere intellectual exercise. The people who have strived hard to build the quality image probably think of themselves as guardians of quality. They may have taken their present jobs as an opportunity to express this feeling about quality. Such values and commitment obviously decrease the adaptability of the persons holding them.

Managers may also be valuable because of their special *skills*—skill in labor negotiations, skill in financial analysis, skill in product styling, or skill in another function. Because those skills helped them advance, they cherish them and tend to see their future as related to their uses. Naturally, their feelings about a reorganization tied to a new strategy will be colored by the importance of their skills in the new setup. If their special talents drop in importance, then both they and the company face a question of whether to attempt to switch emphasis to some other activity where they have less-outstanding track records.

Because executing a new strategy involves redirection, a manager's *ability to promote change* is especially significant for our purposes. This calls for a willingness—perhaps eagerness—to upset old ways, to rearrange power and status, and to learn new patterns. The outcome may be uncertain, and there will be costs in terms of short-run efficiency and friendships. Up to a point, these costs rise with the speed of the change. Individuals vary widely in their capacity to tolerate and manage transitions.

Obviously the need for adaptability depends on the content, magnitude, and speed of the particular strategic change we seek. Thus the extension of established United States operations into Brazil will require only minor adjustments by most of the present executives. In contrast, converting a research organization into a production company will sharply alter the roles of a majority of the key people. But in every strategy shift there will be at least a few individuals whose adaptability is crucial. For these people we must carefully predict whether they can acquire necessary new knowledge, modify their attitudes—values—and commitments, focus on different skills, and pay the price of promoting a new alignment.

BUILDING NEW GROUP COMMITMENT

Two broad steps toward staffing to execute a new strategy have been outlined—carefully determining the capabilities needed and matching the talents and/or adaptability of present executives against the prescribed needs. Let us assume for the moment that we have a reasonably good match. The task is not yet done. We have the players, but we may not have a team.

There is danger that the group as a whole is not committed to the new strategy. The executives and staff people whose jobs are not reshuffled are likely to do "business as usual." When interacting with peers who do have revised missions, this status-quo group will be inclined to stick with old practices. For example, changes in cost accounting standards or personnel routines will probably be resisted in that company which is expanding into Brazil. Even an adaptable executive with a modified job will find life easier by carrying forward much of past practices. In this climate the new strategy is a painful necessity, with many managers being more sensitive to the pain than to the necessity.

Somehow, the old guard has to become enthused and committed to the new strategy. This feeling of rebirth may be generated by one or two individuals with missionary zeal. If they have influence or power and are active promoters, they may succeed in building a group commitment. When success of the strategy has become a group goal, the necessary voluntary coordination and allocation of effort will be forthcoming.

Another approach to attaining group commitment is group formulation of the strategy itself. Group involvement starts before any new strategy is devised and long before personnel assessment is considered. The process involves several steps. First, the total group confronts facts and predications about industry environment, competition, and company prospects. Second, from this objective interchange about the facts of life arises a consensus that remedial action is necessary. Third, alternative courses of action are frankly discussed (based on studies commissioned by the group), and again consensus is developed. Fourth, an assessment of necessary tasks and decision on who should do what (the first two broad steps outlined in this chapter) are agreed on. Adizes and other consultants who assist companies (or self-contained divisions) to go through this process report that, in the proper setting and with modest nudging, executive groups usually do reach consensus. And when agreements emerge there is strong social pressure on everyone to pursue the new program vigorously.

Typically, this self-assessment by the existing managerial group works best when (a) the need for some kind of redirection can be quickly established, (b) workable remedial action does not deviate much beyond or below capabilities already within the group, and (c) persons with formal power have confidence in judgment of the group.

LIMITATIONS OF NO SHAKE-UP

The likelihood that present executives will select and aggressively push a *sharp* change in strategy is low. This conservative tendency is a normal inheritance from past relationships. The old ways are easier and less uncertain. Having advocated those practices, most managers tend to defend their past judgments. Good personal relationships with outsiders often reflect prolonged cultivation and are currently valuable assets; there is an understandable reluctance to discard or upset such relationships, which were so hard to develop. Every manager over the year builds up informal debts and commitments to associates; these constrain future action.

For reasons such as these, responses to opportunities and threats may be slow, and there will be reluctance to change very much at any one time. Consequently, a person who is concerned with the execution of a new strategy must decide how urgent more vigorous action is. Perhaps one or more outsiders should replace present managers. The choice of executives strongly affects what, in fact, happens and how fast.

BRINGING IN OUTSIDERS

Many seasoned executives believe that the fastest and surest way to change strategy is to bring in one or more dedicated managers specifically charged to move the company in the new direction. The proverb "a new broom sweeps clean" expresses the feeling that a fresh start is desirable. The new manager(s) may be recruited from other companies or transferred from a sister division; they are outsiders in the sense that they are not part of the present team which has been working hard to carry out the old strategy.

REASONS FOR USING "NEW BROOMS"

Bringing in an outsider has several potential advantages:

o An outsider who already believes in the new strategy can be selected. This avoids the hurdle present executives face of switching internalized commitment from the present to the new mission. Also, the outsiders may already have industry knowledge or skills that will be valuable. In these respects, the outsider is likely to be *better prepared, sooner* than an insider who has to "retool."

o The challenge of a new assignment typically stirs up *excitement and vigor.* The urge to make a showing can lead to creative effort.

o The newcomer is unhampered by previous commitments—on budgets or to other people. The *slate is clean*—at least with respect to the new appointee personally.

o Moreover, bringing in an outsider *sends signals* to the entire organization and outside that something different and important is expected to happen. Especially when a manager who has been powerful is replaced, associates and subordinates recognize that they may have to modify their own behavior.

When present executives are either too busy or clearly unsuited for new thrusts, calling on an outsider is the only way to move ahead. The inside versus outside choice becomes much harder when there is an insider who might do a tolerable, but not outstanding job.

DRAWBACKS TO INJECTING OUTSIDERS

Like the execution of strategy generally, bringing in outsiders may prove difficult to do successfully. Possible drawbacks deal both with the individual(s) recruited and with side effects:

o Candidates who are suitable in all respects may be unavailable. For each job we want a very specific combination of values, skills, knowledge, energy, and compatibility. And we are constrained in the inducements that we can offer. Thus *compromise* to some degree is inevitable, and dealing with a stranger increases the *uncertainty* of how the marriage will actually work out.

o Some time and expense is always involved in *learning to work together.* The newcomer has to become well acquainted with the new associates, and they with him or her. Local feelings, values, strengths, loyalties—all affect cooperative action.

○ Appointees from a different industry will require even more time *building external contacts* and credibility.

○ Usually an outsider takes a job that several insiders would like to have had. Maybe someone was moved out of the job, and certainly several insiders feel they were passed over. Naturally, these disappointments create *morale problems.* If the displaced or passed-over people are popular with their colleagues, the poor morale—even resentment—can be widespread. (Of course, if the company situation is desperate, the incoming executive can be viewed as a savior.)

○ Especially prickly is what to do with *"poor old Bill."* His long, loyal service—and large block of stock—does not offset an inability to perform the new job well. Being both humane and courageous in such situations may call for lots of ingenuity.

The number of successful transplants in the annals of American business testifies that problems of the sort just listed often can be overcome. However, the failures and examples of mediocre results are so numerous when bringing in "new blood" that the need for great care is compelling.

Political Aspects of Appointments

Inevitably, selection of people for key positions has political overtones. Changing executives always shifts power, and such shifts in power help some causes and friends while hurting others. When an outsider is brought in, the range of potential appointees is greatly expanded, and the possibility of making a politically inspired selection is correspondingly increased. Here are three angles to keep in mind.

Occasionally a special-interest group has a strong feeling for or against a specific selection. For example, bankers and other lenders may doubt the financial competence of some candidates and insist that the new treasurer be someone in whom they have confidence. In troubled times labor unions or a large customer may exert a similar sort of pressure on appointments directly concerning them. The realistic question is how a particular selection will affect the continuing cooperation of a vital resource supplier. (See discussion of resource converter model in Chapter 1.)

A more general sort of pressure is for a group to be represented. Currently the appointment of women and blacks carries legal as well as social sanctions. The appointment of a member of the faction is desired partly to assure that career opportunities are available and partly to assure that a cherished viewpoint is considered in decision making. Many kinds of groupings can be seeking representation—geographic regions, branch offices, a function such as manufacturing, the handicapped, war veterans, and so on. On the negative side, there may be concern that some faction is getting too many jobs and thereby creating a powerful clique. For instance, several years ago widespread comment told of "the Humble Oil crowd taking over Exxon."

More directly related to strategy are coalitions supporting a cause. Within a company a cause may be "keeping production plants in Akron" or "moving into cable television." For the coalition, each proposed appointment is evaluated in terms of helping or hurting the cause.

Political effects of a new appointment rarely should be the dominant considerations, but to ignore them would be a serious mistake. Longer-run success in executing a strategy requires a supportive political climate.

Shaping a New Team

Using outsiders to fill key positions has both benefits and limitations, as is clear from the preceding discussion. How, then, do we decide when to do it? The key is to compare the capabilities needed to execute our new strategy with existing personnel—the first two steps recommended in this chapter. Any gaps or deficiencies should be filled by persons not now in the organization. However, the process is not so simple.

The total complement of senior people in the business-unit must be viewed as a team. These people interact. The strengths of one should complement the weaknesses of other members. This means that compromises from ideal specifications that may seem wise for one manager affect adjustments that are feasible with respect to his or her associates. Thus if the existing sales executive, whom we would like to keep for political reasons, is weak on product planning, then the general manager should be a strong planner. Similarly, an enthusiastic marketing manager who is clearly committed to the new strategy can usually pull along several other team members who are indifferent. All sorts of combinations are possible, reflecting need, individual adaptability, and judicious selection of outsiders.

An added variable is the organization structure. Within limits, the scope of jobs, the use of staff, and the degree of decentralization can be adjusted to capabilities of individuals. Also, as noted in Chapter 9, organization can be treated as an evolving arrangement—changing with the development of key people and with external opportunities.

These opportunities to improve the dovetailing of people and organization have severe limits. Increasingly, competition and other external pressures on business-units require rapid response and the best setup that is known. Sluggish adjustment is not a realistic option for most firms. Instead, strategic anticipation has become a more practical way to secure time for individual growth and team-building. In fact, such long-run anticipation is a key element in human resource strategy.

DISTINCTIVE ISSUES IN ACQUISITIONS

Business-units are the focus in the preceding discussion—as they are throughout most of this book. Before turning to executive compensation, we should note briefly the special staffing problems that arise when a corporation decides to expand through acquisitions.

Basically, when a company is acquired by a corporation we recommend that managerial personnel problems be approached in the manner already outlined. (a) Use the strategy that the newly acquired unit is expected to pursue as the basis for deciding on the array of managerial talents needed. (b) Decide to what extent acquired managers have, or can develop, those talents. (c) Bring in outsiders, if necessary, to fill gaps and to provide committed effort to new directions.*

Difficulties do arise in applying this common-sense approach. Some shake-up is likely. The financial job will change if for no other reason than to use the parent company as a source of capital and to tie into its financial reporting system. Often there are weak spots or fringe activities that the previous top management let slide. A significant contribution of the new owner is insistence that such situations be cleared up. Third, wherever synergies are sought between the new division and the rest of the corporation, local activities msut be modified to some extent.

*Sometimes one of the important assets acquired is individuals whose talents can be used for corporate benefit beyond the acquired division. Obviously, any prospects of transfers out of the division add to the gaps that must be filled.

Many of these changes may be welcome by most of the division executives. Nevertheless, uncertainty arises. Even the top performers and managers with employment contracts are anxious about how they will fit into the new scheme. If this situation lasts too long, good people may leave. Expectations may build up that later have to be shattered.

In an unfriendly takeover, executive tension is even more severe. The acquired management may have resisted the merger—thereby increasing the chances that "heads will roll." Uncertainty is rampant. The morale of managers remaining is likely to be low. Consequently, promptness in establishing a positive program is important. A revised strategy, or convincing reaffirmation of the old one, gives people a sense of direction. If some individuals have to be dropped, the others can feel that they are embarked on a clear, challenging assignment. If possible, for those remaining the acquisition should open vistas that were blocked before.

Fitting in the chief executive of the acquired firm always is delicate. If the acquired unit had been independent (not a division of some other corporation), then in the future the CEO will have to spend more time explaining and seeking approvals. At least some corporate procedures and policies will be imposed. Subtle changes in status are unavoidable. Perhaps the CEO is not adaptable enough to become committed to a new strategy. For reasons such as these, up to half of the CEO's who at the time of the merger intend to stay in fact leave within a couple of years.

Such instability of the senior executive obviously generates uncertainty and insecurity down the line. Yet, the senior executive is the one who normally plays a dominant role in establishing the positive new program recommended above. There is no easy solution. Three measures that at least help are: (a) Discuss with the former CEO early and frankly the typical difficulties sketched above. Have these discussions before the merger, if possible; the acquisition may not be economically sound unless key personnel stay on the team. (b) Have the corporate president (or group vice-president) spend time helping to develop the positive new program for the acquired company, so that corporate executives are known to second- and third-level people and have credibility with them. (c) As soon as it seems likely that the former CEO should not or will not continue in the top position, move rapidly to find and prepare a replacement. A misfit in the top spot during this transition period can be very costly.

INCENTIVES THAT SUPPORT
STRATEGIC ACTION

Wise shaping of strategy and its energetic execution are hard work. Even well-suited and committed managers—like those we have been discussing in this chapter—need encouragement. Faced with competing pressures, they need incentives that reinforce approved programs. The reward system should encourage that extra effort—which is so often necessary when strategy is being shifted.

In practice, designing incentives that support strategic action is difficult. The payoff for strategy is usually long-term. Results cannot be measured quickly. There are genuine risks, and the strategy may be changed in midstream. Managers move in and out of jobs before a strategic cycle is completed. Strategies vary in their targets and in the kinds of actions necessary to achieve them. Intermediate results are often intangible (or may even be negative) and hard to measure. Environmental and other external demands upset tightly phased strategic programs. Such factors as these make it difficult to relate results to individuals and then reward successful action.

To cut through this maze, first our measurements must be improved, and next our rewards must be tailored to the various kinds of results we wish to achieve.

COMMON DISTORTION OF INCENTIVES

Typical executive bonus plans inhibit, if not sabotage, strategic action. In management practice the inconsistency is glaring between the strategic behavior we say we want and the behavior we reward.

The measurement used in most executive bonus schemes is last year's (or quarter's!) profits. Although useful for some purposes, this concentration on the bottom line has four weaknesses in terms of promoting a new strategy: (a) It is backward-looking. Reported results reflect primarily past strategy and past events. (b) The focus is short-term. The span is a single year, even though many of the recorded transactions have impacts over a longer period. (c) Strategic gains or losses are not even considered. To do so would violate financial accounting principles. (d) Usually, investment of time and money in future strategy scores on the negative side. Such outlays are typically intermingled with other expenses, so a manager can improve his or her showing by *not* preparing for the future. All these problems are aggravated where rapid moves or promotions keep changing managers in each slot.

The usual excuse for basing bonuses on last year's profits is one of convenience. "The profits are available, widely understood, and do relate to an important part of a general manager's job." Other considerations such as intangibles and future strategy are hard to measure. Thus the argument runs, "We'll lump those matters into being a good corporate citizen—which we expect of every manager." Many companies have a provision for other factors in bonus determination, but the content is ambiguous. Although there are notable exceptions, the prevailing view of managers who receive bonuses is that, "It's the bottom line that really counts."

Our conviction is that executive incentive plans can and should give much more explicit weight to strategic behavior. Three steps toward this end are:

1. Measure progress toward strategic targets separately from results of established operations.
2. Determine incentive awards separately for established operations and for progress toward strategic targets.
3. Devise a long-term stock-option equivalent to encourage revisions of strategy and entrepreneurial risk taking.

MEASURING PROGRESS TOWARD STRATEGIC TARGETS

Frequently a manager and the organization unit are expected to work on both established operations and strategic moves. A sales manager, for instance, may be asked to sell existing products and also market a new product. An essential step in executing strategy is to measure separately the progress on each part of such multiple assignments. Even if funding is not separated (as suggested in Chapter 11), the achievement to date on each part should be measured.

The translation of a broad strategy into a series of moves and steps is advocated in several parts of this book. Business-unit strategy includes strategic thrusts (Chapter 2). These thrusts can be broken down into programs (Chapter 7). Large-scale programs will have milestone reviews (Chapter 12). The organization assists this process by dispersing the total work to various departments and sections (Chapter 9). In this way strategy is transformed from a grand scheme into a lot of specific assignments. It is measuring progress on these assignments that we are discussing here (and, in the next section, tying that progress to incentives).

Attention to these intermediate steps allows flexibility while keep-ing the strategic change moving. (a) Strategy execution is not cast into a single mold. Instead, the steps for a rapid market expansion that may suit one business-unit will differ sharply from cost-reduction steps that are appropriate for another business. Thus progress measurements must be tailor-made for each strategy. (b) The completion of a step is a natural time for feedback and reassessment of the strategy. The out-come of the step, coupled with other data then available, may suggest modification of the strategy. Any such modification should be promptly reflected in revised assignment of subsequent steps. Thus adaptation to changing conditions is built into the process. (c) In-dividual contributions to strategic action can be measured long before the total change is completed. And the skillful execution of a step (or failure to do so) is counted, even when subsequent events reduce the value of that step. This ability to measure and reward contributions promptly is especially valuable in companies that move their managers frequently, before a change cycle is completed.

The very fact that the performance of each assigned step is being measured will have a noticeable impact on strategy execution. Other managers will know whether a particular person did his or her part in a timely and effective manner, and most of us want to look good to our peers and supervisors. The opportunity for indifferent attention to strategic matters to slip by unnoticed is reduced.

AWARDS FOR STRATEGIC PROGRESS

Once measurements of steps toward strategic targets are obtained, overreliance on profits versus budget can be corrected. Instead, a balanced incentive scheme would be based on:

1. Results achieved in established operations—
   a. Actual financial performance versus budget.
   b. Achievement of nonfinancial goals, such as quality control, personal development, and government relations.*
2. Progress toward strategic targets.

As already suggested, the strategic targets for specific managers would depend on the steps assigned to them, and these steps would un-

---

*Discussion of goals, except when they are an element of company strategy, is outside the scope of this book. Their listing here, however, does reflect our prediction that in the future companies will be forced to pay more attention to external relationships even at the short-run operating level.

doubtedly change as the overall company strategy matured. Thus each manager would be subject to a form of management-by-objectives. Each period a revised set of short-range objectives would be negotiated—including financial budgets, nonfinancial operating goals, and strategic steps. Bonuses and other awards would depend on results achieved in each area.

The *relative* impact on bonuses of results in each area should vary from person to person—depending on the job (for example, production versus R&D) and the strategy of the business-unit (for example, growth versus cash cow). But to be sure that the convenient budget standard does not usurp all the actual payout, we suggest that a minimum of twenty-five percent of awards above base pay be earmarked for results in the strategic and nonfinancial areas.

This incentive scheme is obviously more difficult to use than reliance on just financial budgets plus intuitive feeling about contributions to corporate welfare. However, the benefits from that extra effort include: improved clarity of what is expected of each key manager, removal of the distorting emphasis on short-run financial results, and assurance that desired strategic shifts will not wither from inadequate attention.

Long-Term Stock-Option Equivalent

Two vital steps in tying management incentives to strategy execution have been emphasized in the last few pages. First is clarifying just what results each manager is expected to accomplish as part of the total implementation process. This involves breaking the whole array of necessary adjustments into specific assignments stated in terms of results (output, inputs, time), and then measuring the achievement of these assignments. Second is making sure that awards to managers depend to a significant and explicitly recognized degree on meeting such targets.

This is not enough. The focus in both of these steps is hitting a predetermined target. The strategy, including its major thrusts, is presumed to be settled, and the current task is to make it happen. That kind of focused action is essential. But by itself, it lacks a dynamic and adaptive ingredient. The incentive system should also encourage review and timely revision. Feedback on the success—or lack of success—in the execution of the strategic program, unexpected responses by competitors, new developments in the environment, or the like may make revision of the strategy desirable. Just as an explorer concurrently pushes hard to cross a mountain range and also weighs the wisdom of changing course, so too must strategic planners frequently reassess their position.

Although not all managers will be active in this strategy reassessment, certainly the top executives of the business-unit have major obligations for this activity. They must think in at least three time frames—current operations, pursuit of agreed-on strategy, and other strategies that might be preferable. If incentives are sensitive to only the first two, the third viewpoint is likely to be neglected.

An incentive to foster sound strategic planning at the business-unit level is hard to design. The long timespan and shifting opportunities make specific targets hard to set. However, if the business-unit is a separate corporation with publicly traded stock, then a stock option for those managers who both shape strategy and guide its execution has merit. Normally, a well-designed and executed strategy increases the value of the stock. The payoff will probably be deferred several years, but tax regulations make it possible to build a personal estate through stock options.

The catch is that very few business-units have their own publicly traded common stock. A parent corporation may be able to grant stock options, but the value of such options depends on many factors largely unrelated to a single, specific unit. For incentive purposes we want an award the value of which is closely tied to effective strategic management of each particular business-unit. We want to reward the executives who adjust strategy promptly and wisely and to penalize them for overlooking opportunities.

One possibility is to create a *stock-option equivalent*. The specifics must be fitted to each situation, but the example sketched in Figure 10–2 shows the concept. In this example the number of phantom shares an executive eventually receives is increased in direct proportion to the long-run financial success of his or her business-unit. The payoff, which can be large, is tied to long-run results.

The aim of this long-term stock-option equivalent is to provide a strong incentive for entrepreneurial behavior by one or more senior executives of a business-unit. They should see an opportunity to create a significant estate if they are highly successful. For instance, if the general manager in the previous illustration were granted 1,000 business-unit shares, and under his or her guidance profits rose from $25,000 to an average of $1,000,000 while the return on assets rose

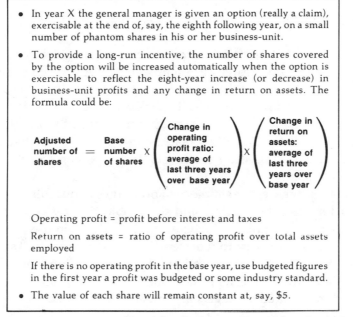

- In year X the general manager is given an option (really a claim), exercisable at the end of, say, the eighth following year, on a small number of phantom shares in his or her business-unit.

- To provide a long-run incentive, the number of shares covered by the option will be increased automatically when the option is exercisable to reflect the eight-year increase (or decrease) in business-unit profits and any change in return on assets. The formula could be:

$$\begin{array}{l}\text{Adjusted}\\\text{number of}\\\text{shares}\end{array} = \begin{array}{l}\text{Base}\\\text{number}\\\text{of shares}\end{array} \times \left(\begin{array}{l}\text{Change in}\\\text{operating}\\\text{profit ratio:}\\\text{average of}\\\text{last three years}\\\text{over base year}\end{array}\right) \times \left(\begin{array}{l}\text{Change in}\\\text{return on}\\\text{assets:}\\\text{average of}\\\text{last three}\\\text{years over}\\\text{base year}\end{array}\right)$$

Operating profit = profit before interest and taxes

Return on assets = ratio of operating profit over total assets employed

If there is no operating profit in the base year, use budgeted figures in the first year a profit was budgeted or some industry standard.

- The value of each share will remain constant at, say, $5.

FIGURE 10–2.   Example of Stock-Option-Equivalent Incentive

from twenty percent to thirty percent, the cash value of the option at the end of the eighth year would be $300,000.

$$1{,}000 \text{ shares} \times \frac{1{,}000{,}000}{25{,}000} \times \frac{0.3}{0.2} = 60{,}000 \text{ shares @ } \$5 = \$300{,}000$$

Of course, the manager might be given such an option in several different years.

All sorts of variations in the scheme are possible. An objective different than operating profit could be used, for example.* To provide for possible transfer to another job, we would vest the option in proportion to the part of the total period that the executive spends in the business-unit. This would increase the executive's interest in training a successor and encourage cooperation after he or she left.

*Another possible variation: If we wished to couple the incentive to *both* the success of the business-unit and of the corporation, the option could relate to actual shares of the corporation. Then the *number* of shares covered would depend on the success of the business-unit, as suggested in the illustration, whereas the *value* per share would depend on the increase in the stock-market price of corporate shares between the granting date and the date that the option was exercised.

CONCLUSION

The suggestions in this chapter for matching and motivating managers to support company strategy are simple in concept: (a) determine the portfolio of executive abilities necessary to execute the selected strategy in the expected environment; (b) decide the extent to which present executives, individually and as a group, can provide these abilities; (c) go outside to fill any gaps; (d) create an incentive system that assures adequate attention to strategic thrusts, to longer-run targets, and to entrepreneurship.

Although apparently simple, adapting these concepts to specific situations requires both effort and skill. Objectivity is difficult. Personal values and political considerations are always involved. Nevertheless, there is no way to sidestep this sensitive task. Other measures—astute programs, focused organization, resource allocations, responsive controls—all help; nonetheless, they are not substitutes. Qualified, motivated managers are imperative for effective execution of strategy.

Resource Allocation—Power of the Purse Strings

T HE OLD SAYING, "He who holds the purse strings has the real power," is an exaggeration, but the underlying point cannot be overlooked. In this chapter we first see how allocation of capital hurts or helps strategy implementation, and then we expand the issue to allotting other vital resources. Unless resources flow to priority programs, strategy will stagnate.

IMPACT OF RESOURCE ALLOCATION ON STRATEGY EXECUTION

Most companies have separate departments to mobilize, protect, and conserve each major resource—capital, manpower, key raw materials, and the like. In their roles as guardians, such departments may place roadblocks in the way of strategic thrusts. They are understandably more concerned with protection than risky use of their resources. The policies and procedures that they sponsor (like those of the SEC and OSHA) stress care and caution with new ventures.

In one electronics company, for example, an appropriation for a pilot plant in the Southwest was delayed for over a year. The pilot operation was part of an off-the-record strategy to move closer to large customers and out of a bad labor situation in Cleveland. However, the proposal was turned down by the appropriations committee because idle capacity existed in the Cleveland plant and estimates for the Southwest operation failed to show savings on an incremental cost basis. In this instance the strategy was not openly discussed in the appropriations committee, and two members who did know the long-run rationale were unsympathetic with the move.

If strategies are to be carried out, ways must be developed that reconcile the planned moves on new fronts with the protective mechanisms of the resource departments. The criteria for approving an investment must be stated in terms of their deployment, rather than as a standard return on investment or minimum cost.

Inputs—Not Outputs

Of course, power over resource allocation relates only to inputs; the projected output may or may not be achieved. Just as the United States sending financial aid to, say, the Sudan does not assure that Sudanese children will be better nourished, likewise an advertising appropriation will not necessarily result in increased sales of a new product. Resources are necessary but not sufficient.

This indirect, enabling character of resource allotments adds to the fuzziness of linkages between allocations and strategy. The people allocating necessary resources can either restrain or permit a project to proceed, but they do not carry out the work. Although they can hold back, it does them little good to "push on the end of a rope." They have learned that even critical problems cannot be solved by throwing money at them. Because their power lies on the constraining side, typically they are more concerned with not making a mistake than with risky successes. They are typically scored on their conservation and low risk exposure—while credits for a spectacular success go to the venture managers.

The Focus on Money

In business firms, money (technically the right to spend money) is the resource that is allotted with the greatest care. Because it is transferable to many different uses, money is a convenient overall planning medium. Also, accounting records already exist to keep track of money flows. As a result, our allocation procedures concentrate on money.

An unstated assumption is that when money is allocated, other resources will follow. One simple theory is that money will buy whatever materials, people, facilities, distribution network, goodwill, or government cooperation that may be needed to carry out a selected strategy. If that were so, financial allocations alone would resolve resource problems. In reality, one or more of these other resources may be just as scarce as money, or it may not be tradeable for money *alone*. For instance, companies often have and can attract only a limited pool of outstanding managers; programs that do not get attention from these managers are very likely to fail. Similarly, a firm's distribution network may have capability of effectively selling a limited number of products; if so, getting prime time of the sales force may be a requisite for success.

The successful execution of strategy in such circumstances depends on how each of these critically scarce resources is allocated. Few companies, however, have formalized their allocation processes for nonfinancial resources. Those that do, such as large construction companies or consulting firms, typically work on a series of big projects and have a matrix organization. For most other companies the allocation of nonfinancial resources for strategic purposes calls for special treatment—often informal bargaining by division managers.

In contrast, our procedures for rationing money are formal and elaborate. The two basic mechanisms, which have the potential for distorting strategy, deal with: (a) capital appropriations for fixed assets and (b) strategic expense budgets. Strategic expenses are current outlays having long-run results that are intended to help achieve strategic targets.

We consider capital allocation first and in most detail, because (a) capital is almost always a significant element in any strategic change and (b) most issues that arise in capital allocation are also prominent in other allocations. Thus the analysis of allotting capital provides a base for briefer scrutiny of other resource allocations.

TWO TRACKS TO CAPITAL ALLOCATION

The point of no return for capital expenditures, normally, is when a contract is signed with an outside supplier. That contract commitment tends to freeze a bit of strategy. However, a long series of proposals, negotiations, and refinements precede the legal commitment, and it is during this earlier planning process that strategy and capital allocation must be harnessed together.

Who initiates specific proposals? Which ones receive continuing study and why? What early screening of proposals takes place? How is support for the remaining refined proposals mustered? What criteria are applied in giving the final authorization to commit the company? These are the points at which strategy must have its impact.

Top-Down Approach

Broadly speaking, there are two approaches to initiating proposals for capital expenditures—top-down or bottom-up. Business-unit managers may identify needs and request their subordinates to work up specific proposals. If the managers have agreed on a company strategy, then ideas for capital outlays are likely to be steps for carrying out that strategy. Of course, the process of spelling out the move may uncover obstacles or opportunities that lead to modification of the original concept, but the initiation and support flows down from the top.

The move of Dover Apparel Company into children's knitwear illustrates this top-down approach. The assistant to the president convinced the president that knitwear was a logical addition to the company's very successful girls' dress line. To make that strategy workable, they decided that Far East production was necessary. This decision, in turn, soon lead to a proposal to invest in a joint venture in Sri Lanka. In this example, a change in strategy is clearly the driving force that will generate several capital-expenditure proposals.

The Dover Apparel Company, however, is distinctive in several respects. It is a relatively small—$50 million—firm in which the top executives know their operations in detail. They are able both to conceive of strategy and to think very concretely of ways to implement that strategy. And without the assistant (and son) of the president with the time and motivation to introduce a change, the risky proposal would never have been seriously considered.

In contrast, senior managers of diversified corporations rarely possess enough knowledge about operations to make specific capital proposals—as occurs in Dover Apparel Company. Instead, they often lapse into a resource conservation mode and merely set up criteria for investments. Such criteria normally will reflect portfolio objectives for the various businesses. If the criteria are ambiguous, they invite padded estimates by operating managers who seek approval for pet projects. Another danger is that a wide separation of strategy formulation from operations will result in capital expenditure proposals that are unrelated to strategy. The larger and more diverse the corporation, the greater is the risk of such disconnection.

Proposals Originating at Operating Levels

By far the largest number of capital expenditure proposals originate in the functional departments of a business-unit and go up the executive ladder for approval. Triggered by a need related to existing activities, few of them deviate very much from the status quo.

Some of these bottom-up proposals are for necessary projects—replacement of a faltering elevator, for instance. Others propose better ways to perform present activities, such as computer control of accounts receivable. Still others may deal with natural expansion—say, a West Coast sales branch or acquisition of an additional coal mine by a utility company. If the business-unit wishes to pursue its existing strategy, such proposals are quite appropriate.

Incidentally, it is proposals of this sort that are the subject of *capital budgeting theory*. In that model the added benefits derived from each proposed investment—compared with present practice or available alternatives—are divided by the incremental investment; this gives a financial rate of return, preferably computed by the discounted cash-flow method. The projects are then ranked according to their rates of return, and the available pool of capital is allocated to top-ranking projects. Note that the model assumes that projects bubble up from the bottom and that selection can be *based on estimated rate of return with little or no attention to long-run strategy*.

Capital budgeting in the pure form just sketched is unrealistic in several respects. First, many potential investments never reach the final screening. The personnel needed to develop the idea may not be assigned by a dubious supervisor, or a departmental manager may not care to sponsor the project. Without both careful analysis and strong sponsorship the proposal is unlikely to be presented to the top allocating body. Second, the model implies that all projects for, say, a year can be held up for a grand ranking. Actually, the need for capital does not fit an annual roundup. Some projects are urgent; others develop in a sequential fashion. Third, the benefits of many projects cannot be expressed in financial terms with equal reliability—nor even in financial terms alone. What, for instance, is the financial return on necessary projects or on environmental-protection investments? What financial return can you show for being two years ahead of your competitors in R&D?

More serious from a strategic-management viewpoint is the absence of a systematic linking of recommended allocations to strategic plans. Some projects may, indeed, support even the newest twist in company strategy, but the typical bottom-up process does not assure such a selection. Nor is there assurance that the best ways to pursue a strategy ever come up for review. The world of operating managers and design engineers is filled with current, local problems, and rewards typically are tied to short-run solutions of these problems. Thus proposals from the bottom naturally have a short-run bent.

Both the top-down and bottom-up viewpoints are needed. The challenge is to devise a system that melds them.

SOURCES OF CONFLICT FOR ALLOCATIONS

A second basic difficulty in linking capital allocations to strategy—in addition to getting good proposals submitted for approval—is the criteria on which the choice will be made—how to decide who gets the money?

WHAT UNCERTAINTY IS ACCEPTABLE?

The outcome of a new strategic move is always uncertain. The responses of resource suppliers, customers, and competitors are in doubt. Secondary effects are even more difficult to predict. So a strategic thrust is usually taken with a degree of boldness and self-confidence. In contrast, the results of capital outlays that buttress present operations are more easily predicted. More is known about the setting, and the proposal will be upsetting to fewer people. The very mechanics of discounted cash flow put a premium on short-term, predictable revenue—but severely handicap longer-term investment-type allocations.

Moreover, the new strategy itself is admittedly subject to change. If it does not work well, something else will be tried. This dynamic quality means that a person strongly advocating a particular investment this year may turn up with a divergent proposal a couple of years hence.

Consequently an executive allocating capital may have to choose between proposals surrounded by uncertainty and perhaps confounded by inconsistency over time, on the one hand, and on the other hand, proposals with a relatively clear short-run benefit. Especially when money is in short supply, the safer, easier choice is the short-run project.

The argument supporting the strategic projects must rest on the *longer-run benefits* of the overall strategy—relative to the status quo. This strategic question raises a variety of issues not normally addressed in a capital proposal, and the person (or committee) making the allocations is not necessarily best qualified to answer the question. Instead, the strategic objectives should have already been settled; most of the uncertainty is absorbed when the strategy is adopted. When the target is thus set, capital proposals can be compared in terms of their contribution to that objective. A project may indeed be risky but its approval or rejection should depend on whether a less-risky alternative to reach the same objective is available.

To cite an example, a few years ago the farmers' cooperative, Agway, made a strategic decision to protect its supply of gasoline and other petroleum products by owning some oil wells. Each well-drilling proposal within this strategy is quite risky—much more so than, say, an expansion of a feed mill. Nevertheless, if Agway is to establish its own crude-oil position, it must accept that sort of uncertainty. Comparison of uncertainty of various drilling proposals is pertinent, but the uncertainty of drilling in general versus other uses of capital has already been absorbed in the strategic decision.

In practice, the uncertainty often involved in strategic projects is troublesome. Just who should decide how much risk may be warranted is often unclear—within a business-unit and even more so among business-units in a diversified portfolio. That lack of clarity can upset the execution of a strategy.

Personal Value Bias

Few of us are as coolly rational as the preceding discussion of uncertainty implies. Each of us has values that, deliberately or unconsciously, color our choices. You may dislike living in the snowbelt, whereas I may have a snobbish preference for dealing with only expensive products. Also, each of us has skills that may be prized under one strategy and of little value under a different strategy. Moreover, we hold beliefs about how rewards are distributed in our company. These personal values inevitably bias the action each of us takes regarding any particular capital-expenditure proposal.

The personal values of individuals who must approve a proposal are especially critical. As noted earlier, supervisors have to assign people and other resources to develop a proposal. Managers in the chain of command and respected advisors must sponsor a proposal, or it probably will be shunted aside. This kind of support depends on a good match between the impact of a proposal and values of the key people. In effect, unpopular ventures do not get proposed.

Of course, personal values often are quite congruent with objectives adopted by one's company. Yet when those objectives and the related reward system are fuzzy, individualistic ends become dominant. Then, if the proposal doesn't suit personal values, the proposal may receive lukewarm support, or objections may be couched in terms that are considered legitimate. (Winning personal support for company strategy, discussed in Chapter 8, and careful selection of executives, discussed in Chapter 10, are positive ways to increase the congruence of personal values and company strategy.)

Politics of Approval

The allocation of capital for strategic purposes may be further complicated by internal company politics. The flow of capital may be either expedited or hindered by an informal exchange of favors which leads to joint behavior.

We have argued elsewhere * that internal politics are natural and inevitable, that such political behavior may be contrary to company interests, but that managers can with skill harness political forces to support company strategy. The crux is to manage rewards and punishments so that mutual help in supporting company goals is encouraged, whereas deviant behavior is firmly squelched.

Politics may enter the capital-allocation process at two points. Large proposals often affect several departments, and the support of managers in all those departments will help in getting the project approved. Also, review of proposals by a representative committee is common practice. This may be a special capital-appropriations committee or a general management committee. In multidivision corporations, such committees often exist at both the division and corporate levels. Again, the support of people with diverse interests and values is needed.

In such a setting the implicit trading of support is common. Personal integrity need not be sacrificed. A statement such as, "I'll support your new plant if you promise never to argue with the introduction of a

---

* See Chapter 21 of W. H. Newman, E. K. Warren, and J. E. Schnee, *The Process of Management*, 5th ed. (Englewood Cliffs, N.J.: Prentice-Hall, 1982).

new line in Division X" is extreme. Instead, when there are wide areas of subjective judgment—as we have already noted are common in new strategic moves—deferring to one member who has a major interest or expertise creates some obligation for that member to defer to us when we need help! The American pioneers helped each other build barns by such a social practice. But the distinction between constructive coalitions and political wheeling-dealing is not always clear.

Unfortunately, political dealing can overwhelm sound judgment. When agreement on overall objectives is lacking, coalitions pulling in different directions may form. In one commercial bank, for instance, approval of bank lines for a new customer increasingly reflected political jockeying among lending officers. A subsequent recession forced serious write-offs of several of these loans, depleting the bank's capital to a point at which its chances for future growth are now undermined. In this instance, if an expansion strategy had to be carefully devised, the political maneuvering could have been minimized.

INCOMPLETE STRATEGY

In some companies, strategy consists of little more than lofty goals. The real formulation of future direction occurs in decisions about specific capital requests. For example, the metal-fabricating division of a corporation recently was authorized to build a second plant in a new location. This division is in a mature industry and supplies less than ten percent of the total market. In a BCG matrix (see Chapter 3), it would show up as a dog and be a candidate for liquidation in some manner.

Local management, however, has devised an improved production process. This process gives low cost for serving one thriving niche in the market. (Thus the division could be placed at least temporarily in the middle of the nine-cell matrix shown on page 45.) The new plant is designed to exploit the improved production process. It is not very clear how the division arrived at its present position—except for resourcefulness of a local engineer—nor just what future moves should be. The current strategy was, in fact, clarified only when funds for the new plant were approved!

Incrementalism—that is, step-by-step feeling one's way—worked out well in the preceding example, but it does place a heavy burden on the capital-expenditure approval process. When the strategy is incomplete, each request has to be evaluated on where it might lead and the desirability of being there.

Summarizing: Conflict may arise when allocating capital, as the preceding discussion suggests. The four potential sources noted—high uncertainty, personal bias, internal politics, and unclear strategy—all open the way for serious gaps between a selected strategy and actual allocation of capital. In these situations strategy fails to play its guiding role and does not get implemented because it lacks funds. Figure 11–1 highlights these allocation hurdles as well as obstacles to obtaining good proposals.

WAYS TO CHANNEL CAPITAL SUPPORT FOR STRATEGY

The need for stronger bridges between strategy and capital spending is pressing. Top-down and bottom-up approaches to capital allocation should be melded, and costly conflicts for grants caused by loose guidance should be minimized—as just noted. Thus we turn in this section to what managers can do. These suggestions move from simple devices to more difficult and powerful ones.

POLICY CONSTRAINTS

One way to tie capital allocations to strategy is to establish policies. Here the term policy refers to a "thou shalt not" guide in the use of capital. For instance, if company strategy insists on flexibility in channels of distribution, a policy prohibiting investment in retail properties would support the strategy. If product strategy is to shift from heavy steel to reinforced plastic bodies, a derived policy might block large investments in metal-working equipment. Similarly, if strategy calls for high leverage through a high debt/equity ratio, then a policy to shun high-risk projects would be reasonable.

Such policies override criteria such as return on investment. Any proposal that violates a policy simply is not considered. If a lot of unusually attractive proposals have to be passed by, then reexamination of the strategy may be called for, but until the strategy is modified, the policies keep the capital allocation within bounds.

The formulation of such policies is not easy. One approach to finding useful guides is to review each facet of company strategy with policy constraints in mind—the domain, the differential advantage sought, the strategic thrusts, and the target results. Of course, this ap-

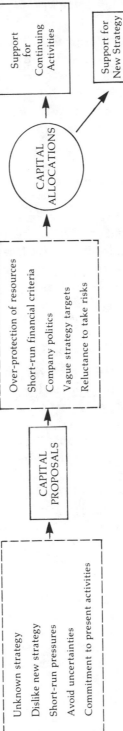

OBSTACLES TO
GOOD STRATEGIC PROPOSALS

Unknown strategy
Dislike new strategy
Short-run pressures
Avoid uncertainties
Commitment to present activities

CAPITAL
PROPOSALS

NEGATIVE FILTERS
AT ALLOCATION STAGE

Over-protection of resources
Short-run financial criteria
Company politics
Vague strategy targets
Reluctance to take risks

CAPITAL
ALLOCATIONS

Support
for
Continuing
Activities

Support for
New Strategy

FIGURE 11-1. *Typical Barriers to Capital Support for New Strategy*

proach implies that most policies will differ from business-unit to business-unit, because each has its own strategy; only policies derived from corporate input strategies will have multiunit application.

A further difficulty in preparing policy constraints is that some kinds of investment are not clearly black or white. For example, a company may sorely need a few computers or wind tunnels, but an additional supply would be a costly burden. The attractiveness of more of such equipment depends on how much of it we already have. For this kind of investment, policy constraints may become too complicated to be useful.

Although they require care in framing, policy constraints can screen out proposals that are gross misfits with strategy. Especially when a new strategy is being introduced, several of its implications can be spelled out in capital-expenditure policies. Being known in advance, the policies should nip out-of-bounds projects early, before a lot of preparatory labor has been spent.

Explicit Links with Strategy

A second linking device is to require with each capital request a written statement of the impact the proposed expenditure will have on the execution of current strategy. Unless a significant contribution can be predicted, the proposal is rejected.

The prime effect of this procedure is assuring that strategy execution is at least included among the criteria for granting a capital request. Return on investments and other numerical and short-run results will still be considered, of course, but the strategic impact is also on the agenda. Assuming that the value and reward systems support the strategy (see Chapters 8 and 10), this explicit linking of each proposal to the recognized strategy is a potent step.

A related gain is forcing the people designing and supporting each proposal to consider strategy in their planning. Even though bottom-up proposals may not originate as strategic moves, the tie to strategy cannot be overlooked. This recurring need to prepare a strategy-impact statement prods a wide range of managers and planners to connect their operations to officially endorsed longer-range goals. Strategy now is relevant!

Such tying of capital grants to strategy does not assure full strategic planning. Important moves may be omitted. At most, money is not spent unless it aids strategy; whether enough of the right steps are being taken is a different issue not covered by the strategy-screening procedure. Like cheese for a sandwich, the linking is fine, but it is not enough by itself.

STRATEGIC PROGRAMS

Strategic need for capital outlays ideally should come directly from the strategy itself. Strategic thrusts are the starting points. They specify the nature and sequence of major moves. Each thrust, in turn, can be laid out in a series of steps—or subgoals—to be achieved. Programs for each step will indicate target dates and predicted resource inputs (costs of investments). Often a variety of subprograms for mobilizing raw materials, training personnel, building offices or plants, obtaining legal clearances, creating market acceptance, or the like will be necessary.

A summary of these programs and subprograms will show, among other things, the new assets (both tangible and intangible) that will call for investment of capital. Thus through this top-down programming a whole series of needed assets are identified. These assets are described in terms of performance requirements, or asset roles. Capital-expenditure projects can then be planned to create or acquire assets having these performance capabilities. By defining needed assets in terms of desired performance, or role, their linkage to strategy should be clear.

As we noted in Chapter 7, however, strategic programming is rarely so neat and orderly as just outlined. Central planners must obtain realistic estimates from people close to concrete action, and a lot of give-and-take about program design must take place. This interchange takes time and opens the door for bias and conflict. Also, dynamic changes and new knowledge lead to modifications of strategy during the time it is being carried out. Consequently, the asset roles are rarely as sharp and fixed as is desirable for capital allocation.

Three practices help managers to obtain the benefits of deriving asset roles from strategic programs while also retaining flexibility to adapt to uncertainty and change:

First, as soon as strategic programs or subprograms are approved, *treat the asset roles they stipulate as settled.* In other words, for purposes of capital allocations and specific asset planning, the need for the asset is established by approval of the program. If alternative ways of meeting that need can be found, a choice among these alternatives is an appropriate issue for subsequent review of capital-expenditure proposals. However, a distinction is made between the need for the performance capabilities—which is determined by a decision to go ahead with the program—and the choice of how best to meet that recognized need.

Note that the basic capital allocation is made by senior managers when they approve the strategic program. That approval presumably weighs alternative uses of capital and other scarce resources. Moreover, if the uncertainty surrounding the program is judged by management to be very high, they can (a) insist that flexibility be included in any asset plan—such as staggered construction, provision for multiple use, or the like, and/or (b) insist on program reviews as outlined below.

Second, include in the program a statement of *key assumptions* regarding maximum dollar outlay for each asset role and also regarding environmental conditions. Then, if during the developmental period management discovers that any of these key assumptions probably will not be met, the program goes back for review by the persons who approved the program initially. Thus if the assets as described just cannot be put in place for the predicted amount, or if a foreign war cuts demand in half, the managers take another look.

Third, even if no warning flags are raised, provide for a *milestone review of the entire strategic program* just before contracts are signed for very large dollar outlays. The risks entailed in such investments could wreck the company—or unexpected opportunities may have opened up. Typically, such large outlays are projected to have a long life; their operation will soak up other resources in addition to the initial investment. Thus prudence requires a review utilizing the most up-to-date information available.

The programming activity implied in these three recommendations obviously requires substantial inputs by senior executives of the business-unit and prompt availability of corporate officials who join in program approvals. Annual meetings will not be enough. Nevertheless, when the system is followed, capital outlays and strategic action are closely coordinated. Flexibility is provided by people whose values and concerns are strategic in scope. In this regard the corporate strategic-planning staff can perform a useful service in monitoring key assumptions and participating in milestone reviews.

Separate Budgeting for Strategy Development

Texas Instruments uses an even more sophisticated system for launching new strategies. Each strategic program has a budget and temporary organization of its own. By concentrating authority to act (and to spend money) in a new-venture unit, strategic programming and capital investing are merged.

This unique arrangement is especially effective in reducing conflicts over short-term outlays; thus it is described in the next section. However, it embraces capital outlays also. Once the idea of separate venture units is adopted, control over capital outlays becomes a natural part of the package.

Summarizing, to tie capital allocations to strategy we have proposed four methods—policy constraints, explicit links to strategy, strategic programs, and TI's separate budgeting for strategy development. The first two are devices any company can adopt with only minor adjustments in existing systems. Every business-unit and corporation concerned about its strategy should adopt them. Programming down to the asset-role level and TI's venture budgeting call for more disciplined managerial behavior. They assure a tighter link, but at some price in executive free-wheeling.

TREATMENT OF STRATEGIC EXPENSES

The execution of strategy requires money for current expenses as well as for capital investment. The chief problems with these strategic expenses involve both record keeping and actual use of funds. Allocations intended for strategic purposes may be "borrowed" to make short-run results look better, and activities with longer-run profits may be shunted aside to meet today's emergencies.

SCRAMBLED ACCOUNTS

All sorts of expenses may be involved in putting a strategy into action. Some of them are not clearly separable from ongoing activities. Arranging for customers to test a new product, training salespersons and calling on new distributors, devising new production methods, testing products for safety, establishing output standards, setting up new accounts, preparing computer software, securing legal approvals and copyrights—the list could go on and on. Because no tangible asset emerges and the future value of the effort is uncertain, normally the cost is simply charged as an expense in the current year.

In an established company this kind of work is mostly done by existing personnel. It is an assignment—at least for the section manager—on top of work on the present business. As a consequence, typically separate expense accounts are not established, nor is there a separate expense budget (as there will be for capital outlays). Instead, the regular expense budgets may be increased by a small amount to recognize the extra workload. The result is that costs of working on old and new strategies are scrambled in the current expense accounts. The annual budget allowances are similarly scrambled.

The Squeeze on Strategic Activities

Short-run needs freeze out long-run action. Engineers assigned to new-product development, for example, are often interrupted to fix a current processing problem or to help a customer. A telephone call from the outside auditor takes priority over a study of growth trends in Brazil. Keeping Susan's even hand on labor negotiations seems more urgent than sending her to a six-week executive development program.

Such preference for dealing with immediate problems is normal. A decision is needed today. The results of attention or inattention are likely to show up soon—maybe in crisp, clear numbers. Managerial incentives typically pay off sooner on short-run performance. In contrast, both the outcome and the reward for strategic action, in most companies, is deferred and uncertain.

Managers normally have many more tasks than they can do completely. They must allocate their own time and the resources at their disposal among these tasks. And then pressure builds up. Total expenses are too high. The CEO wants a good financial report for the third quarter. Or incoming orders take an unexpected spurt. The allocation is hard to make; some things must be squeezed down.

Over and over it is the strategic activities that are deferred. Today's problems soak up available energies and resources. The scrambled accounts and budgets fail to reveal the shift in allocations away from strategic actions to currently squeaking wheels.

Texas Instruments' Separation of Strategic Action

Texas Instruments follows a specially designed system for strategy formulation and execution that assures attention to this important aid to TI's success. Two features of the system are (a) separate accounts and budgets for specific strategic activities and (b) separate ad hoc organization for each strategic venture.

The TI accounts are *not* scrambled. Rather, expense accounts and budgets for existing products focus only on profitability of current activities. And *separate accounts are maintained for expenses and capital expenditures for each new venture.* Budget allocations are made by senior executives for each stage of the strategic planning and implementation; then disbursements and progress are checked at milestones. The progress and prospects of all strategic ventures TI is working on are compared periodically and revised allocations made at that time. This *project budgeting and accounting* enables TI executives to keep close tabs on strategic activities actually taking place.

A corresponding distinct organization is created for each new venture. Like an engineering consulting firm, a venture is broken down into separate studies or steps, and *each step is assigned to a unit or team.* Thus responsibility for completing that step on schedule within its budget allocation is clearly defined.

An unusual aspect of the TI organization is its use of the same cadre of managers for supervising current operations and for special assignments to new ventures. Often managers wear two hats. They are pushing for profits on some existing product, and during the same period they carry a special assignment on a new venture. Nevertheless, the accounting and the measurement of success for each job is sharply separated.

Clearly, then, TI has designed a system that overcomes many of the difficulties we have just outlined. By creating separate accounts, separate organization, and separate allocations, the tasks of operating profitably today and of preparing for tomorrow proceed in parallel. A manager cannot cut back on strategic outlays so as to make current operations look good. If the records are maintained honestly and accurately, one time frame is not short-changed for the benefit of the other, and a mechanism exists for channeling managerial effort in ways that senior executives believe will best serve the total company.*

The TI system is unique. Probably no other company should attempt to adopt all of it. However, the concept of maintaining separate accounts for strategy development is feasible for any firm that has a tradition for keeping records of time spent on different projects. (Advertising agencies, consulting firms, and engineering departments do so routinely.) The concept of organizing around steps in a program is likewise familiar to sophisticated companies. Systematic management of task teams is a fairly common form of matrix organization,

*For a published description of the TI system, see P. Lorange and R. F. Vancil, *Strategic Planning Systems* (Englewood Cliffs, N.J.: Prentice-Hall, 1977), pp. 338–361.

and the combination of separate accounts with separate ad hoc organization enables managers to fine-tune the allocation of effort to strategic matters.

Loose-Coupling of Budgets and Strategy

A variety of ways to make sure that financial allocations support strategy have been recommended in this chapter (see Figure 11-2). Now a qualification is in order.

Experience, especially with long-range planning, shows that when financial budgets are negotiated in the same meetings that new strategy is considered, strategy generation gets little attention. The inevitable concern with exact amounts and with comparisons with previous period injects a precise, critical frame of mind. Exactness crowds out creativity. For this reason, several students of strategic management urge that strategy be considered in separate discussions—three to six months prior to financial budgets. They call this *loose-coupling*.

Our position on this issue is: (a) Yes, strategy should be *considered first*—in an atmosphere in which opportunities, alternatives, and possible consequences are freely aired. Hard evidence is welcome, along with intuitive judgments. Weighing uncertainties and contingencies is part of the process. In such a discussion rarely is there time and detailed information to set next year's budget. (b) On the other hand, the idea of loose-coupling is a high price to pay for imaginative strategic analysis. Too long a separation between strategy decisions and budget decisions runs the risk that strategy will be pushed into the background when tough negotiations over budgets take place. The danger is that strategy will be regarded as wishful thinking, whereas "budgets deal with (short-term) real life."

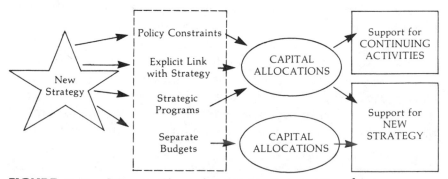

FIGURE 11-2.   Ways to Channel Capital to Support New Strategy

Instead of loose-coupling, we urge that promptly after basic directions and thrusts are agreed on, financial budgets reflecting these decisions should be prepared. These budgets need cover only the next cycle of actions (typically a year or two), with extended estimates for long-cycle activities. For the next cycle the tie to agreed-on strategy should be tight.

As in football, once a play is called the entire team works on its execution. There will be opportunities to change the strategy later—in milestone reviews and in response to control warnings. But the need for such flexibility does not justify loose, ambiguous financial allocations.

Strategy and budgets can be linked by the same devices as recommended for capital expenditures: policy constraints on acceptable activities, explicit ties to strategy, and clear-cut budgets for strategic thrusts and similar programs.

ALLOCATION OF NONFINANCIAL RESOURCES

Just as money is the universal medium of exchange in civilized countries, it is also the widespread medium of planning in companies. Money can easily be transferred from one use to another. Because it is a necessary (though not sufficient) resource for most activities, its allotment is a convenient regulating device. The power of the purse strings is strong.

Money has shortcomings, however. The ease of shifting its use robs it of qualitative power. To carry out strategy we have to devise much more selective guidelines—as have been recommended in this chapter. Moreover, possessing money does not guarantee availability of all other resources. In fact, some other resource may be so scarce that its availability is more critical than money.

During World War II, for instance, the major war-production effort was regulated by the allocation of metals (steel, copper, and aluminum), not money. To change the strategy of a university, the critical variable is faculty appointments. The future of a very large missile company, to cite still another example, is clearly being determined by the way its outstanding R&D capability is allocated.

When a resource such as managerial personnel, raw material, or R&D capability is critically short relative to a company's needs, its allocation can seriously affect strategy execution. The pressures and the dangers are quite similar to those surrounding capital allocations. Local managers will prefer to use the resource in ways that yield prompt, clear results rather than on uncertain, longer-run strategic projects. The resource department probably will be self-protective, if not arrogant, and establish criteria for resource use that minimize risks for the department. Political jockeying is likely. If a new strategy is unpopular, delaying tactics obstruct actual availability of the resource.

Consequently, as with financial allocations, measures are needed to make sure that assignment of the scarce resource is consistent with company strategy. Basically, the same tools are available.

1. *Policies can be set that prevent use for sidetrack activities.* A West Coast electronics firm, for instance, has decided to pin its hope for fast growth on proprietary, state-of-the-art components. For this strategy, R&D is clearly the critical resource. To ensure full effort behind this commitment, a policy of no R&D support for subcontracting business has been adopted (much to the consternation of the production manager who liked subcontracts to keep his plant busy).

2. *Project approval can be withheld unless support of strategy is clear.* For example, a family-owned insurance company is relying on professional managers (three young MBA's) to switch company emphasis from fire to environmental hazards. Proposals to underwrite other kinds of risks, even though probably profitable, are rejected, because senior executives believe that the professional managers will have all they can do to succeed in the environmental domain.

3. *Resource allocations can be derived directly from strategy programs.* The Aluminum Fabricating Corporation uses this approach. It has long-term contracts for a fixed quantity of aluminum ingots priced twenty percent below the current market. The board of directors has decided not to seek new contracts at today's prices; instead, the strategy is to use its low-cost aluminum to build a strong position in selected product markets. Product managers receive an allotment of aluminum—a slice of the pie—based on the outlook and their program for penetrating each market.

4. *Separate allocations can be made for old and new business.* The Sierra Shoe Company, for instance, is facing reluctance of its distributing organization to push its new line. Long known for its hiking, outdoor, and special work shoes, Sierra finally entered the canvas-top athletic shoe field. The primary aim is to better utilize its strong selling organization. But the sales force clearly prefers to sell "real shoes" not "tennis shoes." The company is now trying separate quotas and separate bonuses at all levels, to get the desired effort on the new line.

As these examples suggest, tying resource allocation to new strategy takes different forms, yet it is clear that resource support is often crucial to the successful execution of a new strategy. Somehow, by the methods described or more ingenious ones, the reallocation of critical resources must be achieved.

Two broad conclusions stand out in our analysis of resource allocation:

First, it is entirely possible—in some circumstances even likely—for resource allocation to undermine the execution of strategy. However, managerial techniques are available to prevent direct sabotage. Policy constraints, explicit links with strategy, strategy programs, separate budgeting for strategic development—when wisely administered—will forge close linkages between allocations and strategy. This managers can do if they will.

Second, the most careful building of such linkages, however, does not assure maximum support for a strategy. Resources are indeed necessary; still, they are not sufficient. They are inputs that make strategy execution possible, but other conditions are necessary to employ these resources effectively. Programs, organization, key personnel, controls, and commitment—to name elements examined in other chapters of this book—must breathe life into the resources provided.

Controlling the Dynamic Process

C ONTROL OF STRATEGY is both important and elusive, yet few companies have thought through how to keep their strategic planning and
execution on track. In this chapter we describe four basic steps that
managers can use for this purpose.

CONTROLLING THE FUTURE

Most managerial control concepts deal with existing businesses. Comparison of actual results against a standard is the usual practice. The
work is done, it is past, and then we evaluate the result. But such post-
action review does not suit strategy. Instead, strategy is concerned
with events that have not yet occurred. It is forward-looking. Moreover, it frequently deals with new businesses or with modifications
that are still to be made of existing businesses. Consequently,
customary control concepts and techniques require adjustment.

STEERING CONTROL

Control of strategy is similar to that used to guide the Apollo ship to the
moon. NASA officials did not wait until the space capsule either

reached or missed the moon. Rather, they computed trajectories as soon as Apollo was in flight and predicted the outcome. All along the course, corrective action was based on predictions, not on final results.

Under *steering control* for strategy, in contrast to post-action control, both the target result (standard) and the predicted result lie in the future—as emphasized in Figure 12-1. Corrective action is initiated before the event. Of course, each updated prediction is based on progress to date (and this part of the process relies on the customary comparison of actual achievement against standard). To this data is added the latest information about environmental conditions. Then a new prediction about the most likely outcome is made. If the expected result is unsatisfactory, corrective action is started immediately. The whole process is completed long, long before any CPA sanctifies a report for the SEC.

Here is a classic example. When Prudential Insurance Company decided to use regional home offices as a differential advantage in its drive for top position in the life-insurance industry, it exercised steering control. Experience at the first regional offices was used to project overall expenses and income. In fact, the predicted expenses were so high that the location and original schedule for converting other regions had to be modified. Conversion of corporate headquarters was sharply revised on the basis of other early feedback. Note that steering control altered the strategic thrusts long before the total plan was in place. In this example major objectives remained unchanged, but in other cases steering control may spark adjustments in objectives as well.

DIFFICULTIES TO SURMOUNT

Steering control of strategic action faces four difficulties. (a) The *lead-times* between starting action and the desired outcome is long (and the stakes are high), so we often start controlling on the basis of only a small parcel of experience. (b) *Predictions* of outcomes are surrounded with *uncertainty*. We are unsure of the favorable and unfavorable consequences of our own actions. Meanwhile, changes in the external environment may upset our predictions. (c) The original *strategy* is likely to be *changed* because of dynamic shifts during the long lead time, before the strategy is fully executed. Thus the control target (standard) keeps moving. (d) *Objective evaluation* during the battle is difficult. Often the managers doing the steering control are also actively committed to executing the strategy. Because of this dual involvement, it is

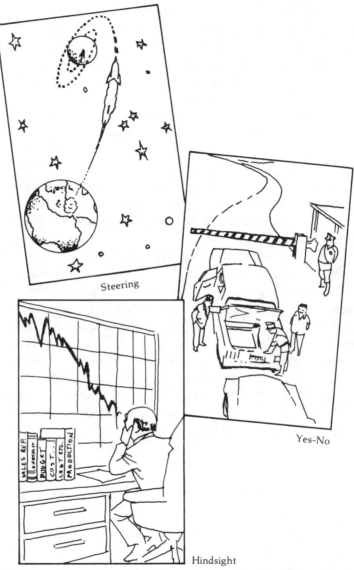

Steering

Yes-No

Hindsight

FIGURE 12-1.   Three Types of Control—For Strategy, Steering Is Most Suitable. From W. H. Newman, Constructive Control (Englewood Cliffs, N.J.: Prentice-Hall, 1975). Reprinted by permission of Prentice-Hall.

difficult for managers to be objective about rather debatable predictions, and strong pressures are needed to provoke sharp redirection.

These inherent difficulties make the application of steering control more delicate than the basic idea suggests. What to measure? When?

How to convert measurements into predictions? Who decides that strategy modifications are needed? Where do corrective action ideas come from? How can changes be made without upsetting morale? Typically, such questions as these must be answered amidst swirling action and nagging uncertainty.

The following four steps will help. They will, at least, generate vital control data and introduce orderliness into the steering-control process.

WATCH PROGRESS ON STRATEGIC THRUSTS

The action front in strategy execution is located in a series of specific, localized programs and moves. Each strategic thrust should be translated into steps, and detailed programs should be developed for those steps to be taken first—as proposed in Chapter 7. In addition, resources (finance, people, materials, facilities, and so on) should be mobilized and allocated for these early moves—as outlined in Chapter 11. In other words, by moving down means-end chains managers convert broad strategic thrusts into quite concrete planned actions and results for individual people.

Steering control can start by watching the outcomes of these specific early actions. When the local programs are formalized and measured, data on progress can be fed to the strategy controller as well as the local manager. Similarly, when separate expense and capital budgets are set up for strategic moves—as in the TI system—copies of the local control reports can go to the strategy controller. Strategic moves that are scrambled with current operations are harder to follow. For these, someone must identify what results related to strategy are expected by what dates, and then periodically check on progress being made.

This watching of progress at the action level serves two purposes. The first is to assure that the total program is moving ahead and that actions taken in various locations remain consistent with overall concept. For example, a few years ago Motorola adopted a strategy to regain its position in the C.B. radio field. A check on the engineering design of a new transmitter revealed that its size and cost exceeded the assigned specifications that had been carefully tailored to a desired niche in the market. Top executives insisted that the engineers redo their work until the specifications were met. Otherwise, various parts of the strategy would have been incompatible.

The second purpose is detecting early a need to revise the strategy. A United States instrument firm did just that. Its expansion strategy called for a series of licensees in Europe who would make simpler equipment and parts and import delicate and complex parts from the United States firm. Experience during the first year cast doubt on the wisdom of the strategy. Several desirable licensees were reluctant to take up the offer; they wanted to manufacture everything or nothing. One company that did enter the agreement was having difficulty maintaining quality standards, and the United States firm lacked power to impose its ideas on how to achieve quality. On the basis of this new data the forecast of European business through licensees was far below hopes. Consequently, the United States firm changed its strategy from licensees to joint ventures (with much better results).

Early experience may be difficult to interpret, but it does have the great virtue of providing hard data. The practical difficulty seems to be (a) clearly identifying and measuring early steps, and (b) promptly reevaluating strategy in light of this early experience.

Internal programs started specifically to support strategy should, of course, be watched closely. But when strategic moves are mixed in with short-run operations in an ongoing business, what to watch is not so clear. A good way to start is to pick the *crucial factors for success* of the plan—those developments that will have major significance in achieving strategic thrusts. Single these out from other current activities and observe them frequently.

MONITOR KEY EXTERNAL VARIABLES

Every strategy is based on an assumed (predicted) setting. Consciously or unconsciously, assumptions are made about future demand, technology, prices, government regulation, competition, and an array of other *external* variables. These assumptions are planning premises; company strategy is designed around these predicted conditions.

RELIABILITY OF PLANNING PREMISES

A crucial part of steering control is checking on the continuing reliability of these premises. If a vital assumption is no longer valid, our strategy may have to be changed. The sooner a revised premise is recognized, the better are chances that an acceptable shift in strategy can be devised. Therefore, each company should flag and systematically monitor its key external variables.

A small electronics firm, for example, concluded that it had to expand to maintain its lead in its market niche. A strategic plan involving technical, legal, and marketing moves was launched. The plan also included a public issue of stock after about one year of growth. Unfortunately, no provision was made to monitor financial markets. The stock issue that would have been easy when the strategy was conceived became impossible. In fact, the firm was so extended financially it had to sell its know-how and liquidate. Whether financial monitoring would have enabled the firm to refinance before the market broke we will never know, but it undoubtedly would have led to restraining the heavy financial commitments until sources of funds were arranged.

What To Watch

The need to monitor external variables is much clearer than knowing just which ones to focus on. Hundreds of variables might have some effect on any one company. However, to attempt to keep track of all of them would be extremely expensive, and the resulting data would swamp the analytical capacity of company managers. For steering control we must be highly selective.

Key variables are of two sorts—impersonal forces and key actors. Impersonal forces bearing on a steel company, for instance, include new technology such as continuous casting, changes in fuel costs, shifts in government import protection or other subsidies, additional ecological restraints, reduced demand for steel in automobiles, and the like. Each company must judge for itself which of these kinds of variables to watch. Major factors bearing directly on the company's differential advantage should always be included. In general, monitor variables that (a) are likely to change and (b) would have a major impact on the company if they did change.

A second set of variables to monitor is key actors—as we used that term in Chapter 5. Leading competitors, suppliers, unions and other powerful pressure groups, and government regulators are in this category. Their long-term behavior can have significant impact on the practicality of our strategy.

Note that identification of key external variables, both impersonal forces and key actors, is best done during the strategy-planning stage. When the analysis is being conducted, we are more aware of the assumptions we make. Thus part of planning should be the designation of variables that will be monitored as part of steering control. This list can, of course, be modified in subsequent milestone reviews when the total situation is reassessed and new predictions made.

LINKING PREDICTED CHANGE TO COMPANY STRATEGY

Monitoring of each variable that has been selected involves (a) gathering full, up-to-date information about the force or actor, (b) predicting future behavior, and (c) suggesting where in the company the predicted behavior could have significant impact.

To illustrate, assume that the Citizens Bank of Northern New Jersey has decided to monitor federal banking laws. (a) The analysis of active legislative proposals might lead to (b) a prediction that "national" banks would soon be permitted to place electronic tellers in out-of-state locations. (c) For Citizens Bank this would mean that large New York City banks would offer localized service, which might upset Citizens' branch setup.

Of the three components of monitoring, the second—(b), predicting—typically receives the most dicussion. Indeed, predicting is rarely easy. Nevertheless, our observation is that most companies are weaker in the other two components—(a), deciding what to watch and then systematically gathering data on that factor and (c), identifying impact linkages so that a forecast can be quickly related to specific features of company strategy. Most major external changes take time to develop and to the well-informed person do not appear as a surprise (scientific discoveries often take a generation to change technology actually in use). If you know what to look for, you often can subscribe to or purchase a suitable forecast. Recognizing the handwriting on the wall and grasping its significance are the common troublemakers.*

The nature and frequency of reports from monitoring depend largely on the typical use of the reports. Sometimes, as on a firetower lookout, no news is good news. Only unusual threats (or opportunities) need be reported. In contrast, a report on major variables that often alters action—as in wildcat oil drilling—should go regularly and quickly to the operating division. For special circumstances in which a quick choice among a few known alternatives is necessary, a report that triggers contingency plans is appropriate. (Contingency planning

---

* A sophisticated approach to these variables is SPIRE (systematic probing and identification of the relevant environment). See article by H. Klein and W. H. Newman in *Journal of Business Strategy*, Summer 1980.

is further discussed in Chapter 14.) A primary use of all sorts of monitoring reports, however, is as an input to milestone reviews—the subject of the next section.

FULL–SCALE REASSESSMENTS AT MILESTONES AND ALERTS

The steering concept in strategy control requires adaptability to new conditions. Dynamic adjustments are part of the very nature of strategy. Consequently, the control system must include opportunities to reappraise plans and progress in light of the latest developments. *Milestone reviews* serve this purpose.

Milestone reviews should include a searching look at the total strategy. A dramatic example was Boeing's assessment of its planned entry into the supersonic tranpsort (SST) market. Millions of dollars and years of scarce engineering talent had gone into designing an SST. The potential market for rapid intercontinental flights was believed to be large, and European competition threatened to get a jump on the market. To continue as planned represented a billion-dollar decision for Boeing. In fact, after thorough review, Boeing quit. The new predicted cost of an SST that would meet performance specifications became much higher than originally estimated. Also, the relatively small number of passengers combined with rising fuel costs made predicted operating expenses per passenger-mile very high. Further government subsidy was unlikely. So, in spite of its pride, patriotic pressure, and large sunk-costs, Boeing withdrew. Its revised projections and its reluctance to gamble caused the abrupt change in plans. Only an objective, full-scale reassessment could have led to this unpleasant decision.

This action stands in sharp contrast to another major aircraft decision. A few years earlier, Convair chose to continue its bid for commercial jet aircraft by shifting from its 880 plane to the 990 plane *without* a full, objective reexamination. A complete milestone review at that time could have prevented a loss of hundreds of millions of dollars.

SCOPE OF REASSESSMENT

A review of the kind being proposed takes another look at the total picture. Fresh data come from the two control steps already discussed.

The progress reports on strategic thrusts provide a basis for revised projection. These new forecasts should include estimates of (a) internal capability to complete the thrusts planned within acceptable time frames, (b) projected total costs based on costs-to-date plus revised estimates of additional costs necessary to complete the plans, and (c) revised statements of probable outcomes—in terms of both target results and undesignated side effects. Of course, many uncertainties about outcomes will remain, but the recently acquired experience and knowledge will almost always change the probabilities and risks.

Updated forecasts on future behavior of key actors and environmental changes, provided by monitoring reports, will flag significant shifts in opportunities and threats. Comparisons with competitors will show relative strength and often suggest ways to differentiate our strategy. Of course, external data need not be restricted to topics being monitored. A perceptive ear to the ground often turns up unexpected news. For steering, knowing how the terrain has changed is crucial.

The external and internal forecasts just described can be used in several ways. The expected results may be closely in line with planned strategy; at most, fine tuning is needed. Or perhaps the thrusts can be speeded up. More likely, no reason to change the basic strategy appears, but adjustments in effort, timing, or method are required. This leads to coordinated adjustments on several fronts.

Nonetheless, a full-scale reassessment also includes opportunity— indeed obligation—to reconsider the soundness of the strategy itself. Normally, a cumulative series of small changes takes place both within and outside the company. The total situation evolves as the months or even years pass. Occasionally, then, responsible executives should stand back and ask themselves whether the prevailing strategy is the best way to serve company interests. There are times when the outlook is so bleak that the situation cries out for corrective action.

Senior managers in each business-unit or division play the major role in these full-scale reassessments. They are the best informed; they are deeply concerned with the outcome; and they are in the best position to act. In multibusiness corporations, the senior executive assigned as outside director should also be an active participant. This person can assist especially in pushing for a thorough and objective analysis and may be the "spark plug" for change. Also, this person is the main communication link with corporate strategy.

1. Corporate strategy, like business-unit strategy, evolves. The corporation's desire for low risk or synergy or cash or growth from a specific unit may have altered since the business-unit's strategy was established. These readjusted corporate values obviously should be

reflected in any modification that the business-unit makes in its action plan.

2. As an outgrowth of a milestone review, the business-unit may need more resources from the corporation, or, its predicted future may have shifted so that its contribution to the corporate portfolio is altered.

The normal, constructive time to rebuild consistency between corporate and business-unit strategies is at milestone reviews. It is the occasion when redirection and rededication—if a change is needed—should occur.

What Triggers Total Reassessments?

Full-scale reviews, such as we have just described, consume time and energy. They also raise disconcerting questions for managers who are striving hard to carry out the existing strategy, so they should take place only when formal reassurance about the wisdom of the next actions is needed. Typically, three kinds of events trigger a full reassessment.

Milestones in Major Programs. Every program reaches points when large commitments of resources must be made—for example, a contract for a new plant must be signed, an issue of bonds sold, a new product placed in production, or an acquisition approved. These milestones—just ahead of the next big step—are natural times for a full-scale review. Before undertaking the commitment, the risks and probable benefits are reexamined. Another kind of milestone occurs when key uncertainties are resolved—at the time of an important court decision, report of an oil gusher (or dry hole) on the continental shelf, or completion of a market test. Strategy should be reviewed in light of this vital information.

An Alert Flashed by External Monitoring. A political coup in the Middle East may threaten our fuel supply; a leading competitor probably will go bankrupt; the FDA will soon announce that salt may be injurious to health. When such news is unexpected and, if correct, would have a significant effect on the strategy we should pursue, a full reassessment may be wise. To cite a specific illustration, information about a new tie between BBC (British Broadcasting Corporation) and Bluebird (a new pay cable network) prompted the Public Broadcasting Service to undertake a full strategy review. For years, BBC programs contributed to Public Broadcasting Service's ability to compete with commercial networks. A reduction in this advantage, coupled with already announced competition in performing arts broadcasts, meant that Public Broadcasting Service had to rethink its distinctive role in the television industry.

A Maximum Period since the Last Full Review.   Note that neither of the previous two trigger points are tied to the calendar. Instead, they provide help when it can be most effective. Only rarely does strategy advance in regular annual cycles. Nevertheless, even a stable situation should be reappraised from time to time. Creeping changes do occur. So, General Electric—for example—conducts a strategy review in each of its strategic business-units every two years, unless a review has already been triggered for a more pressing reason during that period.

Those companies and corporations that make a regular practice of full strategy reassessments—at any or all of the three kinds of trigger points—gain several benefits. The mechanics of preparing for the review and the process itself are known and can be simplified. There is less threat to morale when reviews are a normal event. Reviews are more likely to be held promptly, when needed, and—as with any recurring control—an anticipation of the evaluation prompts early voluntary self-corrections.

The strategy adopted will, of course, have an impact on short-run plans and budgets—especially when allocations for strategic moves are not separated from those for current operations. In the annual preparation of financial budgets, the preceding strategy decisions (made by top business-unit managers) should be accepted as settled. The main impact will be (a) inclusion in the annual budgets of provision for strategic moves assigned to the operating units, and (b) respect for policy constraints established during the strategy review. Clearly, our position is that strategy decisions, once made, are not subject to renegotiation during the annual budgeting process. If the strategy is felt to be unworkable, it should go back for full reassessment.

MAINTAIN INTEGRITY OF THE STRATEGIC MANAGEMENT PROCESS

The three control steps outlined thus far in this chapter go a long way in keeping a company's strategic action on track. Watching progress on strategic thrusts, monitoring external variables, and making full-scale reassessments at key intervals serve the double purpose of (a) checking on how effectively existing strategy is being pursued and (b) providing a built-in mechanism for adapting strategy to changing conditions. The *steering* control concept, with its emphasis on prediction, fits this control activity into a dynamic mode.

Even under the best conditions, however, such control is far from tight. The measurements are mostly updated forecasts, and the standards keep shifting as the strategy is revised. These limitations are inescapable. Furthermore, we want to keep the door open for creative leaps and risk taking; we want a vibrant strategy. That is why the three control steps proposed serve primarily to force managers to confront the future; how the managers respond is left open.

There is still another alternative in the wise manager's toolkit. In situations—such as legal or public relations work—in which standards are subjective and output measurement difficult, we often focus control on the *process* rather than on the results. The underlying assumption is that if the proper process is followed, the outcome should be good. This viewpoint can be applied to strategy formulation and execution.

CONTROL OF THE PROCESS

The strategic activities within a company can be judged in terms of practices recommended earlier in this book (or your refinement of them). Such an evaluation would consider:

1. What *steps* are systematically taken *to design* company strategy? Is provision made for objective and perceptive identification of opportunities and threats, for conceiving of ways to gain differential advantages, for weighing the company's relative strengths to pursue alternative strategies, for projecting outcomes in terms of risks and benefits to key actors, and for clearly defining the official choice?

2. Are provisions made to *change behavior patterns?* Is the laborious task of adjusting work habits and standards undertaken? And is this coupled with persistent, enthusiastic management support of people who do adjust their behavior?

3. Does the company's *organization aid* the strategy? Do appropriate business-units have freedom to move quickly, and is bureaucracy of support departments held in check?

4. Are qualified, committed *people* in strategic posts, and does the *reward system* encourage them to give approved strategy top priority?

5. Are *resources allocated* to nourish strategy? Is the linkage between strategy and local allotments clear? Or can approved programs be sabotaged in the capital appropriation and operating budget process?

6. Do *controls* watch progress on strategic programs and monitor key external variables? Is a system of milestone reviews in effect?

Positive answers to this imposing set of questions will provide a substantial degree of control. A majority of strategic blunders by typical companies can be avoided through process control of this sort. Wise strategic management is not guaranteed, however. Intuitive judgment remains a strong ingredient. Nevertheless, following the right steps will significantly improve the odds for success.

Reaching Back*

None of the strategy controls suggested above ties strategic decisions to individuals. Personal accountability is absent. This lack is serious, because controls on short-run results are often strong, and individuals give much closer attention to areas that are more tightly controlled. A cavalier attitude toward strategy decisions can easily develop: "Make it look good. The plan will be changed three or four times before the results show up, so why worry now? Besides, I'll be transferred long before the day of reckoning."

To overcome this tendency, a few companies *reach back* in time to tie specific decisions to specific individuals. Three steps are involved. (a) For each key decision, write down who decided and who approved. (b) Wait until results are "known." (c) Then reward or punish. For example, in a large telephone company, when a serious blunder in inadequate expansion of facilities became evident, top officials examined the records to find out who had made the decision and under what circumstances. In this instance, potential need for expansion had been pointed out by some (not all) of the staff reports, but the chief operating executive chose a lower figure. Five years after the decision he was retired early, from a different position. Similarly, a large electronics firm transferred a man out of a key job for a mistake he made four years and two jobs earlier. In each of these instances the reason for the personnel action was circulated through the executive grapevine.

One company goes a step further. *Both* the operating executives and the corporate staff people involved must concur in writing on major moves. This record is then available for audit when results are known.

Obviously, such reaching back cannot correct the mistake. Nor is the purpose to find a scapegoat. Rather, the impact lies in the attitude

* This subsection is taken from W. H. Newman, *Constructive Control* (Englewood Cliffs, N.J.: Prentice-Hall, 1975), pp. 116–117. Reprinted by permission of publisher.

generated in other executives; namely, "It could happen to me, so I'd better take seriously my decisions that have long-run effect." The aim is to create a climate that maintains the integrity of the strategic management system.

The reaching-back technique has significant limitations. Substantial historical analysis is necessary to pick out critical decisions and to reconstruct the conditions under which they were made. Did the people involved act wisely with the priorities and information available to them at that time? Unfortunately, mistakes are easier to single out than wise decisions, so the technique tends to be negative and punitive. If pursued too vigorously, executives will become too conservative and spend valuable time concentrating mainly on building a safe record.

Occasionally, reaching back can help overcome a casual attitude about strategy decisions. To be fully effective, however, it should be coupled with high rewards for persistently searching out attractive opportunities and for sagacious risk taking.

CONCLUSION

Controlling the execution of strategy is indeed difficult. (a) Pressing short-run problems tend to crowd out attention to strategy. Strategic deadlines—if they exist at all—do not seem to be as urgent as events that must be completed by next week. (b) Signals of the need for a change in existing strategy are often passive. They do not clamor for immediate remedial action. (c) The strategy itself is subject to modification. This moving target tends to obscure progress and failure. Yet this softness in the warnings only adds to the need for systematic control. Purposeful direction in the midst of crosscurrents can be sustained only by persistent efforts to keep on course.

Fortunately, steering control provides a practical means for regulating strategic action. Four ways have been suggested in this chapter— watching progress on strategic thrusts, monitoring key external variables, full-scale reassessments at milestones and alerts, and maintaining the integrity of the strategic management process. When regularly pursued, these measures both maintain efforts on an agreed-on course and also provide for timely adjustment of that course. Without such control the chances that strategic action will languish are high.

The execution of strategy—especially a new strategy—requires stong, positive support. In Part II of this book we have recommended

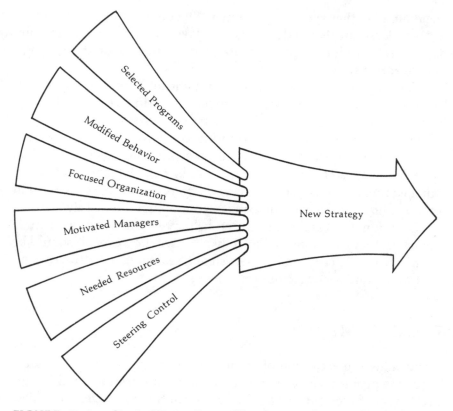

FIGURE 12–2.   Six Activating Forces That Support Strategy Execution. For recommended action see Chapters 7 through 12.

six kinds of actions that managers can take to build such support. These activating forces are: selected programs, revised behavior patterns, focused organization, carefully selected and motivated managers, appropriate resources, and steering control (see Figure 12–2).

Each of these supporting forces plays a distinct role in the total managerial effort. As we have seen in Chapters 7 through 12, each faces hurdles that must be approached with care if effective action is to emerge. Consequently, there are potential benefits from separate, concentrated examination of each area.

On the other hand, the six areas of action are interrelated. Often synergistic effects can be gained by wise combinations. It is achieving this synthesis that we probe in Part III.

PART III

INTEGRATION
Strategy as a Moving Game Plan

Fitting Pieces into a Synergistic Whole

A VARIETY OF AIDS to carrying out strategy have been advocated in Part II. Programming, behavior patterns, key personnel, rewards, resource allocations, controls—each can make a particular contribution; but to be fully effective, there is a further requirement. These aids should reinforce each other. An *integrated* system is necessary.

Here again, the spaceship analogy holds. To reach the moon Apollo had to be more than a set of parts. The parts were combined together into a balanced unity, and actions of the various subsystems were synchronized to keep the ship on the desired trajectory.

We have discussed various aids for executing strategy separately to highlight the nature and importance of each. In reality, however, they interact—the impact of one depends on how the others are being used. To implement a strategy successfully the separate pieces must be fitted together into a synergistic whole. The building of such a total system is our main focus in Part III.

Such mutual reinforcement is not always achieved. For instance, a video-deck firm failed to match its production plans with corresponding controls over marketing and engineering design; the resulting losses almost bankrupted the company. A medical-instruments company, to cite another example, chose decentralization as a way to achieve diversification; however, its resource-allocation procedure and its financial incentives continued to support strongly its traditional business. Because of this lack of integration, the decentralized divisions have had little success in launching new products.

WHAT MAKES A WELL-INTEGRATED BUSINESS?

In practice, trying to think about a business-unit or a corporation as a whole is difficult. There are so many pieces and so many relationships, we don't know where to start and where to stop. However, for purposes of strategic management, one useful approach is to consider (a) how well various parts of the management system *fit* together and (b) how the internal parts, the external impacts, and our actions can all be kept in *balance*.

Fit and balance are vital. They don't completely describe good in-

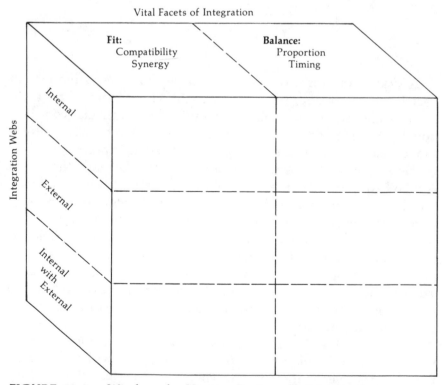

FIGURE 13–1.   *Windows for Viewing Business-Unit Integration*

tegration, but thinking carefully about fit and balance will flush out most of the important aspects. We explore these two concepts more fully in the next section.

An additional way to view integration is in terms of scope—that is, what set of activities should be balanced and fitted together? What should this interlocking web include? For a business-unit there are three sorts of webs. (a) The internal management system has many interdependencies that should be carefully merged. (b) The external relationships with different key actors must be reconciled in a way that supports the business-unit strategy. And (c) conditions agreed to in the external alignments may require modifications in the internal system, or vice versa. Of course, the process of achieving a total integration may create tugs and pulls on any of these webs.

Use of these two approaches will go a long way toward assuring integration of efforts to carry out a strategy in a business-unit. The procedure is to seek fit and balance in each of the three webs—as suggested in Figure 13-1.

To explain this process further we shall first explore the meaning of fit and then the meaning of balance—as they apply to a business-unit. In a final section of this chapter we relate these same integrating concepts to a diversified corporation. This arrangement leaves for the next chapter consideration of a dynamic, changing environment and the added demands it makes for integration over time.

BUILDING FIT INTO AN INTEGRATED MANAGEMENT SYSTEM WITHIN EACH BUSINESS-UNIT

Just as the strategy selected for a particular business-unit should be tailored to its unique history and resources, so too should the managerial design to execute that strategy be suited to the strategy and to the local setting. Thus when Michelin decided to manufacture tires in the United States, more than a new production plant was necessary: also vital were a form of organization and a set of controls that would preserve its quality image. In fact, centralized planning, very tight controls, and unusually high secrecy surround its plants. In contrast, foreign (and domestic) production of Coca-Cola is highly decentralized to licensees, and the bottling process is widely known. Here the initiative of local distributors is considered so important that organization and operations management is localized—with only product formulation and quality and some aspects of sales promotion regulated from corporate headquarters.

MANAGEMENT DEVICES THAT FIT TOGETHER

A vital aspect of both the Michelin and Coca-Cola systems is that each has its own combination of features that are harmonious. Each selects executives and provides incentives that are consistent with its pattern of organization. This fitting together is so important that we should understand what "fit" involves. Actually, we can distinguish two levels of fit.

○ The simplest form is *compatibility*. Like electronic equipment that is incompatible, some management devices create dissonance or conflict when they are placed side by side. A high-technology coated-optics company, for instance, ran into trouble when it tried to impose tight schedules and cost controls on its scientists, who had joined the company for the opportunity to do pioneering research in an informal atmosphere. In contrast, tight scheduling and cost controls are accepted as normal in television assembly plants. The issue is whether such planning and controlling fit with established behavior patterns, personnel selection, and expected rewards.

○ More potent than just compatibility is *reinforcement*. Here, two or more devices management uses to implement strategy have a combined effect that is *synergistic*. Part of IBM's strength, for instance, arises from its combining prompt repair service with customer orientation in product design. Also, in the human resource area IBM not only hires able people; it then adds stable employment, internal career opportunities, and an outstanding array of training at all levels. The repair service compounds the benefits of the product design. The internal career opportunities multiply the value of attracting strong people.

When thinking about how a particular managerial tool—such as personnel selection or organization—can aid strategy execution, the potential of that tool per se should be carefully analyzed—as we suggest in the chapters of Part II. But, before charging off in one direction, the compatibility and perhaps reinforcement of other tools must be weighed. A move that lacks compatibility can cause more trouble than benefit, whereas a reinforcing move generates power for the new strategy.

MULTIPLE DIMENSIONS OF FIT

The introduction of a new strategy into an established business creates many tensions. Values are upset; power and influence are realigned; political maneuvers are inevitable. Fit must deal with such social and behavioral issues—in addition to the more-explicit management devices just discussed.

For example, economic analysis may strongly support the addition of a casino to a resort hotel. The addition of gambling, however, shifts the atmosphere and the clientele. This change runs into *personal values* of employees. The new thrust may undercut the pride that long-service people have in the distinguished resort. Similar value and attitude frictions arise in trying to hold local country dances in a ski lodge.

The adding of a go-go product to a mature product line raises still other problems of fit. The *tempo* of action and the attention to small items of expense differ. The relative status of product developers, marketers, and production supervisors shifts. A reverse situation raises comparable tensions. Trying to turn one product into a cash cow—while the strategy for the rest of the line is building market share for popular items—requires a sharp shift in viewpoint. Not many managers or organizations can concurrently play both roles well!

The nature of competition and who bears what risks affects the way business is conducted. For instance, aerospace companies accustomed to working on government contracts are adept in contracting procedures and renegotiation. They often run into trouble, however, when they try to add a commercial product. Similarly, companies normally doing commercial business have difficulty with the process and pace of government work.

Internal politics is still another dimension of fit. A leading university, for example, decided to establish a Pacific Basin Institute that would draw faculty support from several established departments. The project received substantial backing from business firms, but internal cooperation was weak. The ambitious plans of the institute's director drew fire from entrenched department heads; the director resigned, and finally the entire venture was abandoned. An otherwise sound strategic thrust just did not fit the politics within the university.

These examples show that a good fit often has several dimensions. Our opening discussion of fit focused on managerial devices—kind of planning, organization, control systems, rewards, and the like—

because managers have more power to rearrange these. Nevertheless, questions about compatibility and reinforcement of values, tempo, risk taking, and politics also call for attention. These are all aspects of good internal integration within a business-unit.

THE SEARCH FOR EXTERNAL EQUILIBRIUM

To survive every business must obtain an array of resources, and simultaneously generate enough products, services, and other "values" to keep the resources flowing in. In Chapter 1 we called this the resource conversion process, noting that separate arrangements had to be negotiated with *each* resource supplier (and customer group) for a two-way flow: (a) the resources coming in under attractive conditions and (b) in exchange, "payments" flowing out in a manner that continues to appeal to the supplier.

Each of these deals has lots of angles: volume, timing, stability, risk level, price (often in different currencies), side effects, provision for change, and the like. They are enmeshed in laws, customs, institutions, trust, and informal obligations.

Obviously, managing all these external relations of a business-unit gets very complex. Some way of simplifying the task is necessary. Broadly, the relationships fall into three categories: (a) the major key-actor ties that must be *managed continually*—external strategy is primarily devoted to these; (b) relatively stable relationships—nevertheless potentially involving thrusts or opportunities so that *regular monitoring* is prudent; and (c) relationships with stable suppliers that involve relatively minor inputs and/or have ample alternative sources—so they can be handled on a *routine* basis.

Strategy helps managers decide which relationships to manage, which to monitor, and which to treat routinely. The choice also depends on whether each resource supplier will accept our preferred kind of relationship with him or her. It takes two to tango.

A critical issue is whether a change with one supplier will *fit* with our agreements with other suppliers. For instance, will our bank financing permit us to extend long-term credit to a foreign supplier of raw materials? Can we agree to burn coal instead of oil without running afoul of local moves to reduce air pollution? Will granting a union request for staggered hours enable us to maintain delivery service expected by our customers?

Often a move to improve one relationship upsets another—as just illustrated. But sometimes a synergistic fit can be found. For example, the Japanese contend that lifetime employment not only adds flexibility in labor practices; it also contributes to economic stability and to customer service.

External integration, then, requires that attention be given to multiple fits—to the total set of relationships a business-unit has.

COORDINATING EXTERNAL RELATIONSHIPS WITH THE INTERNAL SYSTEM

The provisions of each arrangement with an external supplier (or customer group) must be fitted into the internal system. The amount, quality, timing, and the like of inputs (of work, capital, materials, advertising service, and so on and so on) must correspond to the internal processing needs. Likewise, the internal creation of jobs, working conditions, side benefits, and the like must correspond to the external payments we have agreed to make.

When the United States government embarked on a policy of deregulating airline operations, it opened up a wide range of opportunities for new initiatives. Texas International, which had been operating exclusively in the Southwestern states, decided to enter the lucrative New York–Washington market. Taking advantage of this external opportunity required some major internal adjustments. A separate corporate entity, New York Air, had to be formed and funded. Equipment suitable for short-haul, quick-turnaround trips had to be acquired, staffed, and managed. Head-to-head competition with a solidly established Eastern shuttle operation called for new and aggressive pricing, promotion, and advertising. Almost every phase of the airline's internal structure and operating practices was affected in some way. Of course, the adjustments in one function or operational aspect had to be tailored and fitted to changes in others.

The manager of the internal system, then, faces two sorts of pressures when seeking a neatly integrated total system: (a) a good fit of managerial devices (planning system organization, incentives, and the like) discussed in an earlier section of this chapter, plus (b) workable adjustments to the diverse requirements of resource contributors. Like the space-shuttle, Columbia, the combined total must be so skillfully integrated that it will actually fly in the manner desired. Good parts are essential, but they must be compatible—and preferably synergistic—with one another.

ADDING BALANCE TO THE INTEGRATION OF EACH BUSINESS-UNIT

NEED FOR BALANCE

Balance, as we use the term here, is a refinement of fit. It has at least two dimensions: (a) the *proportion* or relative emphasis among activities, inputs, or outputs and (b) the *timing* of moves—as in walking a tightrope.

The manager of every business-unit faces the issue of relative internal emphasis to place on marketing versus R&D versus finance versus personnel, and so on. Such emphasis will be reflected not only in the allocation of funds and other resources; it is also expressed in relative power, status, and influence. For instance, a manager of an electric utility may decide to expand the number of company lawyers who deal with external pressure groups, but at the same time to keep the primary power to make final decisions on such matters with line officers.

Similarly, there must be a proper proportion among resource inputs. This relates not just to quantities received, but also to attention devoted and concessions made to various suppliers. Obviously, this balancing of the potency of external agents and of the internal departments should support the current strategy. The combined, interwoven effect is of critical importance to the results the business achieves.

There are more subtle aspects of balancing, in addition to the clear issues just noted. A manager must frequently weigh the emphasis given to:

- Short-term versus long-term problems and results.
- Internal versus external pressures.
- Continuing business versus new ventures.
- Stable, well-understood action versus flexible, unfamiliar, risky action.
- Thinking, analyzing, and planning versus getting in motion.

The way these allocations are made affects the tempo and direction of the united effort. Such balancing bears directly on the degree of integrated support a selected strategy receives.

Impact of a Strategic Thrust

The nature of this balancing act can be suggested by a brief review of a specific strategic thrust.

In the Texas International airline case cited above, the thrust into the New York–Washington commuter market on a low-price basis requires: no-frill service, stripped-down equipment, and a totally new advertising approach through radio and the daily press. Such an effort has both *direct* and *indirect* effects.

The balance among resource inputs has to be reestablished. Capital must be allocated to the East Coast venture, and this may crowd out capital requests from the established Texas division. Temporarily at least, some equipment will be reassigned; how much and when will depend on the way traffic develops in both the new and old territories. Shuttle pilots, fast-check-in clerks, and other personnel must be transferred—which opens up negotiations on both short- and long-run employment terms. Perhaps the new venture plus the old one will justify a jump in scale of operations—such as a new issue of stock—and that new scale carries with it a revised set of conditions to be met.

Any such realignment of inputs obviously requires revision of the internal operating structure. Revised organization, change procedures, new interpersonal relationships, shifts in priorities—all must be developed. There is the normal political jockeying for positions, and individuals committed to the basic Texas operations resent the new fledgling in the nest. Meanwhile, the chairman is engaged in a battle to take over a *national* airline!

Not until both (a) the new balance of external relationships and (b) the associated modifications in the internal structure have been worked through will a strategic thrust be fully effective. Attention, time, and effort are required to build a new, coordinated whole.

The complexity of all these direct and indirect realignments slows down strategic change. Rarely is the movement on so many fronts all clear sailing. This need to investigate numerous channels explains why strategic change so often is sluggish and why companies often fail to pull the total effort into sharp focus.

As a practical matter, the new system cannot be shaped all at once. The human mind cannot think about so many angles at the same time; uncertain outcomes prevent detailed planning in some areas. Instead, central managers carry out the integration process by *sequential attention* to various moves. For instance, a new product may be market tested before the organization is changed; the organization is revised before new financing is sought; and so forth. Of course, a wise manager does some scenario forecasting and broad-brush programming (see Chapter 7), but the actual implementation is almost always a staggered series of steps.

The very fact that many angles must be adjusted, and that these adjustments are usually made sequentially, creates many pitfalls in the execution of a strategic thrust. Potential sidetracks and delays abound. Inspired effort in one dimension is not enough; instead, a whole series of adjustments that fit together—and balance among these—are necessary. To maintain a sense of direction and continuous trajectory during this process, a carefully selected and persistent strategy is of great value.

Tailored System for Each Business-Unit

The management system for each business-unit should be tailor-made. Each unit has its own unique strategy. Indeed, the need for responsive and concentrated effort to outdo competitors is the primary reason for placing each business in a separate organizational unit. Both the strategy and the operating system to execute it are designed to perform a distinctive service.

Also, the resources, traditions, and strengths of any one business-unit are never just like any other business-units. The people, the history, the size, and the social structure are individualistic. Consequently, a strategic thrust that fits in one unit may be incompatible in another. The multidimensions of fit discussed above underscore the need to recognize such differences between business-units.

This conclusion complicates the management of a diversified corporation. Uniform management practices, although simpler for corporate executives to use, are unlikely to suit all operating divisions. Instead, each business-unit strives for a system fully integrated around its mission and capability. Central executives should have the insight and sophistication to deal with the resulting variations.

We are not suggesting that the management systems of business-units should differ in *all* respects. Some consistency in policy and procedures will be a strength. Indeed, many corporations develop a corporate culture that seeks to establish common values, customs, and styles. But effective strategic management does require that the internal operating system of each business-unit fits its strategy and fits together. Part of the price for strong, localized units, each with a carefully integrated operating system, is coping with differences between them.

INTEGRATION AT THE CORPORATE LEVEL

Corporate strategy, in contrast to business-unit strategy, covers a wider sweep. However, the task of artfully weaving the strands together is usually less complex. At the corporate level the stakes are larger, and each move warrants great care, but the number of interrelations that must be synchronized is fewer than those confronted almost continuously by the general manager of a business-unit.

Three kinds of knitting together do require corporate managers' attention: (a) dovetailing existing business-units within the corporate strategy, (b) fitting newly acquired units into the corporate structure, and (c) balancing resource allocations to the business-units so as to further overall corporate aims.

DOVETAILING EXISTING BUSINESS-UNITS WITHIN CORPORATE STRATEGY

From the viewpoint of senior managers, each business-unit in a diversified corporation has a role to play. So a primary step in overall integration is developing a mutual understanding of just what those roles entail. This process involves communicating the corporate strategy and the expected contribution from each business-unit. Normally, there should be some negotiation of goals, resource inputs, and constraints—a *business charter*—within which each unit formulates its own strategy. For a good fit of the business-unit into the total corporation, more than a periodic memorandum or order is necessary; a two-way exchange of facts and feelings should lead to a mutual agreement on goals, dominant values, and commitments to intermediate targets.

Once the charter and broad targets are set, corporate officers have an obligation to help make the plans come true—as outlined in Chapter 9. This continuing close relationship creates a base for sustained integration.

In addition, for those business-units involved in *corporate synergies* the fit and coordination between them become crucial. Economies of vertical integration, for example, will be achieved only if the supplier and receiver dovetail operations closely. Here the integration is similar to that needed within a business-unit, but it is more difficult to maintain because of the otherwise independent lives the business-units lead. Often some hands-on coordination from the corporate office is provided.

Likewise, the provision of *corporate services* to business-units— such as centralized R&D or centralized marketing—calls for a careful fit. Frequently the business-units are completely dependent on the corporate service unit for functions it provides, so responsiveness to local needs is critical. At the same time, people in the service division probably feel that they know best how their function should be performed. To secure integration requires a full understanding of each other's problems, sharing the same objectives, and open communications. As with corporate synergies, *organizational distance* makes difficult this kind of knitting together of effort.

In our observations, most diversified corporations have room for significant improvement in the extent to which all their business-units are integrated around corporate strategy. Improved fit is often possible through use of business-unit charters, spelling out desired synergistic action, and promoting better understanding between corporate services and business-units.

Fitting Newly Acquired Units into the Corporate Structure

Acquired business-units are even harder to integrate into a corporation's social and management structure. They already have an independent existence. Indeed, this going-concern characteristic is probably one of the main reasons for acquiring an established business rather than building one from within.

It is most unlikely that the goals, values, and practices of this new member of the family will coincide closely with those the corporation prefers. Thus, in addition to agreeing on the business-unit charter, perhaps fitting into a corporate synergy, and learning to live with centralized corporate services—the areas noted above for integration of all business-units—newly acquired units also have to merge into the corporate culture. They have to learn the subtleties of new working relationships. The new unit may prompt some modifications in the corporate culture, but this way of meshing usually takes even more time and effort than adapting to current mores of the new owner.

For instance, when the magazine publications division of the Delaware Corporation absorbed the Perlman Publications, a major hurdle was inducing Perlman employees to accept Delaware's aggressive approach to securing advertising. In another example with a different outcome, Cadbury Chocolate Company (England) successfully resisted a takeover attempt by General Foods Corporation because Cadbury directors feared that General Foods would not maintain Cadbury's famous reputation for quality, fairness to employees, and social responsibility.

Such personal values cannot be changed simply by the announcement of a new strategy. If full integration is to occur, a long process of shifting attitudes and values must be undertaken.

BALANCING RESOURCE ALLOCATIONS TO BUSINESS-UNITS

Scarce resources create another sort of corporate integration problem. Although conglomerates may be free to withhold investment in any one of their unrelated operating companies—or even sell off a subsidiary to obtain cash—corporations with interdependent activities face more complicated choices. American Can, for example, is so involved in the can business that it cannot back out. During the past decade, when it closed more than fifty inefficient old plants, it also spent $200 million on new plants. Staying in the industry requires heavy investments in at least some areas. The American steel industry is in a similar fix.

In this kind of situation, resource allocation has to be based on its impact on several different units and several different publics. The repercussions are both direct and indirect. The good of the total corporation often differs from the results shown by a single business-unit. Only by having an awareness of the total corporation can sound strategic choices be made.

CONCLUSION

Although basically a simple concept, strategy bears on almost everything that transpires in a company. Because of its permeating character, converting strategy into action runs into a series of roadblocks.

Broadly, three approaches for moving from strategy to action are advocated in this book. In Part I we stress the importance of translating broad strategic goals into strategic moves and targets. These latter parts of strategy are sufficiently concrete and immediate for managers to act on now. Then in Part II we focus on six basic procedures or steps managers should take to put the strategy into effect. Each of these is part of the make-happen phase. Important, indeed essential, as all these measures are, they are not quite sufficient.

The third approach is putting the pieces together into a workable whole that supports the strategy. Thus this chapter concentrates on the elusive concept of integration. Two aspects of this weaving the parts together are fit and balance. When thinking of fit, managers should seek at least compatibility among their diverse moves, and if possible they should push for synergistic results. Then managerial pressure will be in a direction consistent with strategy. In addition, to maintain the trajectory a balance in terms of effective proportions and timing of actions is necessary.

This kind of integrated effort should be sought at several levels— within the management structure of each business-unit, among the relationships with key actors, at the corporate level, and among all three. The aim is a workable, reinforcing set of forces that intertwines to carry out the selected strategy.

Hitting a Moving Target in a Rough Sea

S TRATEGY MANAGERS face a double task. We must build an integrated system around today's strategy—as urged in the preceding chapter—*and*, at the same time, we must be searching for ways to change and improve that strategy. In a dynamic environment the well-arranged integration that is so valuable sooner or later becomes obsolete. Thus while we are striving for balance and synergy for our current strategy, we should also be plotting yet another synthesis.

In industries such as computers or aircraft, for example, the next generation of products always lurks around the corner. Likewise, providing electrical energy (or education) is a continuing, unfolding task. Fulfilling today's needs with today's strategy calls for tremendous united, coordinated effort, but the needs, the available resources, and the ground rules are sure to change. Tomorrow the successful coalitions and technologies will probably be a redesign, a shift from what is considered optimum today.

This kind of readjustment in the midst of a balancing act is hard to do. Much effort is required to develop a carefully integrated business-unit—with its internal structure and its external relationships fitted together into a synergistic, balanced system. Because such a synchronized system has so many interdependencies, it tends to be inflexible. Managers are reluctant to upset the finely tuned relationships they have worked so hard to establish. Yet, adapt they must. It is like asking a long-distance swimmer to start in a new direction before he or she has quite reached the first shore.

In this chapter we confront the dynamic side of that dilemma. Here we recognize that strategic targets often do move and that the environment may be unfriendly and rough. Nonetheless, the moving target can and should be pursued.

EVER-CHANGING PRESSURES FOR ACTION

Strategic action is always based on some assumptions about the future and on predictions about how key actors will behave. Actually, all such predictions are uncertain. The demand for gasoline made from coal, for example, is surrounded with if's, as is governmental subsidy of higher education.

Unfolding Opportunities and Risks

The uncertainties faced by many businesses involves more than, say, a dry summer or cold winter. Several interrelated variables may be in doubt; they might move at the same time, but more likely one will change and then after an unknown interval a second move could affect a third; even the rules of the game may shift.

Commercial banking illustrates this unfolding process. On the technological front, electronic equipment for the handling of checks and depositor accounts has already forced small banks into multiunit chains; automated tellers permit customer contacts at locations where branches are impractical; within a decade two-way display terminals may bring banking into the home. Meanwhile, legislation permitting multistate banking is under serious discussion. Such new rules plus the new technology could lead to very large national banks and could otherwise change the structure of the industry.

But that structure is already being challenged by new competitors. Stockbrokers are offering the equivalent of checking accounts. Insurance companies are buying up stockbrokers. Mail-order houses and credit-card companies perform several functions that banks might do. And inflation—yet another uncertainty—is so undermining normal interest-rate relationships that savings banks are turning to commercial banking functions to stay alive. Varying state and national regulations compound the uncertainty.

Such shifts as these create opportunities for those who can position themselves to provide a synergistic group of services with a differential advantage. Obviously, the risks are high and are sure to change as the new structure unfolds. Executing a strategy in such a hostile environment calls for unusual adaptability—a quality not traditionally stressed in conservative banking!

Contrasts Among Business-Units

Not all businesses face as drastic a set of changes as do banks. For example, the formulation and method of sale of Mentholatum has continued with very little modification for over half a century. Nevertheless, a close look at most industries reveal some significant shifts in technology, competition, or markets. Even cement manufacturers had to modify their preferred production process when OPEC skyrocketed energy costs.

Because the nature, severity, and frequency of change vary widely between industries, each business-unit requires separate consideration. Status quo may be smart strategy for some units that are well positioned. A cash cow may lack glamor, but such business-units make vital contributions to their owners and to society. For the strategic manager, however, there is always a question about how long to stay with a winning pattern. At some point, tranquility—with its natural stodginess and inertia—turns into a storm—as the banking example cited above illustrates. Then strategic change is a matter of life or death.

KEY TO ADAPTABILITY: PROGRESS REASSESSMENTS

When a company's environment shifts significantly—or preferably as soon as such shifts can be predicted—it should reassess its existing strategy. The unfolding of opportunities and risks may offer—or perhaps require—some modification in plans. The sequence of moves previously preferred may be upset; a slowdown or an acceleration may be called for; new external developments may force a reevaluation of risks; earlier alternatives may become unfeasible; possibly, entirely new alternatives may emerge.

A *progress reassessment* takes a total look at the current situation, company progress to date, and future prospects. The reassessment includes:

○ Review stakeholders—the resource suppliers, major customers, and other key actors whose continuing cooperation is vital or who could undercut company progress toward strategic goals. Has the attractiveness of our domain changed? Has our ability to establish the selected differential advantage changed? Do we have more or fewer bargaining chips with each stakeholder?

○ Decide where action is most needed. In light of current and anticipated developments, what sequences and lead times now appear best? This adjustment of priorities relates to major fronts and to moves within fronts.

○ Adjust strategic thrusts to reflect any revision of priorities and internal capabilities. Internal strengths and values evolve during the same period that the outside environment changes. New action programs should take into account both current capabilities and reformed opportunities.

○ Modify the allocation of scarce resources to fit any adjustments in strategic thrusts.

Such a progress reassessment is similar to a milestone review which, as noted in Chapter 7, is a basic feature of programming. However, a progress reassessment may be triggered by more subtle shifts, often leading to new perspectives on the entire strategy of a company. Redirection is certainly an alternative that should be considered.

LEARNING TO USE FULL-SCALE STRATEGY REASSESSMENTS

When executing a strategy in a hostile environment with high uncertainty, obviously the probability that the strategy will be altered is large. An electric automobile, for instance, might fit a different niche than the one originally sought. Electronic teaching machines may find a much larger market in industrial training than in public education. Possibly Mexico will become a friendly source of foreign crude oil. If progress reassessments are used in such settings, several zigs and zags are likely before a strategy reaches final fruition. *

This emerging at a different point than initially planned poses problems in motivation. We build excitement and commitment around a

---

* For a description of this process see J. B. Quinn, *Strategies for Change* (Homewood: Richard D. Irwin, 1980).

strategic mission, but then midstream we alter the course. For example, the original crew who dreamed of satellite communications with the Eskimos may find on-line commercial banking less appealing, and employers in operating departments may wish the big shots would make up their minds on where they want to go.

The challenge is to maintain enough continuity and persistence of effort to benefit from momentum while at the same time recognizing that some adapting to changing opportunities will undoubtedly be necessary. Living with uncertainty calls for a capacity to learn—and adjust—en route.

Strategic thrusts are the chief mechanism for this adaptive behavior. They permit focused attention on one or two steps at a time. Strategy is achieved by a sequence of such steps. In uncertain situations flexibility is attained primarily by adjusting the nature and timing of the steps. At any given moment, however, the immediate tasks are clear—and expressed in operational terms. We continue flying, purposefully and disciplined, even if the trajectory has been adjusted to a different arrival point or time.

FACTORS AFFECTING AMOUNT OF REDIRECTION

Dramatic external events are the most obvious causes of changes in strategy. Oil discovered on the North Slope, Congress slashing a foreign-aid program, interest rates at twenty-five percent, and the like may raise problems or opportunities. Competitors' actual and likely moves are also widely recognized causes. Most systematic screening devices, including the analysis of key actors outlined on pages 74 to 77, will flush out this sort of information for a progress reassessment.

A variety of other factors should also be weighed. Often these relate to feasibility and political backing. Figure 14–1 suggests the kind of considerations that enter into a decision to modify a strategy. Significant changes in any of these dimensions may lead to redirection, especially when coupled with recognized external shifts.

SEQUENTIAL MOVES IN FACE OF UNCERTAINTY

Progress reassessments provide enough flexibility for most companies. When necessary, strategy can be modified as the dynamic environment and competition unfold. Some businesses, however, face great

---

INTANGIBLE FACTORS BEARING ON
MODIFICATION OF STRATEGY

A. Boldness of existing strategy
      Its fit with existing company strengths and executive attitudes
      Its difference from previous strategy
      Replacement vs. add-on of activities
      Perceived uncertainty and risks

B. Source of new alternatives (modifications)
      Externally imposed vs. internally generated
      Derived by analysis vs. proposed by missionary for idea
      Participation in formulation by those who carry out proposal

C. Timeliness of alternatives
      Unique and fleeting opportunity
      Importance of a head start
      Defensive move vs. offensive
      Other commitments of existing resources

**D. Commitment of respected, charismatic, powerful leaders within
company to present strategy and to alternatives**

E. Congruence with aims of resource suppliers
      Fit with values of key employees and political factors within company
      Acceptability to outside reference groups (banks, neighbors, regulators, etc.)
      Personal opportunities for self-actualization, achievement, etc. at key places in
      the organization

F. Fit with total company operations
      Compatibility with internal operating system
      Compatibility with other external relationships

Note: This list is intended to be suggestive rather than comprehensive.

FIGURE 14-1.   Intangible Factors Bearing on Modification of Strategy

uncertainty, and the magnitude of their risks is severe. The production of liquid fuel from oil shale, for instance, still confronts major technological and economic unknowns, yet the magnitude of investment required for commercial oil-shale ventures is very large. Biological engineering of human characteristics is even more hazardous.

How can strategic management cope with such high orders of insecurity? Rash gambling on the future is an unsatisfactory answer, yet many of us believe that private enterprise is the best instrument to explore business frontiers. Some means of feeling one's way is needed. Two variations of strategic management serve this end: *advance by stages* and *prepared opportunism.*

ADVANCE BY STAGES

A basic way to confront complex, uncertain situations is to take one hurdle at a time—once the general direction is agreed on. Instead of attempting to lay out a complete program in detail, one or two thorny problems are tackled first. If and when workable answers to these problems are found, then another obstacle is examined. Thus the various facets of the situation are dealt with one after another—not all at once.

Typically, for orientation, all aspects of the situation are considered sequentially but promptly. Some broad-brush plans will be developed, recognizing that many unsupported assumptions were made. This preliminary overview (a) gives a rough estimate of potential benefits and costs—an estimate that indicates whether further work is justified. The overview also (b) guides the choice of where to start digging in more deeply. Perhaps improved technology is crucial, or legal constraints must be removed. These early moves are then set up as strategic thrusts.

Because the outcome of these first moves is so uncertain, little planning of other steps is done. The venture is moved through first one stage, then another. The early work proceeds on faith that if the immediate problem can be overcome, ways will be found later to deal with other facets.

Such advance by stages has obvious drawbacks. Much of the work is experimental, with the final use very tentative; consequently, it is poorly suited for building high personal commitment. The "facts" regarding feasibility and external cooperation keep changing, and the choice of future directions often changes opportunistically; this is confusing to a variety of people who will be affected by the final outcome. Risk is compounded because optimum solutions to a facet being studied may not fit with other, later thrusts. Perhaps secrecy will be imposed for tactical reasons, and this further restricts understanding of what the work is all about.

Nevertheless, a stage-by-stage approach may be the only practical way to narrow down the uncertainty. In spite of its staggered progress, moves toward a potentially attractive domain are being made. When a practical way to deal with one uncertainty is found, then the total situation is reassessed, and if it is still attractive, another uncertainty is confronted.

To control the advance by stages, specified milestone reviews are important. (a) They create occasions when bail-out decisions can be made, if results to date are unattractive. (b) They call for judgments on success that is adequate to justify starting on the next stage—rather than waiting until everything is complete and only then moving to the next stage.

PREPARED OPPORTUNISM

For some uncertainties, only the passage of time will unveil the practical opportunities and obstacles, yet senior managers may believe that the potential rewards are so attractive that the company should not merely wait.

Prepared opportunism is one answer. The principle is to take steps now that will place the company in a position to move rapidly—ahead of competitors—when opportunities do appear.

Several companies are pursuing this approach to trade with the People's Republic of China. The probable volume of their business during the next two or three years does not warrant the effort required to establish rapport and learn how to deal with the Chinese government. Those firms that invest such effort now will be poised to act promptly, if and when trade attractive to them opens up.

A construction company in the Northeastern United States is using a prepared-opportunism strategy toward urban renewal. The company foresees slow growth in its present domain—school and commercial buildings. On the other hand, transportation costs and a variety of other factors suggest that conversion and modernization of existing urban structures may become much more common. Currently, few of the larger construction companies know how to do this kind of work. A host of unresolved problems exist—financing, taxation, rent controls, neighborhood rejuvenation, and the like. So the construction company now seeks only a few projects to learn and to establish a reputation. With this background, however, it will be prepared to grasp opportunities when they do unfold.

Prepared opportunism involves risks, as both the China trade and urban renewal examples suggest. No one knows when large expansion will take place nor the specific strengths that will then be valuable. But it is a way of staking out a position before the fog lifts.

Clearly, prepared opportunism presumes that we can identify some factors that will be crucial for success *if* and *when* the opportunity does arise—because these are the areas we should develop in advance of future competitors.

Strategy, then, can be adapted to varying degrees of uncertainty. Careful programming of a series of strategic thrusts is wise when uncertainty is low. If the future and outcomes become more murky, progress reassessment, advance by stages, and prepared opportunism can be used. The final strategic mission will probably differ from that initially conceived—as indicated in Figure 14-2. Nevertheless, the company's

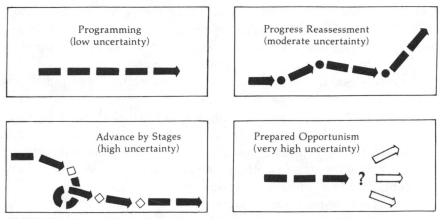

FIGURE 14-2.   Ways of Adjusting Strategic Planning to Uncertainty

fit to its environment should be much better than the fit of companies that change strategy only when the future is clear.

CONTINGENCY PLANS

A preset alternative course of action permits quick response. We use this device for emergencies—fire, snowstorms, power failures, and the like—and also for rerouting an airplane or spaceshuttle. So, why not apply the concept to a wider variety of uncertain conditions?

Note that contingency plans are particularly helpful:

1. When the nature of the uncertain conditions can be *forecast with considerable specificity*. The timing and one or two other variables are decided at the moment, but most of the action is already laid out on the basis of a host of assumptions regarding conditions and alternatives.

2. When the *cost of delay will be high or ruinous*. The contingency plan, we hope, snatches assets from destruction or grasps a fleeting opportunity. However, if time is available to reassess and replan, then a preset plan is unnecessary; the response can be suited to actual conditions instead of assumed conditions.

3. Or, when the *particular conditions are likely*—as is rain at a June wedding.

For strategic action by a business-unit, these prerequisites for contingency planning are rarely met. With so many variables in motion, specific forecasts several years in advance are very difficult. Also, typically some time is available for a progress reassessment. Consequently, strategic managers seldom deal with a situation like a powerless space shuttle coming in for a pinpoint landing.

Nevertheless, the concept of contingency plans does emphasize several features of strategic management.

○ Organization skill in replanning is critical when the domain of a company is highly dynamic. Such skill—which grows out of frequent and thoughtful recycling of strategic plans—enables the company to respond promptly to new contingencies. Prompt response, rather than preset plans, has much greater flexibility.

○ Steering controls and progress reassessments should become a normal practice. Such monitoring raises a flag when replanning is desirable.

○ A good time to identify issues to monitor is during the original strategy planning. Then assumptions, doubts, and concerns are still fresh. Potential roadblocks, and the damage they would do, can be flagged. Such an analysis sharpens the preparation for unfavorable events.

○ Possible retreats, that is, alternative use of assets and other ways to limit one's losses, should be incorporated into business plans whenever feasible.

These features will give a company many of the benefits sought in contingency planning, without the expense and inflexibility associated with most formal plans for uncertain events.

FREQUENCY OF PROGRESS REASSESSMENTS

A yearly review of company strategy is typical of many planning systems. Two of the three procedures summarized in Chapter 6 call for annual reassessments. The differences in rates of change among various businesses, noted especially in these last two chapters, may not fall into such a convenient pattern.

STEADY-STATE BUSINESS-UNITS

In highly dynamic industries a review of company strategy at least once a year is often desirable. Rarely will the basic strategy change that often, but thrusts may need adjustment. By contrast, companies in mature industries face fewer pressures to change. The wise behavior of well-established companies in, say, the builders' hardware or wall-paper industries may be diligent pursuit of established strategies.

In fact, frequent strategy reassessments in steady-state companies have drawbacks. A full-scale reassessment takes a lot of managerial effort that might otherwise be devoted to improving operations. Also, unnecessary reviews tend to switch attention to routine issues; the expectation and excitement of tackling a strategic challenge gets lost. When this occurs strategic planning becomes discredited; many managers feel that it is "a waste of time." This attitude is a handicap later when strategic action is really needed.

For steady-state business-units, then, a full-scale strategy reassessment once every two or three years is probably ample. If spaced out widely, a review that reconfirms the basic strategy is a helpful reminder of where and how the company achieves distinctiveness. With the passage of time, one or more new strategic thrusts probably will be beneficial.

If scheduled reviews are widely spaced, an explicit condition should be the obligation of key executives to watch for unexpected developments and to request an earlier reassessment if the wisdom of the existing strategy is in doubt. For example, major moves by competitors, new technology, significant loss in market position, a drop in gross margins, and a large new market are the kinds of events that suggest a prompt strategy review. Both business-unit executives and corporate executives should have this obligation, and the extended schedule should be no excuse for not speaking up promptly.

COPING WITH ERRATIC CHANGES

A more common difficulty with the annual planning cycle is that developments which prompt new strategic action often do not respect the calendar. They may occur (or become predictable) before or after the normal yearly date.

The fullest adjustment to irregular strategic opportunities is a system like that of TI (outlined in Chapter 6). The entire strategy development process is cut loose from the calendar and follows its own schedule. Exploratory work is subdivided into projects, and completion dates for these are set in light of the size of the task, external pressures, and alternative uses for scarce resources. This arrangement gives great flexibility in moving strategic changes quickly or slowly. Speedy action itself may be an element in the strategy.

Successful use of a system like TI's calls for sophistication and experience in strategic management, and for widespread commitment of managerial effort to make it work. Not all companies have this capability, and their environment may not be dynamic enough to warrant the expense.

A more conservative arrangement is to follow a scheduled annual cycle as a normal practice, but to provide for special planning reviews when a prompt decision is needed or when key information becomes available or a breakthrough achieved at a date far in advance of the normal review. If a special assessment has been made during the year, then the discussion at the annual meetings will be abbreviated.

In companies in which the strategic planning process is well understood, exceptions to the pattern can be taken in stride. Exceptions imposed on a weak system, however, add confusion about who should do what, when. Just as a football team has to learn to work together before it tries special plays, so too does a company need an established pattern of strategic management.

Even though annual strategic planning may not coincide with external changes, an established yearly cycle does have several merits:

- It assures that some thought is given to strategy—short-run pressure cannot entirely crowd out strategic thinking.
- Bridges can be built between strategy and shorter-run plans and allocations, which are geared to years, quarters, and months.
- The customary measurements of annual results can be more easily related to strategic target results.

To obtain these benefits strategic action has to be translated into annual bites. Thus even when an erratic, jerky environment forces strategic planning to reassess at irregular intervals, and when strategic thrusts are scheduled sporadically to get a jump on competitors, annual implementing plans have value. They fit more easily to the operating world, where much of the thinking is in terms of what should be done in the next calendar period.

For most corporations, then, an annual strategic planning cycle sets up the basic system. Steady-state business-units may not go through a full reassessment every year, but the existing strategy does provide a base for more-detailed yearly operating plans. Volatile business-units, on the other hand, may step outside of the annual cycle to make prompt decisions—but here also the desired strategic action should be restated in terms of results by calendar periods. These target results provide the basis for specific operating plans. Such translation of strategy into annual bites is a significant step in fitting strategy execution into the total management system.

CORPORATE INPUTS TO PROGRESS REASSESSMENTS

Corporate managers, as well as business-unit managers, help to confront turbulent and hostile environments. They should be active on three fronts.

First, corporate managers help the various business-units adjust to their respective worlds. That operating level is where goods and services are actually made and sold. So the senior executives participate in progress reassessments as *outside directors*. Perhaps they requested that the reassessment be undertaken. They may offer advice as an interested outside observer. Even more important is assuring that the reassessment process is objectively pursued. If the business-unit seems unable to cope with its changing situation, replacement of local executives may be necessary. The aim is to help each business-unit fit its particular environment.

Second, corporate managers should adjust their portfolio aims in light of the changing prospects of existing and potential business-units. For this purpose, progress reassessments should be undertaken, also at the corporate level. Normally, inputs from the existing business-units to the corporate reassessment should flow from reviews the units undertake for their own benefit.

The ever-shifting opportunities for the different business-units sooner or later will lead to a change in the portfolio role assigned to particular units. In the traditional product–life-cycle pattern, stars become cash cows, old cows are sold off (or rejuvenated), and so on. The mechanism for managing these portfolio roles is the business-unit charter. To tie revised portfolio aims into business-unit planning, agreements regarding terms of the charter must be renegotiated.

New roles for business-units should be set realistically. One issue is what can be done in the present and future setting. A second issue is how fast a business-unit can change direction. Because of the need for both external and internal integration—discussed in the preceding chapter—the time required to make a significant change is long, often two to four years. Unless corporate managers take these facts of life into account when they design portfolio changes, the nominal corporate strategy will not be carried out.

Third, senior managers must assemble and reallocate corporate resources in a way that supports new missions. In addition to capital, these allocations may include key personnel, scarce raw materials, or even prime attention by a centralized marketing organization. By no means least is an adjustment of the reward and recognition system so that backing the updated strategy pays off personally.

CONCLUSION

The underlying purpose of strategy is to enable managers to grasp the initiative in a changing, complex, interacting environment. Through strategic management they take advantage of new opportunities, instead of passively reacting to a host of unfriendly forces.

The degree of turbulence faced by managers varies. In this book we have focused first on evolutionary, more-or-less predictable changes. Then in this last chapter we have suggested ways to deal with higher levels of uncertainty.

If the desired strategy is known and accepted, then a manager can carry it out through the following measures: use programs for next steps (strategic thrusts); earmark parts of capital and operating budgets for new development and place constraints on long-term payout expenditures that are not consistent with new directions; review and, if necessary, revise all policies for compatibility with the new strategy; be sure that the organization can effectively stress the activities selected for differential advantage; put competent, committed, and loyal people in all key positions; tie incentives to new, not former, missions; and install controls to track the continuing desirability and effectiveness of the strategy.

Such steps are not easy, especially when fitting them together into an integrated, synergistic system, but the approach is clear and straightforward.

High uncertainty creates additional problems and risks for the strategic manager. In the more volatile situations strategy is not yet clearly formulated, because of environmental uncertainties and unknown responses to our own moves. Here we must plan as we run. Even when the strategy is better defined, it keeps moving. Nevertheless, managers can still utilize strategic management if they: make progress reassessments when significant changes are flagged and advance by sequential stages, or if necessary, rely on prepared opportunism.

To assure that the strategic effort does not get buried in day-to-day maneuvers, the manager can: isolate the development budget from the regular budget so that development is not unintentionally deferred to make a short-run showing; exempt experimental activities from some established policies or constraints; assign new work to individuals known to be sympathetic to potential new directions; establish task forces or subsections to focus on attractive prospects.

The push exerted in any of the foregoing moves should, of course, take the political climate into account. Timing will depend on active opposition, support, and competing claims on resources. These non-economic factors should be included in each progress reassessment.

This chapter, Hitting a Moving Target in a Rough Sea, makes clear that strategic management is very far from a set procedure or a science. Nevertheless, our observations of successful strategic managers convinces us that the approaches summarized in this book do place strategic action within the grasp of those who have the determination to try. If effectively done, strategic management can have even greater pay-offs in rough seas than in clear sailing.

Selected References

CHAPTER 1—THE REALM OF STRATEGY

ANSHEN, MELVIN, *Corporate Strategies for Social Performance.* New York: Macmillan, 1980. Broad analysis of the problems corporations face in dealing realistically with new social pressures and the new social contract.

GLUCK, FREDERICK W., STEPHEN P. KAUFMAN, and STEVEN A. WALLECK, "Strategic Management for Competitive Advantage," *Harvard Business Review*, July 1980. Identifies and describes four phases in the evolution of formal strategic planning, from financial planning to strategic management.

GUTH, WILLIAM D., "Corporate Growth Strategies," *The Journal of Business Strategy*, Fall 1980. Social costs and depletion of resources will affect current growth strategies and change the ways in which corporations pursue growth in the future.

RICHARDS, MAX D., *Organizational Goal Structures.* St. Paul: West Publishing, 1978. Covers such topics as corporate and business goals, environmental and societal goals, and the relationship between goals and formal planning systems.

SETHI, S. PRAKASH and CARL L. SWANSON, Eds., *Private Enterprise and Public Purpose.* New York: Wiley, 1981. A wide-ranging collection of papers on the role of business enterprise in society and on the relations of companies with social issue groups.

CHAPTER 2—STRATEGIC DIRECTION OF A BUSINESS-UNIT

HALL, WILLIAM K., "Survival Strategies in a Hostile Environment," *Harvard Business Review*, September 1980. A study of sixty-four companies in eight mature industries reveals that the strategies adopted by successful firms share some common characteristics.

HOFER, CHARLES W. and DAN E. SCHENDEL, *Strategy Formulation: Analytical Concepts*. St. Paul: West Publishing, 1978. An overview of the field designed for both executives and students. Chapters 5 and 6 offer thorough coverage of strategic analysis and decision-making at the business level.

PORTER, MICHAEL E., *Competitive Strategy: Techniques for Analyzing Industries and Competitors*. New York: Free Press, 1980. Comprehensive coverage of competitive strategy wr''ten for executives. Chapters 9 through 13 cover strategies for competing in emerging, mature, and declining industries, as well as in global industries.

ROTHSCHILD, WILLIAM E., *Strategic Alternatives: Selection, Development and Implementation*. New York: AMACOM, 1979. A General Electric strategic planner writes about finding strategic alternatives and the extension of such alternatives into plans for functional areas. The aim is to stimulate managers to think creatively about their strategic options.

SOUTH, STEPHEN E., "Competitive Advantage: The Cornerstone of Strategic Thinking," *The Journal of Business Strategy*, Spring 1981. An executive discusses competitive advantage and how to get an organization to think strategically.

CHAPTER 3—PORTFOLIO STRATEGY FOR A DIVERSIFIED CORPORATION

HARRIGAN, KATHRYN RUDIE, *Strategies for Declining Businesses*, Lexington: D. C. Heath, 1980. What is the best strategy for a company operating a business in a declining industry? After studying sixty firms in eight industries, the author proposes a contingency approach with high reliability for this sample. Some statistical material, but generally readable.

HOFER, CHARLES W. and DAN E. SCHENDEL, *Strategy Formulation: Analytical Concepts*. St. Paul: West Publishing, 1978. Chapter 4 provides good, basic coverage of portfolio strategy. In Chapter 7, strategic decision-making at the corporate level—and how to improve it—becomes the focus.

LORANGE, PETER and RICHARD F. VANCIL, *Strategic Planning Systems*. Englewood Cliffs: Prentice-Hall, 1977. An interactive planning system integrates strategic management at the corporate and business levels. Case studies show how the concepts apply in different corporate settings.

PORTER, MICHAEL E., "Please Note Location of Nearest Exit: Exit Barriers and Planning," *California Management Review*, Winter 1976. Exit barriers may encourage companies to hold on to unprofitable businesses. Some of these barriers are described, along with their implications for corporate strategy.

SALTER, MALCOLM A. and WOLF A. WEINHOLD, *Diversification Through Acquisition*. New York: Free Press, 1979. After providing a conceptual framework for strategy, product/market, and risk/return analysis, the authors relate this framework to the histories of some well-known diversifiers and close with a discussion of relevant antitrust issues. Written for managers.

CHAPTER 4—CORPORATE INPUT STRATEGY

BLOIS, K. J., "Quasi-Integration as a Mechanism for Controlling External Dependencies," *Management Decision*, January 1980. Quasi-integration is proposed as an attractive alternative to vertical integration under correct circumstances, because it reduces uncertainty of supply at relatively little cost. Author is an economist.

COREY, E. RAYMOND and STEVEN H. STAR, *Organizational Strategy: A Marketing Approach*. Boston: Division of Research, Graduate School of Business Administration, Harvard University, 1971. Analysis of placing marketing activities at the corporate versus business-unit level. Includes case studies and commentaries on thirteen organizations studied in depth.

GLUCK, FREDERICK W., RICHARD N. FOSTER, and JOHN L. FORBIS, "Cure for Strategic Malnutrition," *Harvard Business Review*, November 1976. An engaging case study that demonstrates the need for a corporate strategy to coordinate R&D efforts in a multidivisional company.

NEES, DANIELLE, "Increase Your Divestment Effectiveness," *Strategic Management Journal*, April 1981. A study of fourteen divestments in the United States and Europe shows that, contrary to common practice, inclusion of the manager of the division to be divested in the search for a new owner tends to yield better results.

PITTS, ROBERT A., "Strategies and Structures for Diversification," *Academy of Management Journal*, June 1977. Scholarly comparison of diversification by acquisition versus internal development. Internal diversifiers have much larger corporate R&D departments and are more likely to supply their own business-unit managers.

CHAPTER 5—SHAPING EXTERNAL ALIGNMENTS

ALLISON, GRAHAM T., *Essence of Decision: Explaining the Cuban Missile Crisis*. Boston: Little, Brown, 1971. Penetrating analysis of strategies employed in the Cuban missile crisis in terms of three models: rational decisions made by a single actor, outcomes of organizational processes, and outcome of political processes.

MACMILLAN, IAN C., *Strategy Formulation: Political Concepts*. St. Paul: West Publishing Company, 1978. Delves into such issues as identification of key actors, forming coalitions and alliances, and anticipating strategic countermoves. Three case studies tie together and illustrate the concepts developed.

MAZZOLINI, RENATO, *Government Controlled Enterprises: International Strategic and Policy Decisions*. New York: Wiley, 1979. Applies Allison's (*op. cit.*) framework to business (123 European government controlled enterprises), expanding the political-process model and including non-crisis decisions.

MINTZBERG, HENRY, "Organizational Power and Goals: A Skeletal Theory," in *Strategic Management: A New View of Business Policy and Planning*, Dan E. Schendel and Charles W. Hofer, Eds. Boston: Little, Brown, 1979. Identifies several basic structures of external and internal coalitions and proposes six theoretical power configurations in organizations.

PORTER, MICHAEL E., *Competitive Strategy: Techniques for Analyzing Industries and Competitors*. New York: Free Press, 1980. How to analyze industries and competitors, read market signals, develop advantageous strategies toward buyers and suppliers, and predict industry change.

CHAPTER 6—BIRTH AND NOURISHMENT OF A NEW STRATEGY

HUNSICKER, J. QUINCY, "Can Top Managers Be Strategists?" *Strategic Management Journal*, January 1980. CEO's can play a dynamic role in revitalizing the planning process by influencing the range of issues tackled, questioning assumptions, and striking a balance between advocacy and consensus.

LORANGE, PETER, *Corporate Planning*. Englewood Cliffs: Prentice-Hall, 1980. A complete guide to corporate planning systems as a tool for strategic decision making. Includes analysis of planning needs; the design, implementation and management of planning systems; and the roles of executives.

NORMANN, RICHARD, *Management for Growth* (translated by N. Adler from Swedish). New York: Wiley, 1977. Develops a theoretical framework for corporate growth, including sources of impetus for growth, problems that may arise, and some ways to handle the problems.

QUINN, JAMES BRIAN, *Strategies for Change: Logical Incrementalism.* Homewood: Richard D. Irwin, 1980. A good look at how organizations really initiate and manage strategic change. Based on more than fifty in-depth interviews with senior executives of United States and foreign firms.

ZAND, DALE E., "Reviewing the Policy Process," *California Management Review*, Fall 1978. Presents a model for reviewing and reforming the strategic planning process, along with suggestions for applying the model constructively in an organization.

CHAPTER 7—PROGRAMMING
—TOO MUCH OR TOO LITTLE

CLELAND, DAVID T. and WILLIAM R. KING, *Systems Analysis and Project Management*, 2nd ed. New York: McGraw-Hill, 1975. A nonmathematical textbook written for business and engineering students that equates systems analysis with strategic planning and project management with the programmed execution of strategy by means of such management science techniques as Gantt charts and PERT networks.

DIRSMITH, MARK W., STEPHEN F. JABLONSKY, and ANDREW D. LUZI, "Planning and Control in the U.S. Federal Government: A Critical Analysis of PPB, MBO and ZBB," *Strategic Management Journal*, October 1980. Research-oriented and crammed with references, this article reviews the use of PPB, MBO, and zero-base budgeting by the United States government. Comprehensive tables compare the characteristics of the three systems and organizational factors influencing their effectiveness.

LORANGE, PETER, *Corporate Planning: An Executive Viewpoint.* Englewood Cliffs: Prentice-Hall, 1980. Chapters 4 and 5 contain a general discussion of programming implementation problems and links between programming and other phases of the planning process.

QUINN, JAMES BRIAN, *Strategies for Change: Logical Incrementalism.* Homewood: Richard D. Irwin, 1980. Chapter 4 in particular makes a strong case for introducing change incrementally. Contains many references to real business situations.

STEINER, GEORGE A., *Strategic Planning.* New York: Free Press, 1979. Chapters 12 and 13 list the steps necessary to translate strategy into functional programs, and functional programs into budgets and other specific decisions.

CHAPTER 8—BUILDING REVISED PATTERNS OF BEHAVIOR

BAKER, EDWIN L., "Managing Organizational Culture," *Management Review*, July 1980. Culture misfit during periods of change and culture clash between merging firms can hurt performance. The author lists ways to modify culture and restore harmony.

KOTTER, JOHN P., LEONARD A. SCHLESINGER, and VIJAY SATHE, *Organization*. Homewood: Richard D. Irwin, 1979. Chapter 7 lists several basic reasons why people fear change and suggests methods for overcoming the resistance. The methods are summarized in a table that includes advantages, disadvantages, and appropriate uses of each. Also included are relevant case studies and additional readings.

PASCALE, RICHARD T. and ANTHONY G. ATHOS, *The Art of Japanese Management: Applications for American Executives*. New York: Simon & Schuster, 1981. An absorbing study of management practice in thirty-four high-performing United States and Japanese firms. Shows how management style, staffing, distinctive skills, and superordinate goals are as important as strategy, structure and systems in achieving results.

PETERS, THOMAS J., "Symbols, Patterns and Settings: An Optimistic Case for Getting Things Done," *Organizational Dynamics*, Autumn 1978. Proposes a number of tools managers can use to signal strategic change and suggests manipulation of dominant values to sustain change over time.

SCHLEH, EDWARD C., "Strategic Planning . . . No Sure Cure for Corporate Surprises," *Management Review*, March 1979. To prevent and overcome problems that often arise during the execution of strategies, managers should focus on changing tactics as well.

CHAPTER 9—ORGANIZING TO EXECUTE STRATEGY

CHANDLER, ALFRED D., Jr., *Strategy and Structure: Chapters in the History of the American Industrial Enterprise*. Cambridge: M.I.T. Press, 1962. Classic study of four major firms—DuPont, General Motors, Standard Oil of New Jersey, and Sears—and how their strategies led each of them to create and develop decentralized, multidivisional structures.

CHANNON, DEREK F., *The Strategy and Structure of British Enterprise*. Boston: Division of Research, Graduate School of Business Administration, Harvard University, 1973. A look at how the top 100 British firms responded to environmental changes over the period 1950 to 1970. Traces the evolution of strategies and structures, particularly with regard to diversification and divisionalization.

DAVIS, STANLEY M. and PAUL R. LAWRENCE, *Matrix.* Reading: Addison-Wesley, 1977. Tells when to use a matrix organization and how to make it effective, as well as describing some common problems and how to detect and correct them. Seven case studies are included.

GALBRAITH, JAY R. and DANIEL A. NATHANSON, *Strategy Implementation: The Role of Structure and Process.* St. Paul: West Publishing, 1978. Summarizes a number of empirical research studies on strategy and structure and presents several models of organizational growth and development. Research-oriented, but readable.

NEWMAN, WILLIAM H., *Administrative Action*, 2nd ed. Englewood Cliffs: Prentice-Hall, 1963. A classic discussion of designing a total organization structure is presented in Chapters 9 through 17.

CHAPTER 10—THE RIGHT PERSON AND THE RIGHT CARROT

ADIZES, ICHAK, *How to Solve the Mismanagement Crisis.* Homewood: Dow Jones-Irwin, 1979. To carry out the four essential roles of management, a managerial team is needed. A good fit between each manager's personal style and job will prevent mismanagement.

GALBRAITH, JAY R. and DANIEL A. NATHANSON, *Strategy Implementation: The Role of Structure and Process.* St. Paul: West Publishing, 1978. Chapter 6 reviews recent research linking reward systems and career paths to the organization's strategy.

HALL, JAMES L., "Organizational Technology and Executive Succession," *California Management Review*, Fall 1976. Using a nationwide sample of 155 companies, the author found significant relationships between the type of technology organizations use and the education and functional-area backgrounds of their chief executives.

HAYES, ROBERT H., "The Human Side of Acquisitions," *Management Review*, November 1979. Suggests aspects of management style and process that buyers and sellers should consider before closing the deal, along with guidelines to help managers in the acquired company decide whether to stay or leave.

RAPPAPORT, ALFRED, "Executive Incentives vs. Corporate Growth," *Harvard Business Review*, July 1978. Tying executive incentives to short-term performance may be one reason the United States is lagging in capital and research investment. The author suggests three approaches for tying incentives to strategy to correct this situation.

SCHEIN, EDGAR H., *Career Dynamics: Matching Individual and Organization Needs.* Reading: Addison-Wesley, 1978. Part 3 argues for an integrated human-resource planning and development system, based on an analysis of individual careers and of key job dimensions and considering both short- and long-term needs of the organization.

CHAPTER 11—RESOURCE ALLOCATION— POWER OF THE PURSE STRINGS

BOWER, JOSEPH L., *Managing the Resource Allocation Process: A Study of Corporate Planning and Investment*. Homewood: Richard D. Irwin, 1972. After studying four capital-investment projects from inception to final acceptance or rejection, the author develops a process model that integrates financial and strategic models and calls for both top-down and bottom-up inputs. Includes a useful chapter on managerial implications.

CAMILLUS, JOHN C. and JOHN H. GRANT, "Operational Planning: The Integration of Programming and Budgeting," *Academy of Management Review*, July 1980. The usual three-phase cycle of strategic planning, long-range programming, and budgeting may be dysfunctional for most businesses. Merging programming and budgeting into one integrated activity should increase both flexibility and control.

HALL, WILLIAM K., "Changing Perspectives on the Capital Investment Process," *Long Range Planning*, February 1979. A study of five multinationals suggests that strategic criteria are being used increasingly—relative to financial criteria—as the basis of allocation decisions and that corporate managers now have significant inputs into the allocation process.

LORANGE, PETER and RICHARD F. VANCIL, *Strategic Planning Systems*. Englewood Cliffs: Prentice-Hall, 1977. Chapter 3 in Part 3 makes the case for keeping capital expenditures separate from development expense. A case study on Texas Instrument's system follows.

STONICH, PAUL J., "How to Use Strategic Funds Programming," *The Journal of Business Strategy*, Fall 1980. Links strategy formulation and resource allocation through a seven-step process that assures adequate resources for strategic projects and builds a coordinated portfolio of projects.

CHAPTER 12—CONTROLLING THE DYNAMIC PROCESS

CHRISTOPHER, W. F., "Achievement Reporting—Controlling Performance Against Objectives," *Long Range Planning*, October 1977. Advocates control through an understanding of the organization's identifying purpose, participatively set objectives, and feedback to signal the advent of new trends.

HOROVITZ, JACQUES H., "Strategic Control: A New Task for Top Management," *Long Range Planning*, June 1979. A study at the top-management level in three European countries revealed a prevalence of long-range planning with short-range controls. Control systems should be tied to strategy and include monitoring of key environmental assumptions and critical factors for success, as well as results.

HURST, E. GERALD, "Controlling Strategic Plans," in Peter Lorange, *Implementation of Strategic Planning*. Englewood Cliffs: Prentice-Hall, 1982, Chapter 7. Perceptive analysis of issues in designing controls for strategic management.

NEWMAN, WILLIAM H., *Constructive Control: Design and Use of Control Systems*. Englewood Cliffs: Prentice-Hall, 1975. One of the few basic analyses of the control process. Stresses the impact of controls on future action, the response of people to controls, and the tying of controls to results. These concepts are demonstrated through application to a variety of management situations.

PAUL, RONALD N., NEIL B. DONAVAN, and JAMES W. TAYLOR, "The Reality Gap in Strategic Planning," *Harvard Business Review*, May 1978. Suggests ten actions a company can take to develop forward-looking control systems, among them setting criteria in advance for stopping a project and minimizing forecasting errors through frequent review of assumptions.

STEINER, GEORGE A., *Strategic Planning: What Every Manager Must Know: A Step-by-Step Guide*. New York: Free Press, 1979. Chapters 16 and 17 provide fourteen guidelines for designing a good control system, with a focus on steering controls, and recommend ways to get people to accept control systems.

CHAPTER 13—FITTING PIECES INTO A SYNERGISTIC WHOLE

ANSOFF, H. IGOR, ROGER P. DECLERCK, and ROBERT L. HAYES, Eds., *From Strategic Planning to Strategic Management*. New York: Wiley, 1976. A collection of papers by researchers and executives. Includes an article by the editors with a typology of environments and tables showing the organizational and managerial capabilities required by each, as well as relevant papers by Radosevich and Ullrich.

LORANGE, PETER, ILENE S. GORDON, and RICHARD SMITH. "The Management of Adaptation and Integration," *Journal of General Management*, Summer 1979. Defines the two tasks of planning as adapting the firm to environmental changes and integrating ongoing activities. The balance between these tasks is unique for each company and must be monitored. Includes several short case studies.

MILES, RAYMOND E. and CHARLES C. SNOW. *Organizational Strategy, Structure and Process*. New York: McGraw-Hill, 1978. A study of over eighty organizations in four industries resulted in four strategic archetypes, each with its own distinctive pattern of characteristics, including market orientation, growth strategy, technology, managerial-succession procedures, structure, control systems, and performance appraisal.

PASCALE, RICHARD T. and ANTHONY G. ATHOS, *The Art of Japanese Management: Applications for American Executives*. New York: Simon & Schuster, 1981. In high-performing United States and Japanese firms, a good fit among and between the tools executives can manipulate to influence the organization—style, staffing, skills, structure, strategy, systems, superordinate goals—appears to ensure long-term results.

VANCIL, RICHARD F., *Decentralization: Managerial Ambiguity by Design*. Homewood: Dow Jones–Irwin, 1978. Chapter 4 deals with management systems and their role in executing strategy. Included are human-resource and resource management, the importance of shared values and goals, performance-reporting systems and their limitations, and reward systems.

CHAPTER 14—HITTING A MOVING TARGET IN A ROUGH SEA

ANSOFF, H. IGOR, "Managing Strategic Surprise by Response to Weak Signals," *California Management Review*, Winter 1975. For more effective response to environmental change, the author recommends strategic-issue management, a continual monitoring of and preparing for change by focusing on discontinuities and weak signals in the environment.

LORANGE, PETER, *Corporate Planning: An Executive Viewpoint*. Englewood Cliffs: Prentice-Hall, 1980. Chapters 4 and 5 advocate monitoring both corporate systems and the external environment using steering and contingency controls. Consideration should be given to the predictability of what is being monitored, its importance, and the firm's strategic response potential.

NEWMAN, WILLIAM H., *Constructive Control: Design and Use of Control Systems*. Englewood Cliffs: Prentice-Hall, 1975. Chapter 8 calls for integrating controls with updated forecasts, including a reexamination of planning assumptions during the process of environmental monitoring.

QUINN, JAMES BRIAN, *Strategies for Change: Logical Incrementalism*. Homewood: Richard D. Irwin, 1980. Builds a case for incrementalism to minimize political risk and to allow an organization more flexibility in responding to environmental change.

STEINER, GEORGE A., *Strategic Planning: What Every Manager Must Know: A Step-by-Step Guide*. New York: Free Press, 1979. Chapter 14 deals with contingency planning, including its purpose and disadvantages, and the development and application of the exploration of alternative futures.

INDEX

Index